# VISIONS OF
# AMERICA

# CONTRIBUTIONS IN AMERICAN STUDIES

SERIES EDITOR: *Robert H. Walker*

# VISIONS OF AMERICA

## Eleven Literary Historical Essays

### *Kenneth S. Lynn*

With an Introduction by Robert H. Walker

CONTRIBUTIONS IN AMERICAN STUDIES
NUMBER 6

GREENWOOD PRESS, INC., Westport, Conn. ● London, England

73-460

Library of Congress Cataloging in Publication Data

Lynn, Kenneth Schuyler.
    Visions of America.

    (Contributions in American studies, no. 6)
    CONTENTS: Walden.—Uncle Tom's cabin.—Huckleberry
Finn.—[etc.]
    1. American literature—Addresses, essays, lectures.
2. Literature and society—Addresses, essays, lectures.
I. Title.
PS121.L9        810'.9        72-817
ISBN 0-8371-6386-2

Library of Congress Card Number: 72-817
ISBN: 0-8371-6386-2

First published in 1973

Greenwood Press, Inc., Publishing Division
51 Riverside Avenue, Westport, Connecticut 06880

Printed in the United States of America

*To the memory of F. O. Matthiessen*

# Contents

# Editor's Introduction

This is a collection of eleven essays by Kenneth S. Lynn published originally between 1957 and 1971. Six of them served as introductions to editions or anthologies, two were reviews, two appeared as articles, and one was a chapter in a commission report. They deal with American literature and society in the past 150 years but concentrate on the era from the Civil War to World War I.

Those of us interested in the subjects covered by these essays will welcome this volume as a rescue mission saving us from the inaccessibility of microfilm readers, the awkwardness of various forms of publication, the inevitably missing back numbers of periodicals, and even that funereal status, "out of print." It seemed clear, moreover, that the collection of these essays would serve something beyond convenience and that the sum might easily be more than its heretofore scattered parts. When I asked the author for his thoughts on this subject, his response began:

> My main hope for this collection of essays is that it will justify the interdisciplinary methods of American studies which I first learned as an undergraduate at Harvard in the 1940s from two remarkable tutors, F. O. Matthiessen and Perry Miller.

This statement is interesting from a number of viewpoints. For one thing it helps call attention to the unsuspected longevity enjoyed by something called American studies. Some readers of this volume will doubtless note with surprise that someone could have been pursuing this kind of curriculum in the remote 1940s. In truth, those responsible for this program at Professor Lynn's college date it from 1906.

There is a parallel ignorance concerning scholarship in American studies. It is entirely possible to attend conventions and read symposia of the last few years and to come away with the clear impression that American studies scholarship is a creation of the last thirty years and is confined to the analysis of revolutions, counter-revolutions, symbols, and happenings. A collection like this one reminds us that, although the last thirty years have seen some decidedly valuable as well as some dubiously modish works, there is a kind of scholarship that generously predates the more recent outpourings and that continues to contribute some of the more lasting perceptions of our culture.

American studies grew from, among other things, the conviction that literature divorced from its social setting could not be fully appreciated. Similarly, history must include the study of creative arts, social patterns, and cultural values and not be limited to the chronicling of depressions, inventions, and elections. The direct scholarly ancestors of Professor Lynn's essays are not only the two illustrious tutors, but also Moses Coit Tyler, Vernon Louis Parrington, Thorstein Veblen, and Charles and Mary Beard. American studies is a lively field. It changes. It reveals a handsome diversity and an uncowardly experimentalism. New subjects and altered methods are constantly revealing themselves in shifting combinations: quantification and exegesis, archeology and esthetics, engineering and sociology. It is reassuring to note that new fashions have not been used to cover a desiccated corpus. Here in this work is a clear and useful continuation of the impulse that added American studies as a recognizable aspect of the academy and that justifies itself not merely in refining the simultaneous use of more than one traditional body of knowledge but also in adding helpfully to the total understanding of American culture.

When, in the history of American studies, the social historian became a literary historian, too, he faced a difficult problem in deciding how much of the new apparatus of Freudian analysis of literature he could usefully accept. In an absolute sense, of course, the Freudian critic is the natural enemy of the social critic, since each is looking for different universals: one set emphasizing internal abstractions, the other, external applications. Professor Lynn can hardly be called a Freudian. But he has not let the sometimes frustrating results of Freudian readings of literature deter him from the necessary task of examining family backgrounds, marital relations, sexual attitudes, and mental aberrations. He uses these data with restraint. He uses them as means to a many-dimensioned understanding rather than as ends in themselves.

Joseph Wood Krutch, one of the earlier enthusiasts for Freudian readings, was fond of delivering a humorously self-deprecating recantation in later years. He had given some of his ingenuity and energy to demonstrating that Poe showed many symptoms of having an Oedipus complex. Later, he said, it occurred to him that the important thing was not to prove that Poe had this particular complex but to wonder what set apart the author of "The Raven" from others suffering from this complex who had failed to attain his level of achievement. This statement surely oversimplifies a complicated question; in the end Krutch never oversimplified, and neither has Professor Lynn. These essays use the modern ability to understand the human personality to sharpen the appreciation of a work of art and its setting in time and place. Where "history and literature intersect interestingly," says Professor Lynn, "is in the personalities of authors."

If American studies ever develops a single inflexible method, then it will cease to mean what it has meant to three of four generations of students and scholars: a chance to use new materials to explore a culture; a chance to accept or reject a scholarly method on the grounds of appropriateness to the task at hand instead of the grounds of traditional usage; and a chance to make connections and syntheses that will add appreciably to the useful understanding of American civilization. These essays represent a distinctive variation of a venerable American studies approach in their compounding of a close reading of texts with the insights from biography and psychology and in the application of these findings to a socioliterary context where there is a full and evident command of literary facts and fashions, as well as historical trends and pressures.

Each of these essays carries with it an ever-present analysis of the pertinent cultural mood. In their manner and method, not one is so private as to be unassimilable nor so predictable as to be dull. Each essay, in its close reasoning and careful support, offers something valid within a self-contained limit. Yet, collectively, these works further validate themselves by producing important observations on some of the major themes in our national experience. These themes are among the importantly comprehensive concerns of serious students of American literature and culture. Not all these themes touch each essay, but they appear and reappear with a marked consistency of definition and application.

Remembering that Kenneth Lynn first addressed us on *The Dream of Success*, a study of divergence between social attitudes portrayed in literature and those acted out in the lives of the authors, the reader of this volume should be least surprised by the persistent treatment of the creative writer's place in society. Although the phrase, "the alienation of the artist," has become a cliché, there is no real end to the need for serious understanding of the tension the phrase elliptically describes. These essays explore both its faces: the way in which the act of artistic creation places the writer apart from his subject and the way in which popular acclaim, or lack thereof, affects the writer. The reader may note with some surprise the number of instances when, in spite of a faltering romance with his public, the writer explicitly and determinedly set out to make his own time and place into his own literary subject matter.

To sharpen perceptions of literature as a social phenomenon, these essays include considerations of critical success as distinguished from material success, of social attitudes expressed in fiction as opposed to social values adopted in life. The difficult role of the creative personality in society is a timeless and international question. In these case studies appears a major effort to discover what is American about this dilemma and how the dilemma shifts with time, with family, and within the geography of American culture.

A related but distinguishable theme concerns the degree of social involvement pursued by the writer and his attitude toward protest and reform. How much of the important differences between Howells and Dreiser as novelists can be explained by the fact that Howells called himself a socialist and Dreiser explicitly denied the function of literature as an agent of deliberate social and institutional change? In opening up such questions, these essays come to deal not only with the writer's engagement with the present but also with his attitude toward the past and his hopes for the future. One is forced to realize that, especially in the experience of literary realism in America, a viewpoint on social statics and dynamics may have had considerable impact on the form and structure of art itself.

The discussion, in these essays, of literature and social protest goes far beyond the turn-of-the-century attitudes of Howells and Dreiser. It begins, chronologically, with a treatment of that defender of John Brown and master rhetorician of civil disobedience, Henry David Thoreau. Next comes the discussion of *Uncle Tom's Cabin*, a novel which is certainly the best single argument in American history for the incendiary value of imaginative literature where documentation, oratory, journalism, and even martyrdom had failed to light the larger fire. Touching many other milestones in the history of literary involvement with social issues, these essays culminate chronologically in the twentieth century in such eminent literary activists as Emma Goldman and John Dos Passos. A kind of unity is imparted to this subject by the fact that Edmund Wilson is discussed here not solely for his treatment of Civil War literature. It was Wilson who, taking a page from the handbook of Thoreau, refused to pay taxes in support of a condition he found similarly intolerable to Thoreau's aversion to the Mexican-American war. Neither the focus of these essays themselves nor of the individuals discussed is ever far from the subject of literature and protest.

The use of biographical detail is so strikingly recurrent as to become a minor theme in its own right, even though these details typically contribute, in the end, to a better appreciation of art and the times rather than a psychological diagnosis for its own sake. The personal distance of the family in which Mark Twain grew up, where hands were shaken before retiring for the night, is shown to have accentuated the sternness of the father to the point where the threat of imprisonment became quite real to the son. In the light of this perception, the reportedly chance reading of a page of print dealing with the Maid of Orleans makes it possible for the reader to appreciate not only Twain's otherwise unlikely interest in the martyred French girl but also his literary fascination with scenes of captivity.

Many of the more spectacular aspects of Emma Goldman's career come together only with the exploration of her less distant but hardly more usual relationship with her father. To students of Civil War literature, moreover, the meaning of Abraham Lincoln to Edmund Wilson's father comes to provide a vital interpretive clue. Personal doubts stemming from familial relations are made, in these essays, to fill out an understanding of Frank Norris and to explain the sadness and mental insecurity of a man often shallowly associated with optimism as a way of literature: William Dean Howells. Similar ironies in the internal and personal life of John Dos Passos are used to explain why we must take this remarkable writer as a great deal more than just another rebel-turned-reactionary. The artistic evidence does not exist for the sake of clarifying phobias and family tensions; but fathers and sons, family and close friends, have been used to develop a minor theme on the personality of the American writer and to provide a necessary background for some of the major social and literary understandings.

Each reader, according to his own interests, will recognize certain other recurring subjects. There is considerable attention given to what might be called the focus of literature: the conscious choice between the various kinds of reality and the purposeful adaptation of styles to fit the choices. The treatment of Harriet Beecher Stowe as an early realist brings up problems of literary influences, purposes, and definitions which are mirrored elsewhere. A number of

American myths receive attention, including the preoccupation with violence that gives a common denominator to such otherwise dissimilar works as Mark Twain's *Pudd'nhead Wilson*, Herman Melville's "Benito Cereno," and Richard Wright's *Native Son*. The cultural meaning of America's shift from a rural to an urban nation becomes an explicitly important aspect of more than one of these essays—especially those dealing with Dreiser and Howells.

In setting down for me the collective importance of these essays as he saw them, Kenneth Lynn ended by stressing the common impulse of all of these figures to create their own vision of America:

Whether they focused on the past, the present, or the future of the Republic, whether they wrote autobiography, fiction, or literary criticism, whether they professed optimism or pessimism about what they saw, they all found original and unforgettable ways of defining what Matthiessen once called "the possibilities of life in America."

One theme that unites this book is even more general, more particular, more universal, and more American. It is the theme that Walt Whitman most eloquently identified when he began his life song by inviting the individual soul while, simultaneously, refusing to forget the mass, the body collective. As with Whitman, the tensions that produced great literature in the writers here under discussion arose from reasons both intensely personal and provocatively public. The treatment of this literature and its makers allows one to see how interestingly it has been dominated by this deliberate American paradox: the creative singular and the receptive plural, the lonely conscience and the collective need, the individual versus the democracy.

ROBERT H. WALKER
*Series Editor*

# VISIONS OF
# AMERICA

# *1*

# Walden

Like John Brown, whom he deeply admired, and whose raid on Harp
ers Ferry he defended with unforgettable eloquence, Thoreau was
possessed by a vision of perfect freedom to which he gave his life. In
everything he did and said, he tested what it was like to be one's own
master; his writings both record his experiments and call on us to be
experimental, too.

In the fall of 1837, shortly after his graduation from Harvard
College, when he was living once more with his family in Concord,
Thoreau wrote in the journal he had just begun to keep regularly,
"The world is a fit theatre today in which any part may be acted.
There is this moment proposed to me every kind of life that men lead
anywhere, or that imagination can paint." South African planter,
Greenland whaler, soldier in Florida, navigator of any sea, were
among the occupations he conjectured for himself. Yet when a friend
proposed to him that they work their passage across the Atlantic and
travel through Europe, the celebrator of perfect freedom turned him
down. The decision was characteristic. For if all the world was a
theater to Thoreau, it is important to note that he seldom went on the
road. The only other book besides *Walden* which he published in his
lifetime was a travel book, to be sure, but it only recorded *A Week*

Source: From *Major Writers of America* edited by Perry Miller, © 1962
by Harcourt Brace Jovanovich, Inc. and reprinted with their permission.

*on the Concord and Merrimack Rivers.* That many of his post-humous publications bear place names as titles—*The Maine Woods, Cape Cod, A Yankee in Canada*—is indicative of the fact that occasionally he *did* leave Concord, but his absences were not for long and did not take him far. Even when he was living at Walden Pond he often returned home for weekends.

Part of the explanation for his homebodyness is that Thoreau was very dependent, emotionally speaking, on his family. He lived a great part of his life under his parents' roof and he died in his mother's house. He never married. When he was twenty-six, he wrote a letter to his mother in which he confessed, "Methinks I should be content to sit at the back-door in Concord, under the poplar-tree, henceforth forever." But perhaps the most poignant instance of his attachment occurred when he was a senior at Harvard. He asked his mother what occupation he should choose, and when she replied, "You can buckle on your knapsack, and roam abroad to seek your fortune," he wept until his sister Helen embraced him and said, comfortingly, "No, Henry, you shall not go; you shall stay at home and live with us."

The main reason, however, that he never went anywhere is that Thoreau deliberately lived a life of paradox. He insisted that there was society in solitude, that silence was a mode of communication, that idleness was productive, that one could go far by staying put. Freedom, he said repeatedly, was not what his neighbors construed it to be; he found it difficult, he confessed, to exaggerate their error. To force them to redefine their terms by making them acknowledge the truth of his outrageous paradoxes was his consistent strategy. Like the cow he spoke of in *Walden*, "which kicks over the pail, leaps the cowyard fence, and runs after her calf in milking time," he lived a life of adventure in native pastures.

Thoreau, then, never went in search of his fortune and never, in a certain sense, amounted to anything. For a time he taught school; he worked for the Emersons as a gardener and general handyman and helped to edit the *Dial*; off and on, he was a surveyor; and he made pencils in his father's pencil factory. For a Harvard graduate it was an extravagant performance, and some of those who were witness to his behavior were disgusted by it. James Russell Lowell, who lived for a year in Concord, found Thoreau difficult and unpleasant, thought there was no excuse for his unbounded egotism, and contemptuously dismissed him as a failure who was spending his life picking up the windfalls in Emerson's orchard.

The wisecrack was not only directed against the scandalous means of livelihood Thoreau had chosen but against the independence of his mind as well; in Lowell's view, Thoreau lived off Emerson's intellect as well as his charity. There is no doubt, of course, that Emerson's essays, especially "Nature" (1836)—which was published in the fall of Thoreau's senior year at Harvard—had an enormous impact on the younger man, stirring him to the depths of his being. He imbibed so many of Emerson's ideas that Emerson himself believed that his mind was mirrored in Thoreau's, the one significant difference being that his own was more metaphysical and Thoreau's more concrete; it was right that Thoreau, not Emerson, should write the "Natural History of Massachusetts" (1842) because Thoreau knew the facts of the subject as well as its truth. Yet this difference hardly exhausted the contrast between the two men. Emerson proclaimed that "whoso would be a man, must be a nonconformist," but Emerson's nonconformity had its distinct limits. If the authorities of the Harvard Divinity School turned their backs on him for the heresy of his 1838 address, Emerson was still invited to Boston for meetings of the Saturday Club, an organization which was as proper as it was literary, and he was both a respectable and respected citizen of the Concord community. Although he was prepared to acknowledge that "for nonconformity the world whips you with its displeasure," he was nevertheless distressed at the news that Thoreau had carried his disapproval of America's war with Mexico to the point where he had been put in jail for refusing to pay a tax. Emerson was generous to Thoreau in a hundred ways—he encouraged him in his writing by persuading the editors of the *Dial* to print one of his poems; he gave him permission to live on some property he owned at Walden Pond; and he habitually referred to his lesser-known friend as "*the* man of Concord." But Emerson also patronized Thoreau, and nowhere more so than in his fond assumption that Thoreau's intransigent radicalism and intensity of spirit were merely personal idiosyncrasies and that when all was said and done their ideas of life were the same. As the years passed, the relationship with Emerson became increasingly unbearable for Thoreau. The later years of his journal do not present a flattering portrait of the man who first proposed that he keep it. "I doubt," runs a scornful entry of 1852, "if Emerson could trundle a wheelbarrow through the streets." In 1856 Thoreau wrote of their friendship that it had been "one long tragedy."

For his part, Emerson was finally somewhat disappointed in his protégé. He had taken up Thoreau when the younger man was unknown because he had recognized his rare combination of qualities. Thoreau, Emerson perceived, was steeped in English poetry, especially in the works of the seventeenth-century metaphysicals in whom Emerson was also interested; he possessed a knowledge of languages—of Greek, Latin, French, Italian, Spanish, German, and Anglo-Saxon—that was astonishing; his acquaintance with the writings of the Hindu mystics eventually rivaled Emerson's. In the woods, Thoreau was unsurpassed. He saw everything; he knew everything; he could ice-skate thirty miles a day over the frozen rivers; he could sniff the smoke of a man's pipe a third of a mile away. In the oration which Emerson gave at Thoreau's funeral (subsequently enlarged for publication in the *Atlantic Monthly*), the list of his physical achievements makes him seem almost legendary, like a figure out of a *Davy Crockett Almanack*.

> His senses were acute, his frame well-knit and hardy . . . and there was a wonderful fitness of body and mind. He could pace sixteen rods more accurately than another man could measure them with rod and chain. He could find his path in the woods at night . . . better by his feet than his eyes. He could estimate the measure of a tree very well by his eye; he could estimate the weight of a calf or a pig, like a dealer. . . . He was a good swimmer, runner, skater, boatman, and would probably outwalk most countrymen in a day's journey.

Thoreau also was accomplished in a variety of mechanical skills and could do any kind of handyman's job. He was, in Emerson's eyes, the potentially perfect example of the American scholar whom he had envisaged in his 1837 address, the man of books who was also the man of action, the "helpful giant" who would build a new American culture. But Thoreau never turned his talents to great enterprise and command. "I so much regret the loss," wrote Emerson, "that I cannot help counting it a fault in him that he had no ambition. Wanting this, instead of engineering for all America, he was the captain of a huckleberry-party. Pounding beans is good to the end of pounding empires one of these days; but if, at the end of years, it is still only beans!"

## II

For young college graduates who would engineer for all America, the nation of the 1830s offered two great opportunities: religion and business. The trouble was, as Thoreau said, that "neither the New Testament nor Poor Richard speaks to our condition." The job problem as he saw it was "how to make the getting our living poetic! for if it is not poetic it is not life but death that we get." Christianity, he conceded, conceived of life poetically. "Seek first the kingdom of heaven." "Lay not up for yourselves treasures on earth." "For what is a man profited, if he shall gain the whole world and lose his own soul?" Such statements were so challenging that Thoreau could not believe any Yankee had ever read them. But the hypocrisy of New England churchgoers aside, Thoreau felt that the New Testament did not speak to his generation because it was too exclusively concerned with man's spiritual affairs. Tough-minded and practical, a shrewd Yankee for all his hatred of the type, Thoreau was convinced that Christ had imperfectly taught mankind how to live. Christ's thoughts were all directed toward another world, and for Thoreau this was unsatisfactory. "There is another kind of success than his," he said. "Even here we have a sort of living to get, and must buffet it somewhat longer. There are various tough problems to solve, and we must make shift to live, betwixt spirit and matter, such a human life as we can.''

As for business, Thoreau was graduated from college in the midst of the financial panic of 1837, a time hardly calculated to make Poor Richard's philosophy of life seem attractive. In a commencement debate on the virtues of the commercial spirit, Thoreau chose to speak on the negative side, and he continued to do so all his adult life, most notably in his journals and in *Walden*. Even as a small boy he had known how he felt about the American dream of success. For Thoreau's father, once a prosperous storekeeper, had gone bankrupt and been forced into the business of manufacturing pencils. Thereafter the family took in boarders in order to make ends meet. The son they sent to Harvard was always neatly dressed, but his classmates noted that his clothes were unfashionable and occasionally patched. The Thoreaus, in sum, were shabby genteel. Now, life in America has a way of driving such people into a corner, of draining them emotionally, of sniffing out their pathetic pretenses with cruel skill; their tragedy has been one of the major concerns of the American novel from Howells on, and it has furnished the theme of the two most important American plays of our time, *Death of a Salesman* and *The Glass Menagerie*. Yet the experience of failing in a success-mad society has sometimes proved to be a liberation. For one of the striking facts about American literature is the number of our writers who have emerged from shabby-genteel backgrounds. Irving, Poe, Hawthorne, Melville, Emerson—to take only writers of Thoreau's time—all came from families of declining status, and the triumph of their art is in a variety of ways related to this circumstance. In Thoreau's case, the experience of wearing patches helped him to understand that "wealth and the approbation of man" constituted a hollow definition of success. "The *terra firma* of my existence," he affirmed, "lies far beyond."

## III

In order to reach the firm ground that lay beyond, Thoreau struck upon the idea—the year was 1840—of going to live at Walden Pond. Not until 1845, however, was he sufficiently clear of debts to carry out his plan. By doing a little farming on some acres that Emerson owned near the pond and by cutting his personal needs to the bone, he was able—as he told Horace Greeley—to get a year's living for six weeks of work. There he remained for two and a half years. His move to Walden was for a brief season the scandal of Concord, but the real drama of his sojourn by the pond consisted of an action the town gossips never saw: the play of his mind and imagination. What he proposed to do was to explore the "Farthest Indies," not by actually going there, but by "other routes and other methods of travel."

Thoreau's passage to India began with his intense awareness of himself, with his terrific concentration on the resources of his own personality. So self-conscious was Thoreau that all his life he was aware of a certain doubleness in himself. He could all but literally stand aside and watch himself in action and in thought. "However intense my experience," he said, "I am conscious of the presence and criticism of a part of me which, as it were, is not a part of me, but spectator, sharing no experience, but taking note of it, and that is no more I than you." Along with his self-centeredness went a faith that everything he thought and did was important. As a transcendentalist, he believed that every fact could flower into truth; therefore, each experience of Henry Thoreau could be made to yield up a more heroic significance. It is scarcely accidental that the lines from the Elizabethan poet Samuel Daniel that are quoted both in the *Week on the Concord and Merrimack* and in "A Plea for Captain John Brown" were on Thoreau's lips, according to some of his friends, more often than any other poem—

Unless above himself he can
Erect himself, how poor a thing is man.

To nature he paid as unremitting attention as he did to self. The
naturalist John Burroughs, among others, has not been impressed by
Thoreau as an observer of plants and animals and has berated him
for his sloppy classifications; such criticisms, however, are almost
totally irrelevant because they fail to take into account Thoreau's
real aim in studying the natural world. If there was anyone whom
Thoreau hated, it was the scientific observer who carefully recorded
and classified biological phenomena and did nothing more. He
specifically attacked Humboldt and Darwin for their automatic habit
of minutely careful observation, followed by notebook citation,
followed by nothing. He urged those who loved nature to avoid their
example. "Do not tread upon the heels of your experience," he said.
"Be impressed without making a minute of it. Poetry puts an interval
between the impression and the expression,—waits till the seed ger-
minates naturally." The germination of the seed was an event the
naturalists failed to wait for. They had no sense of awe or delight in
the out-of-doors, and Thoreau dismissed them with sweeping contempt: "Most of our modern authors have not imagined the actual
beasts which they presume to describe."

Underlying the bitterness of Thoreau's attack on the naturalists
was the fear that in his own investigations of nature his imagination
would someday fail him—that he, too, would be caught in a morass
of facts which would refuse to surrender their ultimate meaning to
him. As the later volumes of his journals reveal, this was in fact the
tragedy that lay in wait for him. But in the years of full intellectual
power, and especially in the Walden period, every walk in the woods
became "a sort of crusade . . . to go forth and reconquer this Holy
Land from the hands of the Infidels." His favorite direction for walking was west, because the west meant wildness, and wildness was
"the preservation of the world. . . . From the forest and wilderness
come the tonics and barks which brace mankind." Yet if he literally
walked westward, he reached the wild only by an act of imagination.
Once, in the primeval Maine woods, Thoreau declared that "we have
not seen pure Nature, unless we have seen her thus vast and drear
and inhuman, though in the midst of cities. Nature was here something savage and awful, though beautiful." Concord woods, however,

were not the forests of Maine, and Thoreau knew it. He was fully aware that there were no cougars or panthers or lynxes or wolverines in eastern Massachusetts in the 1840s. As he once admitted,

> I cannot but feel as if I lived in a tamed, and, as it were, emasculated country. . . . Is it not a maimed and imperfect nature that I am conversant with? . . . I take infinite pains to know all the phenomena of spring, for instance, thinking that I have here the entire poem, and then, to my chagrin, I hear that it is but an imperfect copy that I possess, and have read, that my ancestors have torn out many of the first leaves and grandest passages and mutilated it in many places.

But the tameness of Concord woods did not put bracing tonics and barks beyond mankind's reach. "I shall never find in the wilds of Labrador," Thoreau triumphantly proclaimed, "any greater wildness than in some recess in Concord, i.e., than I import into it." Even in a woods where the wolf and the lynx no longer roamed, a walker could penetrate to the anarchic, wild freedom that lay at the heart of nature if only his imagination were sufficiently extravagant; one could apprehend it, for example, simply by listening, with all one's faculties intensely concentrated, to a blue jay:

> The unrelenting steel cold scream of a jay, unmelted, that never flows into a song, a sort of wintry trumpet, screaming cold; hard, tense, frozen music, like the winter sky itself; in the blue livery of winter's bands.

Another route to the farthest Indies lay in reading. Like every other activity, reading for Thoreau involved an absolute self-consciousness. "Books," he said, "must be read as deliberately and reservedly as they were written." He disliked novels and was acquainted with few of them; he preferred travel books (Josselyn's *New England Rarities Discovered* was one of his favorites) and philosophy. If walking took him westward, his reading often took him East, toward Greece, India, and China. Indeed, the classics of Hindu and Buddhist thought absorbed him so completely that they made him feel as if he were living in another world. Thus in May 1841, after reading the book of the Hindu god Menu, Thoreau observed in his journal:

> That title, "The Laws of Menu with the Gloss of Culluca," comes to me with such a volume of sound as if it had swept unobstructed over the plains of Hindostan; and when my eye rests on yonder birches, or the sun in the water, or the shadows of the trees, it seems to signify the laws of them all. They are the laws of you and me, a fragrance wafted down from those old times, and no more to be refuted than the wind. When my imagination travels eastward and backward to those remote years of the gods, I seem to draw near to the habitation of the morning, and the dawn at length has a place. I remember the book as an hour before sunrise.

Thoreau's study of a book was an action that involved his whole being.


## IV


Vividly aware in the face of every experience, Thoreau was more self-conscious, which in his terms is to say more alive, when he was writing than at any other time. His poetry and his prose both reflect a careful, deliberate craftsman whose remarkable ability to detach himself from his work and judge its quality with dispassionate objectivity is best summarized in his remark that an artist's work primarily consists of performing "post-mortem examinations of himself before he is dead." Thoreau's writing can seem spontaneous, but it is not; it is highly wrought, cunningly contrived; it is the supreme expression of his doubleness. His journals, in which he recorded his daily crusades, are more artful than Emerson's, and like the latter's journals they served a larger artfulness. For Thoreau's private works were a great sourcebook, a mine, out of which he extracted ideas and expressions which were then carefully reset, often after an immense amount of lapidary effort, in the mosaic of the more ambitious and more intricate designs of his public essays.

The two full-length books that Thoreau published in his lifetime are the products of the most beautifully disciplined writing talent of the age in America. *A Week on the Concord and Merrimack* is, however, a more experimental, less finished design, inasmuch as it represents the trying-out of the method of presentation that Thoreau would follow in *Walden*. As his masterpiece would, the *Week* recalls an experience of the author's past. In the summer of 1839, Thoreau, in company with his brother John, had taken a canoe trip on the Concord and Merrimack. Two years later, his brother died horribly of lockjaw. Thereafter, Thoreau's recollections of their idyllic river journey had a special poignance. Four years after John's death, Thoreau went to live by Walden Pond and wrote the *Week*. He continued to work on the manuscript, revising and adding to it, after he left the pond. When the book was finally published—at Thoreau's personal expense—in 1849, the *Week* represented ten years of meditation and work.

Purporting to be a simple record of the 1839 trip, the *Week* in fact contains poems which Thoreau had printed in the *Dial*, journal entries, fragments of essays, and whole lectures written in periods both before and long after the journey. Though the actual trip took a good deal longer, the artful trip lasts seven days, with one chapter for each day. The book seems casually organized, and to a certain extent this is true. But if the thought wanders, there is a transcendental, an organic, rationale for digression in the meandering flow of the rivers. The use of a drifting rhythm as the matrix for the thought and action of a book would not be exploited as successfully again by an American author until *Huckleberry Finn* (1885). Besides its streamlike movement, the book is held together by a rising and falling movement, the cycle of sunrise and sunset, which is repeated each day. The subjects which Thoreau discusses en route are not fortuitous, but are organically related to the unfolding panorama of the journey and to the particular day of the week. (World mythologies, for example, are discussed on Sunday.) Beneath its seeming looseness, the *Week* has the tightness and the economy for which Thoreau always strove.


V


*Walden* (1854) is even more artful and more deceptive; the supreme creation of Thoreau's self-consciousness, it lauds simplicity by means of complexity. In substance as well as in mode of expression, the "humor" of the book is paradoxical.

Thus the author asserts that neither the New Testament nor Poor Richard speaks to our condition, but the opening of *Walden* sounds remarkably like Benjamin Franklin's *Autobiography*. There is, first of all, the same disarmingly candid explanation as to why the author happened to write this book; in Thoreau's case, he insists that he has been prompted to authorship partly because so many of his townsmen have asked him questions about his sojourn at the pond, just as Franklin claims that one of the reasons he became an author was that he felt his son might be interested in learning something about his ancestors. And just as Franklin is charmingly frank about his egotistic desire to talk about himself, so Thoreau admits in a delightful phrase, "I should not talk so much about myself if there were anybody else whom I knew as well." The title of the first chapter would surely have been approved of by Poor Richard: "Economy."

What Thoreau is doing, however, is to destroy the enemy with the enemy's own weapons. He deliberately appropriates the language of the success ethic in order to expose it. In the immemorial manner of the businessman, he talks about "conditions," except that he does not judge them by the standard of economic prosperity. Prosperity, indeed, is ruining the country. The mass of men lead lives of quiet desperation. Their fingers tremble from the hard work they do. They are nothing but machines. They are gasping for breath; they must lie and flatter to get ahead. Published two years after Harriet Beecher

Stowe had made Simon Legree a national byword, *Walden* asserts that "it is hard to have a Southern overseer; it is worse to have a Northern one, but worst of all when you are the slave-driver of yourself." The unluckiest of all are those who succeed, for farms, houses, barns, and cattle—in sum, possessions—make horrible demands upon their owners and are more easily acquired than got rid of. As for luxuries and the so-called comforts of life, they have been throughout history positive hindrances to the elevation of mankind.

Against this appalling picture of the economy of his neighbors, Thoreau sets forth his own economy, his personal plan of living, in a series of elaborate financial metaphors which appear at first glance to be an attempt to justify his plan in terms of the Poor Richard civilization he has just been scorning. The decision to go to the woods is spoken of as the determination "to go into business at once." Over the years, he has "well-nigh sunk all his capital" into listening to the wind; therefore why should he not turn to this new "enterprise"? For a long time he had felt that Walden Pond "would be a good place for business, not solely on account of the railroad and the ice trade; it offers advantages which it may not be good policy to divulge; it is a good port and a good foundation." Having always endeavored "to acquire strict business habits," he of course keeps ledgers and accounts during his sojourn. *Walden* contains itemized lists which outdo anything in the collected works of Franklin. The cost of the things Thoreau buys is given in meticulous detail, down to the halfpenny—even the quarter penny. And if Franklin's economies, his ability to cut his meals down to a glass of water and a handful of raisins, seem awesome, Thoreau's tall tale of economy reduces Ben Franklin to a spendthrift. On food for the first eight months of his stay Thoreau spent $8.74; on clothing, $8.40 3/4; on housing, $28.12 1/2. Once again, however, this ruthless application of the principles of Poor Richard to the practical problems of daily living is made with an anti-Poor Richard purpose.

Poor Richard believed that early to bed and early to rise makes a man healthy, wealthy, and wise. Poor Richard was ascetic in the present, kept his shop now, so that in the future his shop would keep him. But the "Yankee shrewdness" of which Thoreau speaks is directed toward avoiding, not attaining, "the splendid mausoleum" where Poor Richard dreamed of living. The asceticism of Thoreau is directed toward the goal of a greater awareness, a superior intensity, a more and more absolute self-consciousness.

> It occurred to me when I awoke this morning, feeling regret of the day before in eating fruit, which had dulled my sensibilities, that man was to be treated as a musical instrument, and if any viol was to be made of sound timber and kept well-tuned always, it was he, so that when the bow of events is drawn across him he may vibrate and resound in perfect harmony. A sensitive soul will be continually trying its strings to see if they are in tune. A man's body must be rasped down exactly to a shaving. It is of far more importance than the wood of a Cremona violin.

Thoreau accepts the frugality of Poor Richard, but to the end that he will achieve the sensitivity of a Cremona violin, not that he will make a fortune. Thoreau cuts down on costs because "the cost of a thing is the amount of what I will call life which is required to be exchanged for it, immediately or in the long run," and, therefore, a cost reduction is not money saved but a life saved. He gets up at sunrise not for the purpose of getting ahead but because "poetry and art date from such an hour." In perhaps the clearest indication that Thoreau had Franklin in mind when he wrote *Walden*, he says that one of his prime motives for early rising was so that he could hear the crowing of the wild cocks in the woods—for to hear those birds "who would not be early to rise, and rise earlier and earlier every successive day of his life, till he became unspeakably healthy, wealthy, and wise?" In this juxtaposition of the wild chanticleer of the woods with the most famous of Poor Richard's aphorisms is contained the essence of Thoreau's defiance of Franklin's America.

The bulk of the chapter "Economy" is taken up with an elaboration of his objections to the way in which his neighbors feed, clothe, and house themselves and of his alternative ideas. His critique is largely centered on the habits of the group which Thorstein

Veblen forty-five years later would call the leisure class. The Poor Richard who has made his pile can think of nothing to do except eat more and richer food, build larger and more splendid houses, and wear more abundant clothing. The result is that the rich are not simply comfortably warm, but unnaturally hot; they are in fact cooked—"of course *à la mode*." Thoreau's concern is to strip away all these superfluities. "Fanciful clothes are our epidermis, or false skin, which partakes not of our life, and may be stripped off here and there without fatal injury." As for housing, Thoreau maintained that "before we can adorn our houses with beautiful objects the walls must be stripped, and beautiful housekeeping and beautiful living laid for a foundation." He wants to get rid of all pretense and display, he wants to get to the heart of things and start growing outward from there. He comes to the pond to confront experience directly, to make a fresh start, to shuck off the dead skin of a materialistic civilization. This is the "private business" he wishes to transact, and *Walden* is the story of his metamorphosis.

In this light, the practical details of economy can be seen to have a transcendental significance. The stripping away of the layers of clothing and housing in which modern man is cooking to death is the symbolic first step in the act of metamorphosis—as nature herself witnesses.

> Our moulting season, like that of the fowls, must be a crisis in our lives. The loon retires to solitary ponds to spend it. Thus also the snake casts its slough, and the caterpillar its wormy coat, by an internal industry and expansion; for clothes are but our outmost cuticle and coil.

Yet if the casting of the old coat and the creation of a new one are accomplished in solitude, this does not mean that the new coat has no significance for society. In one of the first paragraphs of the book, Thoreau remarks that he hopes his readers will accept such portions of his narrative as apply to them and that he trusts "none will stretch the seams in putting on the coat, for it may do good service to him whom it fits." *Walden* itself is a new "garment" for mankind as well

as for the man who made it, and by donning it mankind can accomplish collective rebirth and renewal. For "if there is not a new
man, how can the new clothes be made to fit?"

With that question we reach the heart of the chapter on
economy, the building of Thoreau's house. The conception of
Thoreau's dream house is at the other end of the scale from Poe's
fantastic "Domain of Arnheim," but both are equally removed from
middle-class, mid-nineteenth-century America. Poe had built luxuriously in the name of art and beauty and taste; Thoreau defines
true luxury as the employment of nature as the "raw material of
tropes and symbols" in the creation of an object. In the spring of
1845, Thoreau tells us, he had gone out to Walden and cut down
some "tall, arrowy white pines, still in their youth, for timber." He
bleached and purified the boards in the sun. He dug his cellar where
a woodchuck had a hole. Thus his house had grown from the inside
out, like an organism. If all men built their own houses, says
Thoreau, they would perhaps be poets. But his self-conscious
purification of the boards in the sun is not merely poetic, it is
religious. While Poor Richard did not speak to Thoreau's condition,
*Walden* nonetheless has a Yankee economy to it; the New Testament
did not speak to his condition either, and yet *Walden* has a Christian
economy too. Christ's forty days in the wilderness were a process of
purification, and to Thoreau, who regarded Christ as "a sublime actor on the stage of the world," such a retreat from the world was an
act of supreme self-consciousness which he self-consciously wished
to repeat. The Christian parallel by no means exhausted Thoreau's
awareness of the religious nature of his sojourn at the pond. The
fable of withdrawal and renewal was one which was common to all
the great religions of the world. ("It is interesting to observe," he
wrote in the *Week*, "with what singular unanimity the farthest sun-
dered nations and generations consent to give completeness and
roundness to an ancient fable.") Thus his retreat to the pond had
Hindu as well as Christian overtones. The doctrine of Yoga, to which
Emerson had introduced Thoreau, urged a complete abstraction
from all worldly objects. Work must be done without the hope of
material reward; sacrifice, mortification of the flesh, and controlling

the breath were the indispensable preliminaries to a higher state of being. "Depend upon it that, rude and careless as I am," Thoreau wrote, "I would fain practice the yoga faithfully. . . . To some extent, and at rare intervals, even I am a yogi." On another occasion he said, "One may discover the root of a Hindoo religion in his own private history, when, in the silent intervals of the day or the night, he does sometimes inflict on himself like austerities with a stern satisfaction.

It would be a mistake to think that Thoreau carried these Christian and Hindu analogies beyond the point of general resemblance. Thoreau was not a Yogi, of course, if for no other reason than that the Hindu mystic wishes release from the unending cycle of rebirth, whereas *Walden* glorifies it. But he did act in conscious knowledge of the general similarity between Eastern religion and his own reenactment of a universal fable; his invocations of Christ and the gods of Greece had the same general analogical purpose. While many of the fabulous parallels are drawn in a spirit of self-deflationary humor which rescues the book from the dangers of both egotism and blasphemy, in a very real sense the author of *Walden* is always serious. The prosaic details of cutting down trees and hewing timbers and digging a cellar, of paying an Irishman named Collins $4.25 for the lumber in a shanty that Collins had occupied, are quite deliberately arranged in such a way as to reveal their religious meaning. Thoreau's ideal was—

> Facts should only be as the frame to my pictures; they should be material to the mythology which I am writing; not facts to assist men to make money, farmers to farm profitably, in any common sense; facts to tell who I am and where I 'have been or what I have thought. . . . My facts shall be falsehoods to the common sense. I would so state facts that they shall be significant, shall be mythic or mythologic.

He cuts down young trees in the spring and he bleaches boards in the sun: these are preliminary steps in building a house. They are also part of the religious ceremony of purification and renewal.

The fourth chapter of *Walden*, "Sounds," introduces another major aspect of the renewal theme: the seeding, planting, fertilizing, flowering, and harvesting of crops. The progress of his bean field is a conversational topic of which Thoreau never grows tired; it also furnishes him with a rhythm that finally imposes an order on the entire book. The structure of the *Week* is a sequence of seven days; in *Walden*, the action begins in early summer and ends the following spring; the twenty-six months which Thoreau actually spent at the pond are compressed into the cycle of a year; his account of his life in the woods follows the elemental pattern of the flowering, death, and replanting of a bean crop. Throughout the book one is constantly being reminded of the continuing drama of vegetation. In the chapter "Visitors," for example, after he has talked at some length about the people who have come to see him—the most memorable visitor being the French woodchopper and the most fascinating being the runaway slave, whom "I helped to forward toward the north star"—Thoreau suddenly breaks off the description, and the next chapter begins: "Meanwhile my beans . . . were impatient to be hoed." And in the second half of the book, in the chapters which follow the crucial chapter "The Ponds," the seasonal cycle comes more and more to dominate the action.

Yet, far down inside Thoreau's submission of his life to nature, there is an ambiguity. The chapter "Higher Laws" begins with the famous sentence,

> As I came home through the woods with my string of fish,
> trailing my pole, it being now quite dark, I caught a
> glimpse of a woodchuck, stealing across my path, and felt
> a strange thrill of savage delight, and was strongly tempted
> to seize and devour him raw; not that I was hungry then,
> except for that wildness which he represented.

Here, seemingly, is the statement of the natural man who likes to spend his days up to his chin in a swamp, of the primitivist who wants to tear apart a woodchuck as if he were an animal himself. But there was an invincible fastidiousness about Thoreau, an abhorrence of dirt and filth that was very deep in him. As the chapter "Higher Laws" makes clear, his adherence to a simple diet sprang as much from his loathing of the unclean as it did from any positive belief in the spiritual efficacy of moderation. Despite the fantasy about the woodchuck, Thoreau was a vegetarian; as he says in "Higher Laws," "the practical objection to animal food in my case was its uncleanness." Such food had no ill effect on his body, but it disagreed, as he says, with his imagination. In revulsion, Thoreau compared meat-eaters to the gluttonous maggot and the gross larva of the caterpillar. The same thing was true of his drinking habits. Thoreau found that water was the only drink worth stomaching, again because his imagination revolted at anything stronger.

Thoreau could be self-consciously earthy and announce that "the poet writes the history of his own body," but no description could be more inapplicable to the poet that Thoreau in fact was. As reported in Emerson's biography of Thoreau, one of Thoreau's friends once said, "I love Henry, but . . . as for taking his arm, I should as soon think of taking the arm of an elm tree." Thoreau wrote that "there is no remedy for love but to love more," but he never married. While he carried Whitman's *Leaves of Grass* around Concord "like a red flag," his response to Whitman's sexuality was decidedly squeamish:

> There are two or three pieces in the book which are disagreeable to say the least; simply sensual. He does not celebrate love at all. It is as if the beasts spoke. I think that men have not been ashamed of themselves without reason.

Thoreau worshiped the sun, its life-giving powers; over and over again in *Walden* he contrasts the clear sunlight with the "smoke of opinion" of misguided men which obscures it from sight, or with the "smoke and steam and hissing" of the railroad train which threatens man's whole relation to the sun. He talks of pouring water on the floor of his unfinished house and letting the sun dry it. The sun in all these connections is a symbol of purification and light. But the sun is also a corrupter, the agent of overripeness, taint, putrefaction.

Therefore, the sun, the fundamental source of all transcendental cor-
respondences between man and nature, was for Thoreau an uneasy
subject. Constantly in *Walden*, when Thoreau is talking about the
sun, one has the feeling that he is about to break through Emerson's
formulation that nature is the present expositor of the divine mind
and confront the fact that nature is not always so reassuringly
disposed. But in the end he does not. He is merely squeamish and
averts his eyes from the full import of the solar correspondence.
Thoreau could triumphantly proclaim that he "dreamed of purity last
night," but he said very little about his nightmares. Only a more
audacious voyager like Melville would be willing to stare into the sun
and then tell all that he saw there.

The closest Thoreau came to facing up to the possible existence
of ambiguity within the virtues he celebrated was in his discussion
of poverty. Throughout *Walden* he glorifies poverty. "By poverty,
i.e., simplicity of life and fewness of incidents, I am solidified and
crystalized, as a vapor or liquid by cold. It is a singular concentration
of strength and energy and flavor." But on the Baker Farm near Walden he discovers John Field, an Irishman, and his family living in a
miserable rented hut. Poverty has not crystallized the Fields; it has
degraded them. The roof of the hut leaks; they are all cold and
miserable. Field works hard and so does his wife, but to no avail; the
family is starving and filthy. Yet for all his recognition of what
poverty has done to them, Thoreau clings to the belief that defiance
is the solution. He tells them they must build a simple house of their
own, cut out tea, coffee, butter, and meat, and then they will all be as
healthy, wealthy, and wise as he is. Melville's story, "Cock-a-
Doodle-Doo!" published the year before *Walden*, both prophesies
and parodies the naïve belief that self-reliance is a solution to the
problem of human want.

In the dramatic structure of *Walden*, "The Ponds" is the central
chapter. Coming in the exact center of the book, it looks back on the
more worldly first half and looks forward to the more seasonal, more
mythological second half. In rejecting both the New Testament and
Poor Richard, Thoreau had said, "We must make shift to live, betwixt spirit and matter, such a human life as we can," and "The

Ponds" maintains an exquisite balance between these two realms of existence. Walden Pond, Thoreau tells us here, has two colors. Viewed at a certain distance on a certain day, the pond is "a clear and deep green well." At other times it is a "matchless and indescribable blue, such as watered or changeable silks and sword blades suggest." Blue and green, the color of the sky and the color of the earth, of this world and the next, Walden Pond brings together the rejected values of the New Testament and Poor Richard in a new synthesis which transforms both.

Both the "earth's eye" and "sky water," the pond is also the supreme object of correspondence between the mind and nature, between the soul and God. So profound is the correspondence that, fishing in the pond one dark night, Thoreau feels that he might almost cast his line upward into the air as downward into the pond. Sounding the bottom of the pond corresponds to sounding the soul, for the pond is "God's Drop." "Heaven," says Thoreau, speaking of Walden, "is under our feet as well as over our heads." For a man to whom self-reliance was a Bible, there was profound meaning in the fact that the pond has no visible inlet or outlet; it maintains itself by an inner energy, its own fresh springs. Unlike the ambiguous sun, the pond is an unmitigated "vision of serenity and purity." It is a great crystal on the surface of the earth, a lake of light. It is very old, older than America; Thoreau remembers having heard that a potter lived on its banks before the Revolution; indeed, it is older than mankind:

> Perhaps on that spring morning when Adam and Eve were driven out of Eden, Walden Pond was already in existence, and even then breaking up in a gentle spring rain accompanied by mist and a southerly wind, and covered with myriads of ducks and geese, which had not heard of the fall, when still such pure lakes sufficed them.

The clean, wild ducks still come to the pond in the course of their migrations, and in the fall the loon comes as always to Walden "to moult and bathe in the pond, making the woods ring with his wild laughter." The loon, with whose moulting Thoreau had already identified himself, is the great embodiment of the spirit of the pond. The loon can soar and swoop in the sky; it can also dive under water all the way to the bottom and swim under water for great distances. Quite the most extraordinary event in *Walden* is the game which Thoreau plays with the loon, watching to see where it will dive and then rowing madly to the place where he anticipates the bird will come up, a magnificent game of tag played through the elements of air and water, lasting for an hour or more, while the bird makes the woods ring with its demoniac laughter. As Thoreau once wrote in his journals, "Not by constraint or severity shall you have access to true wisdom, but by abandonment, and childlike mirthfulness. If you would know aught, be gay before it."

If the pond is old, it is also "perennially young." "It has not acquired one permanent wrinkle after all its ripples." The villagers think of piping its waters into Concord, but Walden's inexhaustibility is proof against such desecration. Although the Fitchburg Railway, that "devilish Iron Horse," muddies the waters with its foot, Walden can absorb the engine's soot, wash out State Street in the bargain, and still retain its purity. The woods around the lake may be cut down, but after a season another forest "is springing up by its shore as lustily as ever." Surely such a pond could never die.

But the great drama of the book is that it does. On the night of December 22, 1845, Walden freezes over. To be sure, the ice looks alternately blue and green, just as the water had; and even in the depths of winter a fisherman can bring up on an anchor from the bottom of the pond a bright green weed, a symbol of life and an object of correspondence: "Methinks my own soul must be a bright invisible green." But the ice-locked pond is dying, nonetheless, and the sequence of four chapters beginning with "House-Warming" records its progressive strangulation. As for Thoreau, he slowly retreats into himself as winter sets in. In "House-Warming" he builds a chimney and plasters his house. When the snow covers the ground, "I withdrew yet farther into my shell and endeavored to keep a bright fire within my house and within my breast." The book becomes more and more elemental. Thoreau's movements outdoors are constricted; fewer animals and birds are seen. The book has been full of sounds, but suddenly a silence falls over everything. "Even the hooting of the owl was hushed." There are fewer visitors than before.

But in his shut-in solitude, Thoreau has at last reached the vital center from which true outward growth can begin. He has cast off his wormy coat and woven for himself "a silken web or chrysalis, and nymph-like shall ere long burst forth a more perfect creature, fitted for a higher society." In the chapter called "Spring" the ritual of renewal reaches its climactic stage and Thoreau's transmutation, his recovery of life, is completed. In the warm sun, the ice on the pond rots; here, for once, rottenness does not run counter to the overall symbolism of the book; rottenness here means not decay but fertility, a fertility out of which death flows back into life; soon the air is filled with the cheerful music of "a thousand tinkling rills and rivulets whose veins are filled with the blood of winter they are bearing off." "The symbol of perpetual youth, the grassblade," is seen again, the sun shines bright and warm, "recreating the world." In May, the loon returns to the pond. "Walden," says Thoreau, "was dead and is alive again." With its rebirth, Thoreau changes "from the lumpish grub in the earth to the airy and fluttering butterfly." Gathering together all the metamorphic symbolism of the book, Thoreau concludes *Walden* with the triumphant fable of the bug:

> Every one has heard the story which has gone the rounds of New England, of a strong and beautiful bug which came out of the dry leaf of an old table of apple-tree wood, which had stood in a farmer's kitchen for sixty years, first in Connecticut, and afterward in Massachusetts,—from an egg deposited in the living tree many years earlier still. . . . Who does not feel his faith in a resurrection and an immortality strengthened by hearing of this?

By his refusal to hurry, by the heroism of his patience and his singleness of purpose and his resolution, Thoreau in *Walden* triumphs over the tyranny of time. A gasping, clock-watching, hurrying America is enslaved by time, but Thoreau, like the Hindu artist Kouroo to whom he compares himself, has made no compromise with time, and therefore time has kept out of his way. Kouroo's resolve had been to create one perfect work of art—a beautiful staff —though it take his entire lifetime, and that had been Thoreau's resolve too. By the time that Kouroo had selected the stick on which to begin his carving, all his friends had grown old and died. Before he had given it proper shape, the dynasty of the Candahars was at an end; by the time he had smoothed and polished the staff, Kalpa was no longer the polestar; ere he had adorned the head with precious stones, Brahma had awoke and slumbered many times. But

> when the finishing stroke was put to his work, it suddenly expanded before the eyes of the astonished artist into the fairest of all the creations of Brahma. He had made a new system in making a staff, a world with full and fair proportions; in which, though the old cities and dynasties had passed away, fairer and more glorious ones had taken their places. And now he saw by the heap of shavings still fresh at his feet, that, for him and his work, the former lapse of time had been an illusion, and that no more time had elapsed than is required for a single scintillation from the brain of Brahma to fall on and inflame the tinder of a mortal brain.

The revisions, the years of meditation and devotion which Thoreau had poured into his great book, made it a veritable staff of Kouroo. Of all the gods with whom Thoreau compared himself, he seems perhaps most like Narcissus. At Walden Pond, he gazed down into the deep green well of the water and stared at his own reflection. He stared long and hard; he looked at no one else. But by that intense concentration on himself, his refusal to write about anyone else but himself, Thoreau transcended himself and wrote about humanity and for other people.

# *2*

# Uncle Tom's Cabin

The shame of American literature is the degree to which our authors of the 1830s and 1840s kept silent during the rising storm of debate on the slavery issue. Bronson Alcott and Henry Thoreau protested against the Mexican War as a conflict undertaken to appease the slavocracy's land hunger, as Lowell had done in the first series of *The Biglow Papers* (1846); Whittier published a number of antislavery poems, and Longfellow followed his lead in *Poems on Slavery* (1842); but the overwhelming majority of the poets and essayists of the day did not even acknowledge the existence of the gravest moral question in the nation's history. The record of our writers of fiction is even sorrier. The devastating loneliness to which the Negro slave was subject might conceivably have furnished Hawthorne with a memorable occasion for dealing with his favorite theme of man's essential isolation. But Hawthorne did not wish to expose his characters to a close comparison with the actual events of real lives; he preferred to stage his dramas of lonely people in a

SOURCE: Reprinted by permission of the publishers from Harriet Beecher Stowe, *Uncle Tom's Cabin,* edited by Kenneth S. Lynn. Cambridge, Mass.: The Belknap Press of Harvard University Press, Copyright, 1962, by the President and Fellows of Harvard College.

theater "a little removed from the highway of ordinary travel." In addition, Hawthorne was a conservative on the race issue; as he himself admitted, he was not interested in the slaves, and he paid no attention to their plight, either in fiction or in life. Washington Irving similarly disdained to concern himself with the realities of contemporary America. Fenimore Cooper's characterization of the Negro never went beyond the clownish stereotype he had worked into *The Spy* (1821). Except for a brief passage in *Mardi* (1849), Melville's demonstration of what slavery meant to the slave is a part of the history of a later decade. If one dismisses Richard Hildreth's *The Slave: or Memoirs of Archy Moore* (1836) and the five or six other antislavery novels that were published in the 1830s and 1840s as being too crudely executed to warrant literary consideration, one has to admit that the only fiction writers in America willing to address themselves to the "peculiar institution" were the plantation romancers who professed to admire it.

Although they were at least honest enough to recognize the presence of the Negro in America, the plantation romancers were nevertheless reluctant to write about the slave *as a person* who had a mind and feelings. Faithful servants are often important characters in Sir Walter Scott's famous romances, but it is significant that his American disciples departed from Scott's example in this respect and kept the Negro very much in the background of their plantation pictures. In the stories of William Alexander Caruthers, John Esten Cooke, and William Gilmore Simms, we often see a Negro holding a stirrup for milady or toting a gun on a hunting trip, but we are given very little notion of the home environment to which the slave returned every evening or of how happy he really was behind his smile. Even John Pendleton Kennedy's *Swallow Barn* (1832), the most detailed—and most charming—account of the "old-time society" in Virginia ever written, focuses on the life of the slave quarters for only a few gingerly pages at the end of the narrative. While the Negro characters in the plantation romances may have names, unlike Scott's "low" characters they are not human beings.

The reason is not far to seek. The plantation romancers sought to glorify the society they described, and they did so by emphasizing what Kennedy called the "good fellowship" of the plantation way of life, "its hearty and constitutional *companionableness*, the thriftless gayety of the people, their dogged but amiable invincibility of opinion, and that overflowing hospitality which knew no ebb." Such an emphasis made for an emotionally compelling argument. It permitted Kennedy and company to say in effect that in contrast to the cutthroat competition of northern commercial life, the typical southern plantation was a social harmony; its members, black as well as white, were all part of one big happy family—and the American family, as even William Lloyd Garrison ought to know, was a sacred institution that was not to be interfered with or even criticized. Yet if the argument was appealing, it was also vulnerable. The ironic fact is that the romancers were employing a familial rhetoric to defend the one American institution which permitted—indeed, encouraged—the total destruction of families. As was not true of slavery in the Caribbean and South America, the family organization of the American Negro slave was completely unprotected by law: black children, no matter how young, could be sold away from their parents, or husbands separated from wives, at the mere whim of their owners. This unique aspect of the American slave system haunted the mind of the white South more than any other and embarrassed the myth-making of the romancers.[1] Instead of being able to portray the domesticity of the slave quarters as an integral part of the Southern idyll, they had to avoid the subject like the plague. Their evasiveness on this

---

[1] We can see it troubling Kennedy very severely in the revised edition of *Swallow Barn*, for example. "I think we are justly liable to reproach," he writes, "for the neglect or omission of our laws to recognize and regulate marriages, and the relation of family amongst negroes. We owe it to humanity and to the sacred obligation of Christian ordinances, to respect and secure the bonds of husband and wife, and parent and child. I am ashamed to acknowledge that I have no answer to make, in the justification of this neglect." J. P. Kennedy, *Swallow Barn; or, A Sojourn in the Old Dominion*, rev. ed. (New York, 1851), p. 459.

score, of course, drastically weakened the case they were attempting to make for the plantation way, but they had no choice. The realities of Negro family life were simply too grim for the romancers to touch.

II

The only group of fiction writers of the 1830s and 1840s one might have expected prima facie to be interested in the tragedy of the Negro family were the sentimental novelists, for these masters (more often, mistresses) of emotional manipulation well knew that there were even more withers to be wrung by depicting the forcible separation of children from their parents than by portraying the seduction of innocent virgins. What was taboo for the plantation romancers had long since been the stock-in-trade of Lydia Sigourney, Hannah F. S. Lee, Timothy Shay Arthur, et al.; broken homes, tearful partings, domestic unhappiness of any sort were their literary specialty. These authors, however, were nothing if not unrealistic, and their books—even those which ostensibly dealt with contemporary social problems like alcoholism and juvenile delinquency—were so patently incredible, so wildly improbable, that they could hardly be accused of having to do with life—let alone life among the lowly. Despite their household settings, these books were escapist fantasies the purpose of which was to enable the reader to forget his (more often, her) humdrum existence. In the exotic characterizations of the sentimental novel the reader found excitement; in its homely scenes, reassuring familiarity; in its lachrymose stories, the divine release of tears. No wonder that the only noncomic Negro type who was allowed to appear in this literature was the inevitably beautiful quadroon girl, sold on the auction block and condemned to a life of marvelously exciting hell, of whom Mrs. E. D. E. N. Southworth had written in *Retribution* (1849)! The sentimental novelists had little use for the sordid realities of slavery.

All the same, when *Uncle Tom's Cabin* swept the nation like a cyclone in 1852, it was rightfully identified as a product of the sentimental tradition. As George Sand said in reviewing the French translation for the Paris newspaper *La Presse*, "this book is essentially domestic and of the family." Uniting reality with fantasy, Mrs. Stowe applied the standard throat-catching examples of domestic infelicity on which the sentimental novelists had battened for years to the one area of American experience where the sorrow could not be overdreamed. Striking to the very heart of the slave's nightmare—and of the white South's guilt—she centered her novel on the helpless instability of the Negro's home life.[2] In so doing she also tapped the richest emotional lode in the history of the American sentimental novel. Thus *Uncle Tom's Cabin* is the greatest tearjerker of them all, but it is a tearjerker with a difference: it did not permit its audience to escape reality. Instead, the novel's sentimentalism continually calls attention to the monstrous actuality which existed under the very noses of its readers. Mrs. Stowe aroused emotions not for emotion's sake alone—as the sentimental novelists notoriously did—but in order to facilitate the moral regeneration of an entire nation. Mrs. Stowe was deeply serious—a sentimentalist with a vengeance—and the clichés she invokes in *Uncle Tom's Cabin* are not an opiate but a goad.

Throughout the book the horror of slavery is brought home to the reader in scenes of domestic anarchy (e.g., the suicide by drowning of the slave woman who has just had her child taken from her forever), while the moral degradation of the loathsome Legree is measured by the broken-down, ill-kept dwelling where he has set up housekeeping with his mulatto mistress—and explained by the fact that as a young man he had not had the moral guidance of a mother! Thus do the most time-hallowed situations of the sentimental tradition give form to a tragic story.

Mrs. Stowe's exploitation of the sentimental conventions was brilliantly conceived and brilliantly executed; yet her use of these conventions is not the heart of her novel's vitality. *Uncle Tom's*

---

[2] Mrs. Stowe's only predecessor in this respect was Richard Hildreth, whose *The Slave: or Memoirs of Archy Moore* was the first work in American literature to be concerned with the sexual irregularities of slave life. But Hildreth by his literary ineptitude botched the theme he had discovered.

*Cabin* is not merely a historical curiosity which sold half a million copies in the United States (and a million in Great Britain) in its first five years, stirred up the North, enraged the South, elicited numerous novelistic "answers" and started, as Lincoln half-jokingly said, the Civil War. It is also an unforgettable piece of American writing, and what makes it so is the penetrating and uncompromising realism of its portrayals of American character. If the plot of the novel and much of its diction derive from the sentimental tradition, only a small percentage of the characters do; for the most part, the dramatis personae of *Uncle Tom's Cabin*—black and white, northern and southern—are shockingly believable, no matter how factitious the dramatic situations may be in which they are placed. Augustine St. Clare, for example, is put through the paces of a deathbed act which may have moved nineteenth-century readers to tears but which strikes us today as hackneyed from beginning to end ("Just before the spirit parted, he opened his eyes, with a sudden light, as of joy and recognition, and said '*Mother!*' and then he was gone!''). The personality of St. Clare, however, is so extraordinarily interesting and so persuasively real that the saccharine phoniness of his final scene simply washes off our memory of him. When we come away from *Uncle Tom's Cabin*, we cannot but recall its most celebrated sentimental scenes—Eliza fleeing across the ice, Uncle Tom and Little Eva talking about Christ, the death of Little Eva, and so on—for these histrionic moments are marvelous specimens of a confectionery art. But what really lives in our minds are the people we have met. Those critics who label *Uncle Tom's Cabin* good propaganda but bad art simply cannot have given sufficient time to the novel to meet its inhabitants. If they should ever linger over it long enough to take in the shrewdness, the energy, the truly Balzacian variousness of Mrs. Stowe's characterizations, they would surely cease to perpetuate one of the most unjust clichés in all of American criticism.

The Negroes in the novel constitute an amazing achievement. To be sure, some of them are comic stereotypes out of the minstrel shows, and one or two come perilously close to the "beautiful quadroon" type, but the majority are human beings, with all the individual differences one finds among the white people in the novel.

The key to Mrs. Stowe's understanding of the Negro personality is her awareness of the destruction that the peculiar institution was wreaking on the slave's humanity. In *Uncle Tom's Cabin* we are shown field hands who are shiftless and house servants who are dishonest, black overseers who are even more brutally tyrannical than the infamous Legree, and mulatto wenches debauched by drink and sex. We are instructed in the human dynamics of punishment: "It is a gradual hardening process on both sides,—the owner growing more and more cruel, as the servant more and more callous. Whipping and abuse are like laudanum; you have to double the dose as the sensibilities decline." And we are made familiar with the infinite ways in which the slaves defied and misled their masters. For all its insight into the slave's emotions, Melville's "Benito Cereno" (1856) spins a far less complex psychological web than does *Uncle Tom's Cabin*. A master analyst of egotism, Melville undoubtedly could have portrayed what Mrs. Stowe calls the "smoldering volcano" of George Harris' pride, which the Negro barely troubles to hide beneath a deadly politeness.[3] Hawthorne, the creator of little Pearl, conceivably could have created Topsy, too, for this diabolically amusing child of slavery, whose every perversity incarnates the guilty conscience of her adult owners, is a veritable black Pearl (what allegorical fancies Hawthorne would have conjured up in the scene where Topsy gives two flowers to Little Eva, one white, the other red!). But no American author before Mrs. Stowe had realized that the comic inefficiency of a Black Sam could constitute a studied insult to the white man's intelligence or comprehended that the unremitting gentleness of Uncle Tom was the most stirring defiance of all. In the age of Martin Luther King, Jr., we can appreciate more fully than before the genius of such comprehension. She had an instinct, too, for the consolations that humor offered to the slave. The backstairs persiflage of the servants in the St. Clare household is at once funny and

[3] Melville's work, however, furnishes no evidence that he shared Mrs. Stowe's startlingly prophetic vision of the proud upsurge of modern Africa, its "mighty republics . . . growing with the rapidity of tropical vegetation," that George Harris voices at the end of the novel.

pathetic, a combination which has since become familiar to us in the Negro humor of a number of later writers, but which has rarely been handled more deftly. Religion was also a consolation in a life of misery, and time and again in the course of *Uncle Tom's Cabin* we hear black voices wailing the old-time spirituals. A Beecher, Mrs. Stowe could not help being an expert on hymnology; by introducing into a work of fiction her sure knowledge of the songs that meant the most to the slaves, she enriched the cultural possibilities of American art.[4]

Although Mrs. Stowe's studies of white character are no more powerful than her Negro portraits, they are more subtly drawn. Marie St. Clare, for example, the neurotic southern lady—insecure, self-pitying, forever complaining that she has a sick headache—is a characterization that compares with Faulkner's Mrs. Compson. Although the New England spinster is one of the recurrent characters in American literature, never has she been "done" with more devastatingly accurate comic effect than Mrs. Stowe's Ophelia. An abolitionist in theory, but more than a little squeamish when it actually comes to touching Topsy's black flesh, Ophelia is a personality whom Mrs. Stowe understands completely—and clearly respects, even though she makes fun of her limitations. For better and for worse, Ophelia is New England clear through, and the scene in which she first descends into the chaos of a plantation kitchen depicts a memorably comic clash of values:

> "Shif'less!" said Miss Ophelia to herself, proceeding to tumble over the drawer, where she found a nutmeg-grater and two or three nutmegs, a Methodist hymn-book, a couple of soiled Madras handkerchiefs, some yarn and knitting-work, a paper of tobacco and a pipe, a few crackers, one or two gilded china-saucers with some pomade in

---

[4] A survey of Methodist hymnals of the period and of contemporary collections of Negro spirituals reveals few of the songs included in the text of *Uncle Tom's Cabin*, a fact which suggests that Mrs. Stowe was familiar with the oral tradition of this music, as well as with its literature.

them, one or two thin old shoes, a piece of flannel carefully pinned up enclosing some small white onions, several damask table-napkins, some coarse crash towels, some twine and darning-needles, and several broken papers, from which sundry sweet herbs were sifting into the drawer.

"Where do you keep your nutmeg, Dinah?" said Miss Ophelia, with the air of one who prayed for patience.

"Most anywhar, Missis; there's some in that cracked teacup, up there, and there's some over in that ar cupboard."

"Here are some in the grater," said Miss Ophelia, holding them up.

"Laws, yes, I put 'em there this morning,—I likes to keep my things handy," said Dinah. "You, Jake! what are you stopping for! You'll cotch it! Be still, thar!" she added, with a dive of her stick at the criminal.

"What's this?" said Miss Ophelia, holding up the saucer of pomade.

"Laws, it's my har *grease*;—I put it thar to have it handy."

In the long nightmare of Mrs. Stowe's anatomy of slavery, Ophelia and Dinah furnish us comic relief; always and inexorably, however, the nightmare returns. At the center of it stands Simon Legree, with his glaring eyes and his fists like iron hammers. What makes him so awful is that he forces us to believe such men once lived in America—and still do. For Legree is far from being a cardboard character in an abolitionist morality. He is, despite his beastliness, a human being. While the lesser demons in the novel lack the complexity of Legree's personality, they are drawn with such vividness they, too, compel us to accept the fact of their existence. Take, for example, the slave trader Haley—"not a cruel man, exactly, but a man of leather"—who knows the price of everything, including the exact market value of Christian belief:

"Some folks don't believe there is pious niggers, Shelby,"
said Haley with a candid flourish of his hand, "but *I do*. I
had a fellow, now, in this yer last lot I took to Orleans—'t
was as good as a meetin, now, really, to hear that critter
pray; and he was quite gentle and quiet like. He fetched me
a good sum, too, for I bought him cheap of a man that was
'bliged to sell out; so I realized six hundred on him. Yes, I
consider religion a valeyable thing in a nigger, when it's the
genuine article, and no mistake."

Such revealing likenesses, when taken all together, present an entire
civilization.

## III

To a later generation of American writers, the realists of the
post-Civil War years, Mrs. Stowe was a heroine. As they looked back
on romantic America, she seemed a prophet crying in a desert. In the
age of Hawthorne and Poe and Cooper, *Uncle Tom's Cabin* was an
amazing phenomenon—a literary freak, a sport. As Henry James
said in *A Small Boy and Others* (1913), "Letters, here, languished
unconscious, and Uncle Tom, instead of making even one of the
cheap short cuts through the medium in which books breathe, even
as fishes in water, went gaily roundabout it altogether, as if a fish, a
wonderful 'leaping' fish, had simply flown through the air." In the
influential opinion of J. W. De Forest, who measured all novelists by
Balzac and whose own best work, *Miss Ravenel's Conversion*
(1867), clearly showed the influence of Balzacian realism, Mrs.
Stowe was just about the only pre-Civil War American writer who
was worth the time of the modern reader. He did not like Cooper; he
said of Brockden Brown and Simms and Paulding that "they wrote
about ghosts, and the ghosts have vanished utterly"; and he
dismissed Hawthorne's books as "characterized by only a vague consciousness of this life. . . . They are what Yankees might come to be
who shut themselves up for life to meditate in old manses. They have

no sympathy with this eager and laborious people, which takes so many newspapers, builds so many railroads, does the most business on a given capital, wages the biggest war in proportion to its population, believes in the physically impossible and does some of it." *Uncle Tom's Cabin*, however, was something else again. It was not perfect, in De Forest's view. Uncle Tom was incredibly good and Little Eva totally unreal. But, De Forest said, we have known northerners like this, "and we have seen such Southerners, no matter what the people south of Mason and Dixon's line may protest." The strength of the book, in sum, lay in its realism, in what De Forest called its "picture of American life, drawn with a few strong and passionate strokes, not filled in thoroughly, but still a portrait." As of the year 1868, he felt that no other native novel had painted American life "so broadly, truly and sympathetically."[5]

Thus in an era when American literature was still romantic and the great Balzac had a significant following only among the young and the unpublished, Mrs. Stowe had produced a work that throbbed with the spirit of realism. Instead of depicting nature and the self, she had portrayed character and society. How was it possible that she had accomplished this? It is breathtaking enough to realize that an inexperienced writer, the author of a modest volume of stories and sketches entitled *The Mayflower* (1843), could bring to the sentimental novel such an unprecedented seriousness of purpose as to turn an escapist genre into an instrument of social upheaval. By the early 1850s, the greatest geniuses of American writing, Hawthorne and Melville, were taking drastic liberties with the formulas of the romance; *Uncle Tom's Cabin*, at its vital best, simply transcended them. What was the force that propelled her to such creative audacity?

Certainly her background in literature does not prophesy *Uncle Tom's Cabin*. As a child, she was allowed to read Scott's Waverley romances—one summer she read *Ivanhoe* seven times—and some of Byron's poetry. Later she read Madame de Staël's *Corinne* and a

[5] Quoted in J. W. De Forest, *Honest John Vane*, with an introduction by Joseph Jay Rubin (State College, Pa., 1960), pp. 27-28.

few works by George Sand, but except for her familiarity with the eighteenth-century English novelists her acquaintance with the world of fiction was neither wide nor deep. She seems not to have read any of the masterworks of European realism, and it is not likely that she knew anyone who had. In the home of Lyman Beecher, novels—especially French novels—were not deemed an enlightening topic for discussion. At the meetings of the Semi-Colon Club, the literary society in Cincinnati, Ohio, to which for a time Harriet belonged, the dominant voices were those of Dr. Daniel Drake, the founder of the society and the author of that remarkable literary manifesto, *Discourse on the History, Character, and Prospects of the West* (1834), which called on American writers to take pride in the sublimity of the western forest and the splendors of democratic oratory; and of Judge James Hall, whose *Legends of the West* (1832) had carried the conventions of Irving, Cooper, and Scott across the Alleghenies. The only literary lady capable of making herself heard above the romantic rodomontade of the men was Mrs. Caroline Lee Hentz, a shameless sentimentalist, who in the fullness of time would come to devote her little talent to composing oozy novels in defense of slavery. ("It is true they were slaves," she would write, "but their chains never clanked. Each separate link was kept moist and bright with the oil of kindness.")[6] As for Dr. Calvin Stowe, the seminary professor whom Harriet married in 1836, he announced that he had faith in his wife's writing, but this was an expression of love, not of literary judgment, for Dr. Stowe's interest in reading fiction was scarcely keener than Lyman Beecher's.

Nor does her personal experience do very much to account for the novel. In Litchfield, Connecticut, where she was born in 1811 and grew up, Negroes were a rarity. The South was very far away. What little the young Harriet knew about the moral anarchy of slavery came from an aunt who had married an English settler in Jamaica only to discover that he had a Negro mistress and a family of dark-skinned children. Then in 1832 Harriet's father, the most

[6] Quoted in Helen Waite Papashvily, *All the Happy Endings* (New York, 1956), p. 83.

vigorous Congregational preacher of his day, heeded a call to save the west for Calvinism and moved his family to Cincinnati, where he assumed the presidency of the Lane Theological Seminary. Here, on the north bank of the Ohio River, fugitive slaves from Kentucky could occasionally be seen, and Harriet heard some of them tell of the life they had escaped. She herself once visited for a few days in Kentucky, although she did not stay at a plantation. Her brother Charles, on the other hand, spent a considerable period of time in New Orleans, and upon his return told Harriet of his experiences, including the gruesome story of the overseer with a fist like an oak burl who boasted, "I got that knockin' down niggers." Mainly she learned about slavery from books such as *The Life of Josiah Henson, Formerly a Slave* (1849), *Narrative of the Life of Frederick Douglass, An American Slave* (1845), and above all from Theodore Weld's *American Slavery as It Is: Testimony of a Thousand Witnesses* (1839). Weld was a fervent abolitionist, active in the Cincinnati area, and associated for a time with Lane Theological. Despite the fact that Weld eventually decamped from Lane and went to Oberlin, taking with him some of her father's most promising students, Mrs. Stowe admired him. For the most part, *American Slavery as It Is* consists of advertisements of runaway slaves and other relevant documents Weld had copied from southern newspapers on file in a New York library, yet so effectively were they put together that the book had the impact on its readers of an eyewitness account. Dickens drew heavily on Weld's book for his *American Notes* (1842), and it made a deep impression on Mrs. Stowe. She informed Weld's wife, the Quaker reformer Angelina Grimké, that she "kept this book in her work basket by day and slept with it under her pillow by night, till its facts crystallized into Uncle Tom's Cabin." In Mrs. Stowe's *Key to Uncle Tom's Cabin* (1853) Weld's book is repeatedly referred to. The "personal experience" of slavery which seems to have meant the most to her was a literary experience.

Undoubtedly the realism of Weld's newspaper clippings has something to do with the realism of *Uncle Tom's Cabin*. But a novel is a work of the imagination, after all, not a mere transcript of a researcher's notes; the true key to *Uncle Tom's Cabin* lies in the quality of mind that imagined it, not in the chrestomathy of facts and figures Mrs. Stowe published in 1853 by way of proving she had simply written "the truth." As if she herself knew that her *Key* did not get to the heart of the mystery of *Uncle Tom's Cabin,* she wrote an "Author's Introduction" for the 1878 edition of the novel which attempted a more personal accounting: "The first part of the book ever committed to writing was the death of Uncle Tom. This scene presented itself almost as a tangible vision to her mind while sitting at the communion-table in the little church of Brunswick [the Maine town to which the Stowes had moved in 1850, when Calvin Stowe was appointed to a professorship at Bowdoin College]. She was perfectly overcome by it, and could scarcely restrain the convulsion of tears and sobbings that shook her frame. She hastened home and wrote it, and her husband being away she read it to her two sons of ten and twelve years of age." In still later life she became fond of saying, much as Julia Ward Howe did when questioned about "The Battle Hymn of the Republic," that "The Lord Himself wrote it. I was but an instrument in His hand." If we are to believe Mrs. Stowe, *Uncle Tom's Cabin* was the product of a mystical communion with God.

These statements, however, are as vague as they are sensational. By themselves they explain nothing. Even if we assume that God was indeed her muse, the question still remains, why was her muse a realist? Like the facts of her literary background and of her personal acquaintance with slavery, Mrs. Stowe's religious interpretation fails to explain the achievement which amazed Henry James and impressed De Forest. Yet her interpretation is not altogether useless, inasmuch as it serves to remind us of how important a part of Mrs. Stowe's life was the problem of religious faith. In so doing, it brings us to the impulse that made her, all precociously, the first realistic novelist of any significance in American literature. For the revolutionary literary mode of *Uncle Tom's Cabin* originated in a religious rebellion—in Harriet Beecher Stowe's rejection, on the grounds that it was an intolerable doctrine, of Lyman Beecher's Calvinism.

## IV

In the transition from anti-Calvinism to antiromanticism, the crucial figure was Lord Byron. To Mrs. Stowe, Byron was the most striking man of the nineteenth century. Everything about him fascinated her. As previously noted, she knew his poetry from childhood and she remained fond of it in maturity. His death affected Harriet Beecher as deeply as a personal loss; when she heard the news, she fled into the fields surrounding the Beechers' Litchfield home, wept copious tears, and prayed for the poet's soul. The year after *Uncle Tom's Cabin* was published, she became the friend of Lady Byron, who soon told Mrs. Stowe the full story of Byron's allegedly incestuous relationship with his half-sister Augusta, a relationship which supposedly had continued even after his marriage to Lady Byron. This story, too, agitated Mrs. Stowe to the depths of her being. When Lady Byron's death in 1860 breathed new life into discussion of the marriage, Mrs. Stowe was horrified to find that Lady Byron was being crucified in the press as the villain of the affair. In 1869, unable to hold back her feelings any longer, Mrs. Stowe wrote "The True Story of Lady Byron's Life" for the September issue of the *Atlantic Monthly*, and the following year published a book on the subject, self-descriptively entitled *Lady Byron Vindicated*, which created almost as much of a furor as had *Uncle Tom's Cabin*. Mrs. Stowe simply could not get Byron out of her system. He had the power, even from beyond the grave, to make her care for him very much, although she profoundly disapproved of him. He was talented, and appallingly self-centered; uncommonly attractive and uncommonly immoral. Harriet Beecher and her father would come to disagree about many things, but his response to the news that Byron was dead sums up the mixed feelings of admiration and regret which forever marked her own attitude: "Oh, I'm sorry that Byron is dead. I did hope he would live to do something for Christ. What a harp he might have swept!"

In *Uncle Tom's Cabin*, her ambivalent feelings about Byron are expressed in the person of the most interesting character in the book, the southern aristocrat Augustine St. Clare. With his electrify-

ing entrance toward the close of the river-boat sequence, the pace of
the whole novel quickens with a new excitement. Handsome, sar-
donic, his eyes "clear, bold, and bright" but his "beautifully cut
mouth" perpetually curved in a "proud and somewhat sarcastic expression," St. Clare is a domesticated version of the Byronic hero.
Though realistically portrayed, he is the very image of romantic genius—and despair. For if St. Clare talks marvelously well, what he
expresses is his corrosive sense of guilt at being a slave owner. With a
loquacity that anticipates the monologues of Faulkner's southern
gentlemen, St. Clare speaks of oncoming disasters, of an America
due to explode with volcanic violence, of a heedless world plunging
toward the day of wrath. At the same time, St. Clare will not lift a
finger to save either himself or his society. He is a Hamlet whose
mocking words never lead to action. Even though he obviously fails
to meet Mrs. Stowe's moral standards, she nevertheless views him
with great sympathy. He is not a monster but a man suffering from a
sickness of the spirit; in fact, despite his cynicism, this man named
Augustine St. Clare makes at least one confession which reveals that
he has a soul rather like St. Augustine's:

> "My mother used to tell me of a millennium that was com-
> ing, when Christ should reign, and all men should be free
> and happy. And she taught me, when I was a boy, to pray,
> 'Thy kingdom come'. . . ."
> "Augustine, sometimes I think you are not far from the
> kingdom," said Miss Ophelia, laying down her knitting,
> and looking anxiously at her cousin.
> "Thank you for your good opinion; but it's up and down
> with me,—up to heaven's gate in theory, down in earth's
> dust in practice."

Throughout the book, his potential saintliness is defined by that in-
fallible indication of goodness in the sentimental novel, his love for
his dead mother, and by his susceptibility to the religion of
love—which was the religion of his mother, and of many other
American mothers, as Mrs. Stowe is at pains to emphasize. To St.

Clare, his mother and Christianity are one and the same. He cannot believe, for example, that the Bible justifies slavery because the Bible "was my *mother's* book," and he speaks tenderly of the New Testament because his mother personified it. Nevertheless St. Clare is unable to make his mother's faith his own, despite his worship of her memory. He is ridden by a dream of how men ought to behave and cannot accept a religion based on the forgiveness of sins. Wasting his life on scornful talk, he goes to his death an unhappy, irresolute, doubt-haunted man.

In Mrs. Stowe's subsequent novels, most notably *The Minister's Wooing* (1859) and *Oldtown Folks* (1869), a split personality continues to be the mark of the romantic spirit. And in these later novels the force revealed as driving the Byronic hero into war with himself is Calvinism. Romanticism, as Mrs. Stowe never tired of saying, was the child of Puritanism. Inasmuch as Byron himself had been brought up a Calvinist, his career was thus a paradigm of American cultural history.

Harriet Beecher, of course, was also a child of Puritanism, but at the age of sixteen she found that she was unregenerate—a discovery which, in Lyman Beecher's household, had to be repressed. It was far easier to lie awake at night, "crying and groaning till midnight and wishing she could die young," than to inform her father that she was not among the elect. Try as she would, she could not overcome her revulsion against the rigors of Calvinist doctrine; for all its magnificence, the system was inhumanly harsh. As the years passed, her doubts increased, especially following the death by drowning of young Professor Fisher of Yale, the fiancé of Harriet's older sister Catherine. Because Fisher had died before his conversion, Lyman Beecher believed him doomed to eternal punishment. Catherine refused to accept this judgment on her lover, and her subsequent announcement that she could no longer tolerate her father's religion encouraged Harriet's insurgency. In *Uncle Tom's Cabin* Harriet's private quarrel with Lyman Beecher's God was laid out for all the world to see, although the final break did not come until 1857, when her eldest son was drowned and she was confronted, as her sister had been, with the Calvinist judgment that a loved one was inevitably damned. At that point her disillusionment with Calvinism became bitterly explicit.

With that final break came the mightiest release of imaginative energy she was ever to experience. Beginning almost at once, she poured forth in the course of the next twenty years a multivolume, fictional study of the New England mind that constitutes a major document in the intellectual history of America. Inevitably, her principal emphasis fell on religion and theology, but in the first two volumes of her history, *The Minister's Wooing* and *Oldtown Folks*, she followed the doctrinal complexities of Puritanism through their secular transmogrification into romanticism as well. Thus it is called to our attention that Aaron Burr, who appears as a character in the first book, is the grandson of Jonathan Edwards—which in point of historical fact Burr was. While Ellery Davenport, in the second book, is purely a fictional character, he, too, is given an Edwardsian lineage, and both Burr and Davenport are Byronic heroes. Like Augustine St. Clare, who spent his childhood in his cousin Ophelia's house, they have been bred in New England Calvinist environments, only to rebel against their upbringing. That upbringing nevertheless left its legacy. In a particularly brilliant passage in *Oldtown Folks* Mrs. Stowe analyzed how the magnificent austerities of the New England theology had "the power of lacerating the nerves of the soul, and producing strange states of morbid horror and repulsion." Calvinism could leave a person who rebelled against it secretly uncertain that he might not be opposing truth and virtue itself, and thereby produce in him that same combination of arrogance and self-hatred, as well as the despairing eloquence, which she had already portrayed so memorably in the character of Augustine St. Clare:

> Ellery Davenport was at war with himself, at war with the traditions of his ancestry, and had the feeling that he was regarded in the Puritan community as an apostate; but he took a perverse pleasure in making his position good by a brilliancy of wit and grace of manner which few could resist; and, truth to say, his success, even with the more rigid, justified his self-confidence. As during these days

there were very few young persons who made any profession of religion at all, the latitude of expression which he allowed himself on these subjects was looked upon as a sort of spiritual sowing of wild oats. Heads would be gravely shaken over him. One and another would say, "Ah! that Edwards blood is smart; it runs pretty wild in youth, but the Lord's time may come by and by''; and I doubt not that my grandmother that very night, before she slept, wrestled with God in prayer for his soul with all the enthusiasm of a Monica for a St. Augustine.

If the Calvinistic causes of romantic sickness are insisted on in Ellery Davenport's case, whereas they are only hinted at in Augustine St. Clare's, that is because at the time of writing *Uncle Tom's Cabin* Mrs. Stowe's rejection of Jonathan Edwards'—and Lyman Beecher's—theology had not reached its final crisis. Ellery Davenport also degenerates into a figure of evil, as St. Clare never does, for reasons which have to do with Lady Byron's revelations and the continuing failure of romantic America to meet the moral challenge of the slavery issue. Despite these differences, Ellery Davenport and Augustine St. Clare are clearly the same character: each, like Byron, might have swept a harp for Christ; each was a St. Augustine *manqué*, haunted by ideals he could not bring himself to live by. It is also clear that in studying the romantic agony of men who were reacting against what she called "the merciless terms of denunciation" in Edwardsian sermons Mrs. Stowe was not merely conducting an objective examination of American cultural development. She was also studying herself—for did not she, too, run the risk of becoming infected by the Byronic hero's bitterness against the churches of Christ in consequence of her own recoil from those very same sermons? The romantic personality was an object lesson to all Americans who would deny the religion of their youth.

V

Romanticism was not the only road, however, for those who had turned away from the New England theology. There was the road that Augustine St. Clare had not taken, but which his mother had, and Little Eva, and Uncle Tom: the New Testament way of love. "I sent for you all, my dear friends," says Little Eva on her deathbed,

> because I love you. I love you all; and I have something to
> say to you, which I want you always to remember. . . . I
> want to speak to you about your souls. . . . Many of you, I
> am afraid, are very careless. You are thinking only about
> this world. I want you to remember that there is a beautiful
> world, where Jesus is. I am going there, and you can go
> there. It is for you, as much as me.

If the religion of love was a simple doctrine, especially when compared to Calvinism, Mrs. Stowe affirmed in *Oldtown Folks* that the whole of Jonathan Edwards' *Treatise on True Virtue* "falls to dust before the one simple declaration of Jesus Christ that, in the eyes of Heaven, one lost sheep is more prized than all the ninety and nine that went not astray. . . ." The deliverance of romantic America from the bondage of morbid introspection which it had inherited from Calvinism could be accomplished, like the freeing of its slaves, only through what she termed "that greatest and holiest of all the natural sacraments and means of grace,—LOVE."

Now whatever one may think of the religion of love as a faith or as a social policy, its literary implications were rich. In rejecting romanticism as a sickness of the ego, Mrs. Stowe had naturally turned her back on the romantics' literary concern with the self. This left her with the problem of finding an alternative means of organizing and focusing a work of fiction. In embracing the religion of love she found it. The moral heart of *Uncle Tom's Cabin* is located not in the tortured, Augustinian calculus of a lonely hero, but in a community of love centering on the family——its perspective is social.

Just as scenes of domestic anarchy take the measure of slavery's evil,
so scenes of domestic bliss provide the yardstick for that measure-
ment. Thus we pass immediately from the suicide of the grief-
stricken Negro mother who has lost her child to the chapter entitled
"The Quaker Settlement," which begins with the following description:

> A quiet scene now rises before us. A large, roomy, neatly-
> painted kitchen, its yellow floor glossy and smooth, and
> without a particle of dust; a neat, well-blacked cooking-
> stove; rows of shining tin, suggestive of unmentionable
> good things to the appetite; glossy green wood chairs, old
> and firm; a small flag-bottomed rocking-chair, . . . and in
> the chair, gently swaying back and forward, her eyes bent
> on some fine sewing, sat our old friend Eliza. . . . By her
> side sat a woman with a bright tin pan in her lap, into
> which she was carefully sorting some dried peaches.

Similar descriptions, it is true, could be found in dozens of sentimental novels of the antebellum period, and the plantation romancers, after all, had been defending the South for years by depicting it
as a family. The verisimilitude of the sentimental novel, however,
lacked both the solidity of specification and the panoramic sweep of
Mrs. Stowe's portraiture, while the plantation romancers could never
have thrown the searching moral spotlight on southern families—not
even on white families—that Mrs. Stowe did. What Mrs. Stowe justly
termed the *"living dramatic reality"* of *Uncle Tom's Cabin* had
behind it an author who took an unprecedented interest, a well-nigh
insatiable interest, in the homely facts of American life. A religious
urgency made for her interest. Domestic details were not just details—they had a philosophic meaning; her human comedy was a
new myth by which America might live. Mrs. Stowe organized and
interpreted the comprehensive experience of a vast variety of people
in terms of their home lives, as the title of her masterpiece perhaps
implied it would do, because the American home, whether a mansion
or a cabin, was the altar of the religion of love, where one either

served Christ by serving others or desecrated Him and was judged accordingly. "Woman's nature," Mrs. Stowe would write in *Oldtown Folks*, had "never been consulted in theology. Theologic systems, as to the expression of their great body of ideas, have, as yet, been the work of man alone. They have had their origin, as in St. Augustine, with men who were utterly ignorant of moral and intellectual companionship with woman. . . ." But now it was just possible that woman's nature *was* to be an influence in theological matters. If American literature looked at life realistically, then the national spirit might become gentler, more socially concerned, more feminine, more truly Christian. With *Uncle Tom's Cabin*, the first and greatest of her epistles, Lyman Beecher's daughter launched the task of converting a whole people to her vision.

Oddly enough, she made her main character a man. Uncle Tom has all the feminine virtues, however, that Mrs. Stowe wished to celebrate—gentleness, patience, understanding, devotion to his family, and a taste for religious reading that is "confined entirely to the New Testament." At the same time, he is nothing like the servile, fawning creature of the Uncle Tom plays and the Tom Shows that became popular in the United States during the latter half of the nineteenth century and that are largely responsible for making his name synonymous in twentieth-century America with bootlicking cowardice. Mrs. Stowe's protagonist stands for a set of values he is determined to live by, even if doing so costs him his life. Like Mary Scudder in *The Minister's Wooing* and all the sweet but resolute young women of Mrs. Stowe's later novels; like Sarah Orne Jewett's Mrs. Todd and Willia Cather's Antonia, the best-known heroines of the two writers who have most consciously carried forward Mrs. Stowe's concern for feminine values; like Faulkner's Dilsey, standing indomitable amidst the doom of the Compson family, Uncle Tom never surrenders to the juggernaut of circumstance. If his serene endurance at times taxes our belief, it nevertheless continues to challenge an anxious and insecure civilization.

# *3*

# Huckleberry Finn

By his own account, Mark Twain's career as a writer began on the fateful day when a young printer's apprentice named Sam Clemens read a page torn out of a book that he had found lying in the dust of a Hannibal street and for the first time understood what a power there was in words. The story is charming, and may even be true, although it is perhaps wise to remember that as compensation for our lack of a literary tradition American writers have always tended to enlarge their own personalities into archetypes, and that as a self-mythologizer Mark Twain ranks with Benjamin Franklin, Edgar Poe, and Ernest Hemingway. However, what is significant about the anecdote is not its veracity, but the fact that the page which Twain said changed the whole course of his life was a description of Joan of Arc in the cage at Rouen. Twain is by no means the only comic writer of modern times who has found the Maid a compelling figure, yet there was a special urgency about Twain's fascination with Joan's captivity not to be found in Shaw's or Anouilh's interest in this aspect of her career. The image of an abandoned youngster, locked up and forgotten, haunted Twain's imagination from childhood to death; by

Source: "Huck and Jim," *The Yale Review* (XLVII, Spring, 1958), copyright Yale University Press.

saying that the description of Joan in the cage made him a writer, Twain offers us one of the master keys to his life and work.

The fantasy of being locked up and forgotten was deeply rooted in Twain's experience of growing up in the Clemens household. Although Twain's mother was warmhearted, the family atmosphere was dominated by the personality of his father. Thanks to this strange, austere, loveless man, the Clemenses were reserved and formal with one another at all times; at night, they shook hands before going to bed—a warmer gesture would have been unthinkable; indeed, Twain could only remember one occasion (the death of one of his brothers) when a kiss was ever exchanged between members of his family. The story that Mrs. Clemens married her husband out of spite and was not in love with him has never been satisfactorily verified, but there is no doubt as to the nature of the relationship between father and sons. Twain spoke for his brothers as well as himself when he wrote, "My father and I were always on the most distant terms when I was a boy—a sort of armed neutrality, so to speak."

In such an atmosphere, Twain must have suffered almost daily from rejection, but the instance that seemed to him to epitomize all his experiences of neglect was the time when his family, moving from Florida, Missouri, to a new home in Hannibal, drove off without him. Writing an article in later years for the *North American Review*, Twain could still remember the "grisly deep silence" that fell upon the locked house after his family had gone, and the terrible darkness that descended as the afternoon waned into evening. As the late Dixon Wecter has pointed out, the story is engrossing, but untrue, for Twain was here describing as a personal experience something that in fact had happened to his older brother Orion. So acute, apparently, was Twain's sense of rejection and of isolation from his father that in looking back on his early life he was convinced that it was surely he who had suffered the agony of being locked up and forgotten.

The loneliness of Twain's childhood is reflected everywhere in his work. As has often been observed, loneliness is the peculiar quality of a great deal of American writing and comes out in many forms—one thinks of Melville's renegades and castaways, the solitary men in the stories of Hawthorne and Poe, the sense of "otherness" in Henry James and Henry Adams—but in Twain, loneliness almost without exception takes the form of alienation from the family. In *The Innocents Abroad* Twain describes himself as a "helpless orphan"; Tom Sawyer has lost his father and mother; the prince and the pauper, like the protagonists of *Huckleberry Finn* and *Joan of Arc*, are runaways; the "aristocratic" Tom Driscoll in *Pudd'nhead Wilson* makes the nightmarish discovery that his real mother is a Negro mammy. And for all these orphans and runaways there exists the horror of incarceration. The solitary confinement cells in the Chateau d'If have a fearful fascination for the narrator of *The Innocents Abroad* (indeed, in all of his travel books, prisons, dungeons, tombs, and catacombs are the sights that Twain is most powerfully attracted to); death in a cave lies in wait for Tom Sawyer and for the boys in *A Connecticut Yankee*; Huck's equivalent of Joan's cage is the cabin in the woods where his Pap locks him in while he goes off for days at a time. With the possible exception of Poe's fantasies of being buried alive, there is no other corpus of American writing that reverts so often as does Twain's work to the nightmare of being utterly cut off.

But the obverse of the nightmare of being locked up and forgotten is the dream of release and recognition, of power and glory. Henry James considered that only primitive persons could be interested in Twain, but James' belief in the supremacy of the artist has a great counterpart in Twain's conception of the role of the humorist. The nihilistic vision of *The Mysterious Stranger* is perhaps a strange place to look for affirmations, but that book was for Twain what *The Tempest* was for Shakespeare—a valedictory—and the Stranger is as bold as Prospero in asserting the glory of his creator's life. The human race, says the Stranger, for all its grotesqueries and absurdities and shams, has one really effective weapon—laughter. "Power, money, persuasion, supplication, persecution—these can lift at a colossal humbug—push it a little—weaken it a little, century by century; but only laughter can blow it to rags and atoms at a blast. Against the assault of laughter nothing can stand." For Twain, the humorist was above all else a moralist, in whose hands the ultimate weapon of laughter might conceivably become the means of liberating mankind from its enslavement to false ideals.

Over and over again in his work, Twain plays with fantasies of power that express the scope of his ambition. In *Life on the Mississippi*, he apotheosizes Mr. Bixby, the pilot who reigns over the titanic river that had conquered even La Salle. The hero of *A Connecticut Yankee* doesn't amount to much in nineteenth-century America, but in the world of King Arthur he becomes "the Boss." The pauper from Offal Court becomes the heir to the English throne. Like Poe's Dupin, the detective heroes of *Pudd'nhead Wilson* and *Tom Sawyer, Detective* are the indispensable agents of social justice. Richard Watson Gilder might assure the readers of the "Century" that Twain was not a "giber at religion or morality"; Howells might call him "a humorist who never makes you blush to have enjoyed his joke . . . [and] whose fun is never at the cost of anything honestly high or good"; all America might regard him as a funny man; but for Twain, the humorist was not only a giber, but a destroyer, a Jeremiah preaching the corruption of the state. When he described his books as "sermons," America took it as just another joke—his agnosticism, after all, was notorious—but Twain was in dead earnest. (Perhaps the people who best understood him were not his admirers and friends, but the librarians who banned his books as subversive.) Like Joan of Arc, Twain dreamed of purging society of its pettiness in order that it might become great, and if in the end it was safer to burn Joan, it was manifestly more convenient to regard Twain as a joker who never made fun of anything high or good. Given what society did to him, it is no wonder that the most memorable of Twain's fantasies of power are also prophecies of tragedy and defeat.

Today we lament Twain's taste when he asserted that *Joan of Arc* was his favorite of all the books he wrote. Yet by now it should be as easy to understand this judgment as it is to comprehend why he should wish to have it believed that reading about her was the turning-point of his career. For in a sense, Twain spent his lifetime writing about Joan; the tension between the nightmare of being locked up and forgotten and the dream of liberation is in all his best work. The most exquisitely poised expression of this tension is, of course, *Huckleberry Finn*. If Twain never fully recognized the book's greatness, we nevertheless have him to thank for knowing that we should call it a sermon.

The first episode from *Huckleberry Finn* to appear in print was the chapter about Huck and the raftsmen that Twain casually excised from the still-uncompleted novel and threw—as he phrased it—into *Life on the Mississippi*. The purpose of the transposition was to illustrate "keelboat talk and manners" as they had existed in the 1840s, but Twain could hardly have chosen a more significant chapter for introducing what he liked to call "Huck Finn's Autobiography" to the world, because in his prodigally wasteful American way, Twain improved a good book at the cost of looting his masterpiece of an episode of extraordinary richness, of great beauty and humor, which sets forth in a parable the two major themes of the novel.

The chapter begins immediately after Huck and Jim's terrifying experience of getting lost in the fog. Drifting down an unfamiliar and "monstrous big river," the boy and the Negro decide that Huck should find out where they are by swimming over to a huge raft they have seen in the distance and gathering the information by eavesdropping. Under cover of darkness, Huck reaches the raft, climbs on board without being noticed, and settles down to listen to the talk of the raftsmen, to their colossal boasting, their roaring songs, and above all, to the fantastic tall tale about a man named Dick Allbright and the mysterious barrel that followed him on the river wherever he went rafting, bringing terror and death to his companions. Nothing, the teller of the tale assures his audience, could keep the barrel off Dick Allbright's trail or mitigate its inexorable fatality, until finally a raft captain swam out to the barrel and hauled it aboard. Inside its wooden walls, the captain and his men found a stark-naked baby—"Dick Allbright's baby; he owned up and said so. 'Yes,' he says, a-leaning over it, 'yes, it is my own lamented darling, my poor lost Charles William Allbright deceased,' says he—for he could curl his tongue around the bulliest words in the language when he was a mind to. . . . Yes, he said, he used to live up at the head of this bend, and one night he choked his child, which was crying, not intending to kill it—which was prob'ly a lie—and then he was scared, and buried it in a bar'l, before his wife got home, and off he went, and struck the northern trail and went to rafting; and this was the third year that the bar'l had chased him.''

Crouched in the darkness, naked and afraid, Huck seems utterly apart from these coarse, rough men, but the fantasy of violence and terror which the raftsman has spun for the scoffing delight of his fellows nevertheless vitally involves· the runaway boy, for the story tells, after all, of a man who locked up his son and of a naked child floating down the river in search of its father. That Huck has escaped to his fabulous voyage by making his Pap think he has been murdered only completes his identification with the dead baby who was somehow "reborn" in the river, an identification which he makes explicit when, suddenly seized from his hiding place and surrounded by strange men demanding to know his name, Huck jokingly replies, "Charles William Allbright, sir." Always in Twain the best jokes reveal the profoundest connections, and with the release of laughter triggered by Huck's superbly timed joke, the chapter not only reaches its humorous climax, but we are suddenly made aware that through Huck we have been eavesdropping on a parable of the search for the father and of death by violence and rebirth by water which takes us to the very heart of the novel.

Yet even this awareness does not exhaust the richness of the riverman's story. The symbolic connection between Huck Finn and the tall tale beautifully exemplifies how Mark Twain could exploit for the purposes of high art the tradition of southwestern humor; but it also reveals that behind the novel there stands the Bible. A baby in a barrel afloat on a great, continental river: beyond a raftsman's fantasy we discern the infant Moses in the ark of bulrushes hidden in the Nile. Through that association we can understand that Twain was doing a great deal more than simply setting up a magnificent joke when he began *Huckleberry Finn* with a chapter entitled "I Discover Moses and the Bulrushers," for although Huck soon loses all interest in Moses, "because I don't take no stock in dead people," the humorous introduction of the biblical story effectively announces the somber theme of death and rebirth, with its attendant implications of slavery and freedom, and inextricably associates Huck with the Mosaic saga of an infant who ''died'' and was reborn in the river and who grew up to lead an enslaved people to freedom.

The Moses theme unfolds in a series of initiations. A new life, a fresh start, is constantly being attempted by Huck; in the course of his journey down the river, he assumes a dazzling variety of roles, becoming by turns George Peters, George Jackson, a young girl, an English valet, and, finally, Tom Sawyer. But just as Pap's spiritual rebirth culminates in a quite literal fall from grace (dead drunk, off a porch roof), so Huck's initiations run a cycle from birth to death. His ''new life'' at the Widow's terminates with his simulated murder in the cabin where Pap has locked him up; his identity as George Jackson is concluded by the blood bath at the Grangerford's; his masquerade as an English valet is abandoned in a graveyard. The same cyclical movement marks the drama of liberation. From the time that Tom and Huck tie up Jim ''for fun'' at the beginning of the novel until they make a game out of liberating him from the cabin on the Phelpses' farm at the very end of the book, Jim moves in and out of one bondage after another. But these sine wave movements from birth to death and from freedom to slavery that give the novel its characteristic rhythm take place within the framework of a larger movement that carries Huck and Jim simultaneously toward triumph and tragedy. When Moses led the Israelites to freedom, he also moved toward his prophesied appointment with death; the great paradox of *Huckleberry Finn* is that Huck and Jim's voyage toward freedom takes them due south into the very heart of the slave country and that the triumphant liberation of Jim inexorably enforces the tragic separation of the boy and the Negro. As W. H. Auden has observed, the final meaning of *Huckleberry Finn* is that freedom and love are incompatible, which is another way of saying that the liberation theme and the search for the father theme are tragically at odds.

The search theme is officially introduced when Judge Thatcher and the Widow Douglas go to court to get permission to take Huck away from his Pap. Who should be his parents—the respectable aristocrats who are no blood relation to Huck or his violent, drunken father? Nothing less than a human life is at stake; the decision would

seem to call for the wisdom of Solomon. Echoing Huck's judgment of
Moses, Nigger Jim "doan' take no stock" in the wisdom of Solomon,
yet in the chapter entitled "Was Solomon Wise?" our laughter at
Jim's stupidity carries with it the realization that the search theme also has a connection with the Bible. Jim regards it as utter foolishness
that Solomon should have attempted to settle the parenthood dispute
by offering to cut the child in two—"De 'spute warn't 'bout half a
chile, de'spute was 'bout a whole chile; en de man dat think he kin
settle a 'spute 'bout a whole chile wid a half a chile doan' know
enough to come in out'n de rain." As well as being marvelously funny, the speech throws into biblical perspective the entire problem of
parenthood with which the novel is concerned.

Like Solomon, Huck listens for the voice of truth and the ac-
cents of love as a means of identifying the true parent he seeks, but
neither side in the legal contest so identifies itself, and therefore
when Huck escapes to the river he is fleeing, as Twain once pointed
out, both a "persecuting good widow" and his "persecuting father."
Encountering Jim, Huck is at first amused and exasperated by the
black man's ignorance, but part of the great drama of their relationship is Huck's gathering awareness that Jim is always right about all
the things that really matter—about how certain movements of the
birds mean a storm is coming, about the dangers of messing with
snakes, and the meaning of dreams. But if Jim's relationship to Huck
is fatherly in the sense that he constantly is correcting and admon-
ishing the boy, forever telling him some new truth about the world, he
is identified even more unmistakably as Huck's father by the love
that he gives him. Just as Huck is searching for a father, so Jim is attempting to rejoin his family, and he lavishes on the love-starved
river waif all of his parental affection, calling Huck "honey," and
petting him, and doing "everything he could think of for me." Jim's
ludicrous horror at Solomon's apparent willingness to split a child in
two is, as it turns out, a humorous statement of his loving care for the
integrity of his white child.

The moral center of the novel focuses on the intense relationship between Huck and Jim, but as in Gogol's *Dead Souls*, the

panoramic sweep of Huck's journey in search of his father also opens to view a whole civilization, and the wrath of Twain's judgment of that civilization is the novel's most biblical quality. Entering many houses in his quest for truth and love, Huck calls only the raft his home, a fact which symbolizes at the broadest reach of social implication Twain's massive condemnation of the society of the Great Valley as he knew it in the tragic quarter of a century before the Civil War.

When, at the beginning of the novel, Huck is sworn into Tom Sawyer's gang and introduced to Miss Watson's piousness, he is thereby initiated into the two mysteries of the society which of-fer—respectively—an institutionalized version of truth and love: romanticism and religion. For Tom, life is a circus, a romantic ad-venture story. Turnips are "julery" and Sunday School picnickers are "Spanish merchants and rich A-rabs," and Tom denounces Huck as a "numskull" for his literal-mindedness about these marvels. Huck, however, who understands that the fine spectacle of lights twinkling in a village late at night means that "there was sick folks, maybe," knows that romanticism is a way of faking the nature of reality, and when he temporarily forgets this, when he disregards Jim's warning and boards an abandoned steamboat to have an adventure of which Tom Sawyer would have approved, he comes close to losing his life. (The fact that the steamboat is named the *Walter Scott* is scarcely ac-cidental, for in *Life on the Mississippi* Twain had already blasted the Scott-intoxication of the South as "in great measure responsible" for the Civil War.) But the novel's bitterest attack on the romantic imagination occurs in two interrelated and successive chapters, 21 and 22. In the latter chapter, Huck goes to a circus, sees a drunken man weaving around the ring on a horse, and is terribly distressed, although the crowd roars with delight. But it is not Huck's charming naiveté in not recognizing that the drunkard is a clown that Twain condemns; it is the callousness of the crowd. For this circus scene de-pends upon the preceding chapter, which really does involve a drunk, the drunken Boggs, who weaves down the street on horseback shout-ing insults at Colonel Sherburn. When Sherburn mortally wounds Boggs, a crowd gathers excitedly around the drunkard to watch him die. Everyone is tremendously pleased—except Huck, and the dying man's daughter. Thus by this juxtaposition of episodes, each of which contrasts the boy's sympathetic concern with the gleeful howling of the crowd, does Twain lay bare the depravity of a society that views life as a circus, as some kind of romantic show.

For Miss Watson, life is a moral certainty. Bible readings and daily prayers fill her smug world with assurances. She tells Huck that if he will pray every day he will get whatever he asks for, and when he prays for fishhooks without being able to "make it work," she calls him a fool, just as Tom had called him a "numskull." Yet it is Miss Watson, prattling of providential mercy, who treats Nigger Jim severely, who despite her promise to him that she would never sell him away from his wife and children, can't resist the sight of a stack of money and agrees to sell him down the river. If romanticism is a lie, religion is a monumental lovelessness, a terrible hypocrisy. When Huck goes to church with the Grangerfords, the minister preaches a sermon on brotherly love to a congregation made up of men armed to the teeth and panting to kill one another; when the King pretends he is infused with divine grace in order to con the camp meeting, he is only acting out Miss Watson's hypocrisies on the level of farce. But once again, as in his attack on life as a circus, Twain's most withering blast at lovelessness and hypocrisy is delivered by juxtaposing two chapters with a vengeance.

The last paragraph of chapter 23 is perhaps the most poignant moment in the entire novel, for it is here that Jim relates to Huck how his daughter, after recovering from scarlet fever, became a mysteriously disobedient child. Even when Jim had slapped her and sent her sprawling she refused to obey his orders, but just as he was going for her again, he realized what was wrong: "De Lord God Amighty fogive po' ole Jim, kaze he never gwyne to fogive hisself as long's he live! Oh, she was plumb deef en dumb, Huck, plumb deef en dumb—en I'd ben a-treat'n her so!" On the last page of chapter 24, the King and the Duke launch their scheme for robbing the Wilks girls of their inheritance, with the King pretending to be a parson and the Duke acting the part of a deaf mute. When viewed beside Jim's sorrow and compassion for his deaf-and-dumb daughter, the spectacle of the two frauds talking on their hands is sickening—"It was enough," says Huck, "to make a body ashamed of the human race."

In the end, Huck turns his back on the corruption of society, but his tragedy is that in the very moment of doing so he loses Jim. In one of the numerous sequels to the novel that Twain obsessively sketched out in his later years, Jim has somehow been caught again and Huck fantastically plans to free him by changing places with him and blacking his face. But the sad reality of the novel is that such a masquerade is an impossible dream; once Jim has reached the promised land of freedom, Huck is forever separated from his black father by the tragedy of race. It is scarcely necessary to know that in still another contemplated sequel Twain envisioned Huck as a broken, helplessly insane old man in order to sense that at the conclusion of the novel Huck's voyage has become as doomed in its way as Captain Ahab's, and that in lighting out for the territory without Jim beside him he flees with "all havens astern."

# *4*

# Howells in the Nineties

In the early summer of 1892 William Dean Howells was three months past his fifty-fifth birthday, and to the New York journalist T. C. Crawford he looked like everything that was wrong with American literature. With quietly effective satirical touches, Crawford shaped an image of Howellsian complacency for the readers of the New York *Tribune* which prefigured the plaster bust of "The Dean" that H. L. Mencken would set up for the purpose of smashing in *Prejudices, First Series* (1919) and that Sinclair Lewis would further demolish at Stockholm in 1930. Mr. Howells, wrote his interviewer,

> is of medium height and is quite stout, round, and contented looking. His face is round. Nearly all the lines of his figure are curved. His hands are fat and dimpled. His round face has the look of refinement, experience of the world, the good-natured indifference and the cynically

SOURCE: The original source is "Howells in the Nineties," *Perspectives in American History* (IV, 1970) © 1970 by Kenneth S. Lynn. This essay is included in somewhat different form in *William Dean Howells: An American Life* by Kenneth S. Lynn and is reprinted by permission of Harcourt Brace Jovanovich, Inc.

happy disbelief of a diplomat of experience and high position. . . . His voice is very agreeable. There are certain
notes of contentment in the tone of his voice which argue
that Mr. Howells is satisfied with his career and with the
success he has made in life.

Nowhere in the *Tribune* article was there the least hint that
Howells was suffering from a personal and artistic despair which was
every inch as profound as the more celebrated glooms that gripped
his three greatest literary contemporaries—Henry Adams, Henry
James, and Mark Twain—in the same decade. Nor did the interviewer furnish his readers any reason for guessing that Howells
would have the courage and the imaginative capacity to write, as he
did in the middle nineties, one of the most significantly iconoclastic
novels in all of American literature, *The Landlord at Lion's Head*.
With T. C. Crawford's inability to see anything but the "smiling
aspects" of William Dean Howells, modern criticism's sorry habit
of making simplistic judgments of a very complicated man was
launched.


                                    I


Contributing to the smug, untroubled impression he made on
strangers by his physical appearance in the nineties was the apparently effortless facility with which Howells wrote. Between 1890
and 1900, the pen he clutched in his dimpled hand turned out ten
novels, three novellas, two children's books, a utopian romance, four
volumes of memoirs, a volume of poetry, a book of literary sketches,
a revised version of a travel book, a collection of literary criticism,
twelve plays, and assorted introductions, social essays, and short
stories. In addition, he wrote twenty-seven "Editor's Study" columns
for *Harper's Monthly* in the opening years of the decade; edited John
Brisben Walker's *Cosmopolitan* for a brief season in 1892; con-
tributed a series of essay-reviews to *Harper's Weekly* from March
30, 1895, to February 26, 1898; and between the spring of 1898 and

the fall of 1899 sent an ''American Letter'' to *Literature*, the precursor of the London *Times Literary Supplement*. Clearly, Howells was not an author who suffered from writing blocks, but a remorselessly efficient literary machine—whose output, furthermore, was highly profitable.

In 1893, for example, a year of financial hardship for many Americans, Howells added a column of figures in his notebook and realized that the eight new contracts he had recently signed were worth nearly $30,000. Besides income from fresh projects, Howells in the nineties could count on a 20 percent royalty from Houghton Mifflin on the continuing sale of *The Rise of Silas Lapham, Indian Summer, The Minister's Charge*, and other books he had written in the course of his earlier career in Boston. He had an equally advantageous royalty arrangement with Harper & Brothers for such works as *April Hopes, Annie Kilburn,* and *A Hazard of New Fortunes*. A master of the art of renegotiating contracts, Howells also managed to persuade Harper to pay him a royalty on all the books he would write between 1892 and 1897 of 20 percent of the retail price on the first 5,000 copies sold and 25 percent thereafter. Having haggled successfully for better terms, he then proceeded to pepper Henry Mills Alden at the Harper editorial office with suggestions about book design, retail pricing, and timing of publications, all to the end of increasing the sales of his forthcoming books. In the novelist's own phrase, the man of letters was a man of business, and Howells' thorough knowledge of the literary marketplace brought him an income most businessmen would have envied. When augmented by the fees he received for performances of his plays, and by the money he was paid for editorial work, freelance journalism, and the magazine serial rights to his books (such as the $10,000 Edward Bok paid him to serialize *My Literary Passions* in the *Ladies' Home Journal*), Howells' advances and royalties gave him as much purchasing power in the 1890s as an author in 1970 who earned $120,000 a year.

The pleasure he took in his success was enormous. Ever since his shabby-genteel beginnings in small-town Ohio, Howells had yearned to be in the position to indulge himself in ''the pleasures which other sages pretend are so vapid.'' The remarkable number of houses he had either bought or built for himself and his family in Cambridge, Belmont, and Boston, each one more impressive than the last, was the gauge of his rapid climb up the path of material comfort in the twenty-year period after the Civil War. It is therefore not surprising that in the nineties, when his annual income soared and his net worth increased more than 50 percent in seven years, a certain tone of contentment crept into his voice during newspaper interviews.

Coupled, however, with the contentment was an awareness of strain, which he publicly acknowledged only in his fiction. (As Howells remarked in one of his autobiographical volumes, fiction was the only way to show one's "real face." Thus in *A Traveler from Altruria* (1894), Howells confessed what was troubling him personally when he had one of the characters admit how difficult it was for American writers to be loyal to their art at the same time that they made money the first consideration of their lives: "I should say that it puts such men under double strain, and perhaps that is the reason why so many of them break down in a calling that is certainly far less exhausting than business." Yet if Howells was wary about what his divided attention was doing to his nervous system, he was never able to break free of thoughts about money, for somehow his expenses kept mounting as fast as his income. His aging and improvident father required financial support until his death in 1894. Various sanatariums and physicians, including such high-priced specialists as S. Weir Mitchell, submitted staggering bills to the novelist during the ten years that his daughter Winifred suffered from an inexplicable malady. After Winifred's death in 1889, the health of Howells' wife Elinor gave way to an expensive invalidism that lasted until she died in 1910. Howells sent his son John to Harvard and paid for the young man's architectural training in Paris as well. After 1885, when Howells and his wife gave up their residence in Boston and in effect became gypsies for the rest of their lives, their incessant movements were a grand progress, because Elinor Howells not only liked the good life as much as did her husband, but her frail health needed to be cushioned. In a typical decision, the Howellses took a four-room suite at the Chelsea in New York in the spring of 1888, the cost of which prompted Howells to write to his father that "there are a great variety of ways of living in N.Y., and all expensive." A year later found them installed at the opulent Hotel Vendome in Boston, preparatory to subletting for the summer the "vast" Brooks-Winthrop mansion overlooking Fresh Pond in Cambridge. During other summers of the nineties the novelist sampled—either with or without his wife—the waters of Saratoga (1890) and Carlsbad (1895) and the beauties of Paris (1894) and the Rhine (1897). The purchase of places on the ocean at Far Rockaway, Long Island, and Kittery Point, Maine, added further dimensions of pleasure—and expense—to the Howellses' summers.

Living on a scale that only sages pretended was vapid made it necessary for a writer who was not independently wealthy to find new ways to pay old debts. Hard bargaining, however, created as many problems as it solved. When, for instance, Howells signed on with a New York firm rather than with another Boston firm after the failure of James R. Osgood and Company, his previous publisher, it was because no house in Boston had the resources to match Harper's guarantee to Howells of $10,000 a year—but the price Harper exacted of Howells in return was an agreement to write a new novel every year of approximately 100,000 words and to contribute several pages of literary criticism every month to the "Editor's Study" department of *Harper's Monthly*. The convenient train accidents and other improbabilities that weaken Howells' stories of the late eighties and early nineties directly result from the speed with which these stories were written. Furthermore, Harper immediately began to put pressure on Howells (through his quondam publisher James Osgood) to move to New York. Howells at first resisted the pressure with a plea to his new publisher not to "Barnumize" him. Nevertheless, within two years of signing the Harper contract, Howells was spending long periods of time in New York. Finally, after shuttling back and forth between Boston and New York for several years, Howells in the early nineties shifted permanently to the Empire City, albeit his domiciles continued to be hotels and rented apartments.

That Howells in New York was vulnerable to commercialism

was a fact of which his friends were unhappily aware. When Henry James heard that Howells had put down the burden of the "Editor's Study" only to pick up the editorship of the *Cosmopolitan*, he wrote to his old friend with a distinctly un-Jamesian directness: "But what, my dear Howells, is the *Cosmopolitan*—and why—oh, why (let me not be odious!) are you hanging again round your neck the chain and emblems of bondage? I will be bold enough, at this distance, to tell you that I hate the idea most bitterly, that I hold you too high for such base uses and want you to write only other and yet other American chronicles. *That* is your genius." Howells could not bring himself to answer James' letter in the same spirit of candor, yet in a sense he had already done so before receiving it. Not only did his friends deplore his new, commercial tendencies, but the novelist himself was racked by the guilty knowledge that he had indeed "Barnumized" his genius, after only token resistance. Wherefore in *A Hazard of New Fortunes* (1890) Howells satirized the readiness of Basil March, who has come down from Boston to New York to edit a magazine (and whose last name further connects him with his creator, since it is the name of the month in which Howells was born), to compromise his aesthetic standards for the sake of a commercial success.

The impulse of Basil and his wife Isabel to escape from the sordid reality of city life into the fantasy world of the Broadway theater constitutes another sign of Howells' uneasy awareness of the discrepancy between his literary ideals and his literary practice—and of his consequent need to chastise himself with the lash of his literary wit. The discrepancy arose out of the fact that the proprietor of the "Editor's Study" constantly inveighed against the current American theater as "still almost wholly injurious, through its falsehood, its folly, its wantonness, its aimlessness," while the author of such one-act farces as *Five O'Clock Tea* and *The Albany Depot* spent his imaginative energy on the difficulties of the servant problem, the social complications of polite lying, and other agonies of life in the more comfortable faubourgs of the eastern seaboard, notably Boston's Back Bay. Although such confections may have meant a great deal to sentimental college boys like Booth Tarkington, who "came home at Christmas to be either in the audience at a Howells farce or in the cast that gave it," by the intellectual and emotional standards Howells himself had established for the modern drama, his plays were hack work. The irony with which Howells treated the Marches' taste for theatrical escapism was really aimed at himself.

But while Basil March tells us a good deal about Howells' attitude toward his own commercialism, the novelist could not completely reveal what he thought of artists who pandered to the popular taste through a character who was only an editor. It took Angus Beaton, the cynical young illustrator who fully understands the connection between "the Arts and Dollars" and is fully prepared to exploit it, to round out Howells' self-portrait in *A Hazard of New Fortunes*. In many ways, the hateful Beaton's conduct diverges sharply from his creator's, both personally and professionally. Yet there are several scenes in which the illustrator and the novelist come very close together. In the most telling of them, Beaton, who has no sense of social responsibility and only the faintest sense of family obligation, suddenly thinks of sending some money to his impoverished father. Upon reconsideration, though, he discards the idea, because it conflicts with his desire to buy for himself a conspicuously expensive item of wearing apparel: "He was now often in that martyr mood in which he wished to help his father; not only to deny himself Chianti, but to forego a fur-lined overcoat which he intended to get for the winter. He postponed the moment of actual sacrifice as regarded the Chianti, and he bought the overcoat in an anguish of self-reproach." Howells, of course, would never have denied financial help to his own father. Nevertheless, the heart of this little drama of temptation is autobiographical, harking back to the autumn of 1888 when Howells had come to New York to find a place to live for the winter. Confronted with the social cruelties of the city, he had written a letter to Henry James in which he expressed his feelings of foreboding about the direction that modern America seemed to be taking: "After fifty years of optimistic content with 'civilization' and its ability to come out all right in the end, I now abhor it, and feel that it is coming out all wrong in the end unless it bases itself anew on a real equality." Yet in spite of his recognition of the need for a new spirit of sharing, Howells had concluded the letter with a searingly honest admission of his own selfishness: "Meantime, I wear a fur-lined overcoat and live in all the luxury my money can buy."

The fur-lined figure of Angus Beaton represents, however, only one facet of Howells' troubled mind in the nineties. His letters to close friends and relatives in this period point to the existence of other and darker facets—for these communications repeatedly resort to a language that is simply too extreme to be accounted for as a mere guilt-reaction to his upper-middle-class tastes, or to the artistic concessions he was willing to make in order to indulge them. In the private correspondence of the aging Howells we feel ourselves in the presence not only of an uneasy conscience, but of a profoundly disoriented imagination and shattered morale.

In the beginning, Howells had approached the challenge of New York with artistic gusto. He wanted, so he told Edward Everett Hale in the summer of 1888, to "get intimately at that vast mass of life." The following October, he repeated to Henry James how excited he was by New York, adding that "I hope to use some of its vast, gay, shapeless life in my fiction." Almost in the same breath, however, he expressed in another letter to Hale his sense of futility at being a writer. Words, after all, could not affect life; they could "only breed more words." Expanding upon his feelings of uselessness, he characterized himself as a "creature of the past," whose glimpses of the light of the future had merely illuminated his present "ugliness and fatuity and feebleness." By 1892, Howells could confess to Charles Eliot Norton that he had recently had to ask himself "very serious questions about my power and fitness to go on in the line I have kept so long." In 1894, in the very midst of one of the most productive decades ever enjoyed by an American writer, he informed the same friend that "I don't work much." Indeed, he continued, "I am terribly sick of literature, at times, and would be better content if there were some other honest way of earning a living." As for New York's vast, gay, shapeless life, it soon became so offensive to Howells that he almost felt like exchanging it for Jefferson, Ohio, from whose provincial constrictions he had fled thirty years before. "We are here [in Boston] at the Hotel Berkeley for the month of October," he wrote

his sister Annie in 1891, "and then we go to New York. I confess
that I go with no vivid expectations of any kind, and chiefly to keep
the family together. . . . I am so sick of cities that I should be willing
almost to live in Jefferson . . . but that's impossible." In the course of
the next ten years his sense of being trapped in New York mounted
steadily. By 1901, he could hardly bear the thought of living there.
"Every year I hate the return to the city more," he wrote to Charles
Eliot Norton, "but with each return I feel my helplessness more. My
wife and I had long dreamed of a permanent home in the country: a
little while ago we counted up our requirements and found that the
country would not meet them. . . . So we go back to New York, our
refuge, our ugly exile."

Caught between his revulsion against New York and the im-
possibility of going back to Jefferson, Ohio, Howells conceivably
could have yearned for Boston. But while Isabel March in *A Hazard
of New Fortunes* "lamented the literary peace, the intellectual refinement of the life they had left behind them," her husband silenced her
lamentation with what was Howells' conclusive judgment of the city
he had abandoned: "He owned it was very pretty, but he said it was
not life—it was death-in-life." No matter where he turned, Howells
in the nineties could no longer find a base for a meaningful existence.
He was, as he said, "sick of cities," while the country failed to meet
his "requirements." So lost was he, so confused and uncertain, that
there were times when he even doubted whether he had the authority
to feel pangs of conscience about his hedonism. A conscience, after
all, implied the presence of moral standards—but who could be sure
any longer that such standards were valid? To his father—his closest
confidant—Howells poured out the full truth of how he felt:

> The whole of life seems unreal and unfair; but what I try to
> teach the children is to be ready for the change that *must*
> come in favor of truth and justice, and not to oppose it. Of
> course the world still looks beautiful to them; they cannot
> see it as I do; but I hope they can see the right. In the
> meantime Elinor and I live along like our neighbors; only,
> we have a bad conscience. Sometimes, however, the whole

affair goes to pieces in my apprehension, and I feel as if I had no more authority to judge myself or to try to do this or that, than any other expression of the Infinite Life,—say a tree, or a field of wheat, or a horse. The only proof I have that I ought to do right is that I suffer for my selfishness; and perhaps this is enough. I dare say God can take care of all the rest.

Yet the bizarre fact is that only thirty-six days before writing to his father, Howells published a book which in later years would do more to discredit him as a shallow optimist than anything else he would ever write. In the twilight years of the fin de siècle, when Mark Twain, Henry James, and Henry Adams were all searching their imaginations for symbols of failure, the author of *Criticism and Fiction* called on American writers to concern themselves with the "smiling aspects of life," and in the pickle-weaned judgment of twentieth-century criticism, any writer who could say such a sickly sweet thing at such a sour time was not worth reading. However, as his private correspondence attests, *Criticism and Fiction* is an unreliable guide to Howells' state of mind in the nineties. Put out because both publisher and author wanted to make money, the book was hastily assembled out of the "Editor's Study" pieces that Howells had written for *Harper's Monthly* in the previous five years. One of the pieces included was the "Study" for September 1886 in which Howells had commented upon a French translation of Dostoevsky's *Crime and Punishment*. While lavish in his praise of the novel, Howells had oddly insisted that Dostoevsky's vision of life was not relevant to the United States. Even more oddly, he had based his argument on details of Dostoevsky's own career rather than on the tragic novel he had written. The point Howells was concerned to make was that while Dostoevsky had had the horrifying experience of being sentenced to death and then—following the commutation of the sentence—of being exiled to Siberia, American writers lived in freedom. "Whatever their deserts, very few American novelists have been led out to be shot, or finally expelled to the rigors of a winter at Duluth. . . . We invite our novelists, therefore, to concern themselves with the more smiling aspects of life, which are the more American.'' By way of further justification of his argument, Howells had also thrown in the fact that journeymen carpenters and plumbers in the United States were so far from being oppressed that they were striking for wages of four dollars a day (the outrageous demands of carpenters and plumbers being of course lively in the mind of a writer who had built or done over a number of houses), but basically the identification of America with the smiling aspects of life rested on the assertion that the American artist, unlike his Russian counterpart, was not an alien and helpless figure in his society.

As a political comment on the difference between life in Czarist Russia and life in democratic America, the assertion is straightforward and unexceptionable. But as an autobiographical revelation, it is a fascinatingly complex, highly neurotic denial of social maladjustment on the part of a writer who only a year and a half before the Dostoevsky review appeared in *Harper's Monthly* had suffered a nervous breakdown as a direct consequence of his sense of alienation from the great issues of his age and who by the time of the review's reappearance in book form five years later had become overwhelmed by the conviction that the ''whole of life'' was ''unreal'' and ''unfair.'' Far from being the hallmark of an infinite complacency, Howells' words about the ''smiling aspects'' constituted a short-lived counterattack against an enveloping anguish.

Although Howells' feelings of anguish were intensely personal, they also reflected the cultural tragedy of a whole generation of American writers—which novels as different as *The Princess Casamassima, Looking Backward, Democracy, The Bread-Winners,* and *A Connecticut Yankee in King Arthur's Court* helped to define. But Howells' writings confronted that tragedy more squarely and more continuously than anyone else's. And it was Howells, too, alone of his generation, who finally and painfully broke through the literary formulas that he and his contemporaries had devised in response to their situation and began to deal with American experience in the manner of a twentieth-century naturalist. In a beautiful and melancholy letter to Henry James, Howells in his old age acknowledged that ''I am comparatively a dead cult with my stat-

ues cut down and the grass growing over me in the pale moonlight.''
Self-distrustful as always, Howells refrained from adding that the
fate he had suffered was unjust.


II


Howells could believe that American life was smiling at him in 1886
because his own career had recently begun to satisfy him in ways it
never had before. He was troubled, of course, by the commercial
pressures that Harper & Brothers had begun to exert on him, but for
the most part he was buoyed up by a fresh sense of artistic purpose
that contrasted sharply with the feelings of inferiority he had suffered
from in the seventies and early eighties, along with all the other
young writers of the time. As Howells later recalled, the writers of
the Gilded Age had lost the prestige their predecessors had enjoyed
before the Civil War, when ''the literary fellows had a pretty good
share of the honors that were going'' and ''such a man as Longfellow
was popularly considered a type of greatness.'' The war, Howells
continued, had made the soldier a hero, and for ''a period of ten or
fifteen years . . . he dominated the national imagination.'' When that
period passed, ''the big fortunes began to tower up, and heroes of
another sort began to appeal to our admiration.'' Under such circumstances, the writer not only ceased to be considered a type of
American greatness; he came to be derided as ''a kind of mental and
moral woman, to whom a real man, a business man, could have nothing to say after the primary politenesses.'' To the general fate of
Gilded Age writers was added, in Howells' case, the special hazards
of living in Boston and environs. The apostolic succession that
Holmes and Lowell had held out to a bright young man from the prov-
inces in 1860 was confirmed with astonishing speed after the war by
means of the editorship of the *Atlantic*, membership in the Saturday
Club, an invitation from President Eliot to lecture at Harvard, and
other tribal honors. Yet while Brahmin Boston made room at the
feast for a gifted Ohioan, as it had previously done for Longfellow,
Agassiz, and other outlanders, Howells was famished by the courtesy

as well as gratified. With a flood of feeling that not even his urbane wit could entirely conceal, Howells remarked in *The Rise of Silas Lapham* that with its "comprehensive cousinships" Boston society had the trick of hemming in "the adventurer" and leaving him out at every turn,

> by ramifications that forbid him all hope of safe personality in his comments on people; he is never less secure than when he hears some given Bostonian denouncing or ridiculing another. If he will be advised, he will guard himself from concurring in these criticisms, however just they appear, for the probability is that their object is a cousin of not more than one remove from the censor. When the alien hears a group of Boston ladies calling one another, and speaking of all their gentleman friends, by the familiar abbreviations of their Christian names, he must feel keenly the exile to which he was born; but he is then, at least, in comparatively little danger; while these latent and tacit cousinships open pitfalls at every step around him, in a society where Middlesexes have married Essexes and produced Suffolks for two hundred and fifty years.

In addition to being aware of the limitations Boston imposed on his social acceptance, Howells lived in the consciousness that Boston had literary reservations about him as well. As editor of the *Atlantic*, he suffered from the resentment of in-groupers who regarded editorial decisions that went against them as the impertinences of an arriviste. When, for example, Howells deferred publication to a later issue of an Emerson poem, an icy wind immediately blew in from Concord: "My dear Sir, Please send me back my verses and break up the form. I did not doubt that they were to be printed for the February number, and it would be ridiculous to print so strictly occasional lines after two months, instead of one. Sorry to waste the printer's time, but beg you to return them at once." Similarly, a letter from Brooks Adams about an article of his that Howells had turned down was ugly and aggressive. Further adding to Howells' troubles with Boston was its resistance to his efforts to be a realist. From *The Undiscovered Country* through *A Modern Instance* to *The Minister's Charge*, Howells in the eighties had endeavored to furnish his readers with a sense of the surface reality of modern Boston. In the Howellsian vision, it was a city in flux, where a fashionable neighborhood might go to seed almost overnight—and "every house seems to wince as you go by, and button itself up to the chin for fear you should find it had no shirt on"; where newlyweds recently arrived from the backcountry, like the Bartley Hubbards in *A Modern Instance*, live in boardinghouses, take their meals in restaurants, and tragically fail to put down roots; and where thieves, drunks, and whores throng the ancient common of the Puritans. The accuracy of Howells' observations has never been challenged, but to Bostonians of the period who were still dominated by what Howells would later refer to as the "intense ethicism" of the New England mind, accuracy was beside the point; the purpose of literary art as they understood it was to display ideal models of character and behavior so that readers could be morally edified, and Howells' art studiously avoided the ideal. By 1884, consequently, all Boston appeared to be divided, according to the calculation of the newly arrived Hamlin Garland, "into three parts, those who liked [Howells] and read him; those who read him and hated him; and those who just plain hated him."

Caught between the condescension of a nation which no longer took writers seriously and the suspicions of a city which still did, Howells triumphed over his ambiguous position by dramatizing it. The ruling figure in his fiction of the seventies and early eighties is an observer who starts outside the story's action and tries to join it, despite the hostility he encounters and despite his own doubts about the worthwhileness of joining. What makes the observer an important person is not money or power but the quality of his mind and spirit. As Thomas Wentworth Higginson noted in 1879, the Howellsian observer was vastly different from Washington Irving's sentimental spectator in that the former had "thoughts and purposes, something to protest against, and something to say," whereas Geoffrey Crayon was merely good-natured. Henry James made a similar point when he contrasted the intellectual naiveté of the "mere spectator'' of pre-Civil War days with the critical attitude of the post-Civil War observer—although in doing so James was thinking more about his own literary consciousness than he was about Howells'. For the observer was a ruling figure in James' fiction as well, and in Henry Adams' *Democracy*, Mark Twain's stories of Hannibal, and many lesser works by lesser writers of the period. Henry Adams' observer was, to be sure, a lady, while Mark Twain's were boys (sometimes), but whatever the physical incarnation, the post-Civil War observer was always recognizable by his skepticism, his distrust of passion, and his deflationary humor. Although other people often ignored the observer's moral insights or failed to get the instructive point of his jokes, events generally proved him to be right about things—and thus he salvaged treasure from defeat. In his ability to comprehend but not to control, the observer exemplified the cultural situation of the post-Civil War writers as they themselves understood it.

If Howells artistically transcended the difficulties of his position, he also succumbed to them. As editor of the *Atlantic*, he tacitly agreed with the philistine proposition that literary men were mental and moral women by rarely using his reviewing stand in the magazine as a forum for discussing serious social issues. And when he published the thoughts of other writers on such issues, he generally chose conservative essays like J. B. Harrison's series on "Certain Dangerous Tendencies in American Life," which was designed (in Howells' words) to explode such delusions as "the inherent virtue and wisdom of the people, the injustice of society to the poor, and the tyranny of capital." Only in the final year of his editorship—1881—did he risk running such a controversial piece as Henry Demarest Lloyd's "The Story of a Great Monopoly," and the bravery of Howells' decision to do so was mitigated by his knowledge that State Street investors who had put their money into western railroads were as indignant as Lloyd about the cutthroat efforts of Standard Oil to reduce its transportation costs. The post-Civil War writer's loss of social status also had a narrowing effect upon the scope of Howells' fiction. While the novelist was assertedly enthusiastic about the commonplace details of urban change that he recorded with well-nigh scientific care, his ironical prose style bespoke his acute consciousness of how far removed his realism was from the great, shaping forces of nineteenth-century American life. No matter how shrewdly commented upon or meticulously described, the facts which interested the Howellsian observer were often appallingly inconsequential, and the observer's vaunted understanding thus went to waste on trivia. In order not to alienate his Boston constituency any more than he had to, Howells accepted other limitations on his realism. He never attacked any of Boston's important institutions, and he confined his really probing satirical thrusts at the Brahmin class to peripheral figures like Miles Arbuton, the Europeanized young man in *A Chance Acquaintance*. Howells further protected his position in Boston by making himself almost slavishly useful— whether to institutions like the *Atlantic*, which had never been perfectly proofread until the Ohioan came along with his printshop experience, or to clubs like the St. Botolph which he helped to launch, or to influential people like James Russell Lowell, whose early kindnesses Howells repaid with indefatigable and ultimately successful efforts to persuade President Rutherford B. Hayes, who was Elinor Howells' cousin, to appoint the poet minister to Spain, a post that Lowell had coveted. Socially as well as artistically, Howells worked very hard to build up indulgences for himself in his adopted city.

He was never free, though, of the haunting feeling that he had given away too much in exchange for too little, and in 1884 he entered into a period of psychological crisis which ultimately produced a sea change in his cautiously conceived career. The crisis began in late summer, on a note of elation. Ambitious not only for himself but for his daughter Winifred, whom he hoped would soon be well enough to make her debut in Boston society, Howells purchased a house at 302 Beacon Street in the Back Bay, just two doors away from the residence of Dr. Oliver Wendell Holmes, whom Howells had always considered one of the quintessential figures of the Boston establishment. As a backdrop for a daughter's entrance into society, the house was perfect. In a letter to Henry James written shortly after moving in, Howells endeavored to be casual about his new address, but he was unable to keep a vivid feeling of self-realization from shining through. The onetime printer's apprentice had come a long way from Jefferson, Ohio:

> The sun goes down over Cambridge with as much apparent interest as if he were a Harvard graduate; possibly he is; and he spreads a glory over the Back Bay that is not to be equalled by the blush of a Boston Independent for such of us Republicans as are going to vote for Blaine. Sometimes I feel it an extraordinary thing that I should have been able to buy a house on Beacon str.

Despite the wonderful feeling of having at last arrived at the summit, Howells was vaguely oppressed by his success. It is significant in this regard that in the very months of moving into Beacon Street he began a novel about an outlander named Silas Lapham, whose moral "rise" would require him to sacrifice all hope of social success in Boston. What sort of a moral decision Howells was beginning, semiconsciously, to consider for himself had first been indicated four years earlier in the praise he had bestowed on J. B. Harrison's essays in the *Atlantic*. Howells had admired Harrison because his writings promoted better understanding between the social classes, demonstrating to the rich on the one hand "what excellent types of character exist among workingmen and their wives," and on the other hand teaching "the poor how a capitalist may be necessarily their friend." In so doing, Harrison had bridged the gap of distrust between workers and owners—an important achievement in a decade when observers as diverse as John Hay, Edward Bellamy, and Jacob Riis were coming to fear that Americans had lost the ability to understand one another. Howells shared this rising fear and was affected by it as an artist. In an atmosphere of widening suspicion punctuated by outbreaks of social violence, was it not the duty of the novelist to "widen the bounds of sympathy" by imaginatively entering into all the worlds of American experience, presenting individuals in the context of their social class, and dramatizing both their faults and their virtues—even though "every

Half-bred rogue that groomed his mother's cow'' might reproach the novelist for "introducing him to low company''? Genteel reviewers had been offended by the social realism of John Hay's *The Bread-Winners*, but Howells had written a letter to Hay in January 1884 lauding the novel for its courageous expression of "a fact not hitherto attempted: the fact that the workingmen *as* workingmen are no better or wiser than the rich *as* the rich, and are quite as likely to be false and foolish.'' Hay had set an example which stirred Howells' imagination more and more as the months of 1884 progressed.

The presidential campaign that autumn further increased Howells' sense that the role of the American writer desperately needed to be redefined. For the Blaine-Cleveland campaign was deeply upsetting to Howells. As the son of a newspaperman and minor politician who had been involved with the GOP since its inception, and as the author himself of a campaign biography of Lincoln, Howells had a tradition of Republicanism that was firmer than most. Nevertheless he felt guilty at having to support Blaine—and when he took refuge in the excuse that Grover Cleveland was unfit for the presidency because of his sex life, Howells' discomfiture was increased by the ribald scorn of his friend Mark Twain: "To see grown men, apparently in their right mind, seriously arguing against a bachelor's fitness for President because he has had private intercourse with a consenting widow! Those grown men know what the bachelor's other alternative was—& tacitly they seem to prefer that to the widow. *Isn't* human nature the most consummate sham and lie that was ever invented?'' The best Howells could do by way of riposte was to attack Cleveland's physiognomy. "I don't like his hangman-face. It looks dull and brutal.'' But though the reply was feeble, Howells still felt very strongly that the return of the Democrats to the White House, for the first time since the Civil War, would inevitably coarsen the national leadership. As he lamented to his father in the wake of Cleveland's victory, "A great cycle has come to a close; the rule of the best in politics for a quarter of a century is ended. Now we shall have the worst again.'' Clearly, the nation's need for a new source of leadership was acute.

Still, Howells hung back from trying to make the American

novel that source—possibly because of his habitual caution, possibly because he did not yet fully understand the significance of his own thoughts. As he worked on *The Rise of Silas Lapham* through the fall of 1884 and into the winter, he gave to his spokesman in the book, the Reverend Mr. Sewell (whose last name was as Welsh as his own), a formulation of the novelist's role in American life which merely reiterated the purpose that Howells had set for himself in his fiction ever since the early seventies, namely, helping people to be honest with themselves and with one another by portraying "human feelings in their true proportion and relation." The study of different sorts of people in the context of their socioeconomic grouping was not yet a part of Howells' program for the American novel. Indicative of the transitional state of Howells' thinking in 1884 was the fact that he included in *Silas Lapham* a penetrating study of business ethics in the Gilded Age; but his prevailing conservatism was also indicated by the novel's subordination of Silas' life as a businessman to the Lapham family's efforts to breach the walls of Boston society. As befitted a comedy of manners, the pivotal scene in the book was set in a Beacon Hill dining room, not in an office or a factory. And while the existence of class antagonisms in Boston was referred to during an important conversation in that dining room, it was not directly dramatized. Furthermore, Howells proved willing to modify even the reference when he was asked to do so by an important figure in the publishing business. As originally planned, the Brahmin aristocrat Bromfield Corey was supposed to speculate, in the course of the dinner party he gives for the Laphams, about the possibility of the spacious, airy mansions of Beacon Hill and Back Bay being dynamited during the summer, while their owners are off at Newport or Saratoga, by resentful slum dwellers who have been stifling in the heat of crowded buildings in the North End. In giving this remarkable thought to old Corey, Howells was drawing partly on his disturbed awareness of the recent rise in anarchist violence in the major cities of the United States and partly on a letter about urban housing he had written to his father shortly after settling at 302 Beacon Street. "There are miles of empty houses all around me," Howells wrote on August 10, 1884. "And how unequally things are divided in this world. While these beautiful, airy, wholesome houses are uninhabited, thousands of poor creatures are stifling in wretched barracks in the city here, whole families in one room. I wonder that men are so patient with society as they are.'' If Howells had simply allowed Corey to voice the sentiment he had expressed to his father, then Richard Watson Gilder, who had been serializing *Silas Lapham* in the *Century*, would probably not have been upset. Instead, the novelist crossed the comment to his father with his thoughts about dynamite. The result was that when Gilder, in the process of reading page proofs, came upon Howells' Brahmin idly wondering why slum dwellers did not express their opinion of empty mansions by blowing them up, there was pandemonium at the *Century*. By return mail, Howells received a letter from Gilder: ''I hope you will not think us super-sensitive when we call your attention to page 867 of your April installment. . . . It is the very word, *dynamite*, that is now so dangerous, for any of us to use, except in condemnation. None but a crank would misinterpret your allusion, but it is the crank who does the deed. The other day it was found that dynamite had been built in-to all the hearths in a new house—there is no telling where this sort of thing is going to break out—it is an unknown and horribly inflam-mable quantity, and we don't want, if we can help it, to be associated with the subject, except in opposing it.'' Without a murmur, Howells defused Corey's comment to read, ''If I were a poor man, with a sick child pining in some garret or cellar at the North End, I should break into one of them, and camp out on the grand piano.''

In *Silas Lapham*, then, Howells did not chart a new course for the American novel. The author, unlike his hero, did not rise to the challenge of conscience. But having failed to rise, Howells suddenly collapsed, borne down by the questions and problems of American society that he might have dealt with but had not. A decade later, he told the story of his breakdown to a journalist, who promptly reported their conversation in *Harper's Weekly*:

> They made their demand—these questions and prob-
> lems—when Mr. Howells was writing *Silas Lapham*. His
> affairs prospering, his work marching as well as heart

could wish, suddenly and without apparent cause, the status seemed wholly wrong. His own expression in speaking with me about that time, was, "The bottom dropped out!"

## III

The urbane wit and matter-of-fact realism of his writing and the remarkable steadiness of his work habits had served Howells from the very beginning of his career as a means of clamping a tight control on an extraordinarily nervous temperament. When the bottom dropped out, the demoralized novelist turned to the only therapy he knew. Exactly how much time he lost to his illness is unknown, but it cannot have been very long—a matter of weeks, at most—before he resumed his usual schedule of work. The monthly publication in the *Century* of successive installments of *Silas Lapham* never once faltered, and by the time the final installment appeared in August 1885, Howells was forging ahead with *The Minister's Charge*. Apparently, the collapse of his psychological health had not left any scars at all.

In the autumn of 1885, however, the novelist abruptly began to deviate from accustomed patterns of behavior. He declined the Ticknor firm's proposal to become his publisher and signed with Harper, thereby loosening his cherished ties with the Boston literary establishment. Howells and his wife also let their house on Beacon Street and moved to a hotel in Auburndale, Massachusetts, a shift that was made primarily for the sake of Winifred, whose increasingly precarious health now frightened her parents, but that also had the effect of further diminishing Howells' commitment to Boston. Most important, he acquired a new literary passion. Beginning with *The Cossacks*, Howells embarked upon a systematic exploration of Tolstoi's novels and ethical books, the moral vision of which hit him with the force of religious revelation. Struggling suddenly, in the dying months of 1885, to break free of his old life, Howells found in Tolstoi's presentation of human suffering the greatest literary inspiration of his lifetime. Ten years later, he tried to convey what the Russian's example had meant to him: "I do not know how to give a notion of his influence without the effect of exaggeration. As much as one merely human being can help another, I believe that he has helped me." In the soul of a writer who had been ashamed of the womanish role in which American society had cast its artists, Tolstoi had awakened "the will to be a man." Through his achievements, Howells affirmed, "I came . . . to the knowledge of myself in ways I had not dreamt of before, and began at least to discern my relations to the race, without which we are nothing."

The effect of Tolstoi on the editorial Howells was immediate and considerable. Beginning with his review of William H. White's *Mark Rutherford* in the February 1886 "Editor's Study," Howells reviewed many more novels of social significance for *Harper's Monthly* than he ever had in the *Atlantic* and stepped up his attention to the work of political theorists, economists, and sociologists. In the first three years of his tenure at *Harper's*, he had praise for such varied books as Tolstoi's *Anna Karenina* (April 1886) and *Que Faire?* (July 1887), Hardy's *Mayor of Casterbridge* (November 1886), Gronlund's *Cooperative Commonwealth* (April 1888), Bellamy's *Looking Backward* (June 1888), A. W. Rollins' *Uncle Tom's Tenement* (October 1888), and Stepniak's *The Russian Peasantry* (same issue), as well as for the general achievement of Ruskin and Morris (December 1888).

An even more striking example of Howells' new assertiveness was the public stand he took in favor of mercy for the anarchists who were convicted of first-degree murder for having thrown a grenade in Haymarket Square, Chicago, on the night of May 4, 1886. An act which took the lives of eight men, the bombing brought down on seven of the anarchists a sentence of death by hanging (an eighth anarchist was sentenced to fifteen years in jail). In his endeavor to save the doomed men, Howells sought the support of two holdover figures from the antebellum literary scene, when American writers had been more accustomed to speaking out on public issues, but although both men agreed that the anarchists had been convicted on inadequate evidence, neither George William Curtis nor John Greenleaf Whittier was bold enough to speak out against the vindictive hysteria that ruled the nation for a year and a half. When Howells' old friend from Ohio, Whitelaw Reid, agreed to run an appeal for clemency for the anarchists in the November 6, 1887, issue of his New York *Tribune*, the appeal was signed only by its author, W. D. Howells. A file of newspaper and magazine clippings in the Howells Papers at Harvard University testifies to the coast-to-coast abuse which Howells sustained as a result of his lonely act of courage. Yet Howells was not moved to modify his position in the ensuing days and weeks; indeed, the absence from his correspondence of the expression of any wounded feelings suggests that he was not only unmoved by the criticism but unhurt. Having single-handedly reaffirmed the lost American tradition of the socially engagé writer, a fifty-year-old, neurotically sensitive novelist experienced unprecedented feelings of toughness and self-confidence. Only if we appreciate Howells' new sense of himself as the creator of the social conscience of the race can we understand why he should have chosen to repudiate the relevance of Dostoevsky's experience to American life in the very midst of the Dostoevskyan tragedy of the Haymarket affair. In the United States, a writer could become a champion of human freedom without himself becoming a political prisoner. It was not Dostoevsky's career that had meaning for America but fearless, free-spirited Tolstoi's.

So carried away was Howells by his surging Tolstoianism that two weeks after his appeal for clemency appeared in the *Tribune*, he wrote a letter to his sister Annie which proclaimed that he and his wife were now willing to emulate the Russian aristocrat even in his adoption of the life of a peasant. "Elinor and I both no longer care for the world's life, and would like to be settled somewhere very humbly and simply, where we could be socially identified with the principles of progress and sympathy for the struggling mass." In his thirst for involvement, Howells was soon indulging himself in other utopian daydreams as well, including W. D. P. Bliss's plan for a Christian Socialist mission in Boston and Edward Bellamy's New Nation, but Tolstoi's willingness to share the lot of the Russian peasant loomed largest in his imagination. In a sense, it is surprising that the shrewd and skeptical Howells should have been willing to accept

Tolstoi's renunciation at face value, just as it is fantastic that a man so devoted to the creature comforts of American life could have thought himself capable of adopting the living standard of "the struggling mass." But Howells very much wanted to believe in renunciatory gestures because he felt they lent moral authority to denunciatory words.

Inevitably, Howells found himself unable to give up any of the luxuries to which he had become accustomed, and when he made this discovery about himself, his social guilt predictably increased—until finally he had to write a novel in an effort to exorcise it.

The title of *Annie Kilburn* deliberately recalls *Anna Karenina*, but the novel is actually a rebuttal of Tolstoi—at least in its demonstration that a minister named Peck has paid an intolerable price for his Tolstoian insistence on making his private life correspond to his egalitarian social philosophy. Caught up in an abstract love of all humanity, Peck is not able to relate successfully to people, not even to his own daughter, a parental failing which Howells was particularly sensitive to and always condemned, but nowhere more so than in *Annie Kilburn*—the reason being that the novel was written in the agonizing, terminal phase of Winifred Howells' life. Forgetful of himself as well as of other people, Peck finally steps into the path of a train and is killed, while en route to a factory town where he had intended to establish a cooperative boardinghouse for mill workers. In thus associating self-destruction with schemes for introducing middle-class intellectuals to poverty, Howells tried as hard as he could to break free of the ethical imperative that was casting a shadow across his life.

Howells also confessed in *Annie Kilburn* to a failure far more serious than his inability to imagine himself in a proletarian boardinghouse. For the enormous defeatism of this novel does not center on the minister's death—as important as his death is—but rather on the heroine's inability to put an end to the social hatreds in her native town of Hatboro, Massachusetts. Just as Howells had come back from a nervous breakdown to assume the responsibility of widening the bounds of sympathy between the social classes, so Annie comes back from Rome (after the death of her beloved father) to spearhead the drive of upper-class Hatboro to establish a social union for the town's factory workers. The fund-raising effort, it is expected, will in itself be socially healing, because the effort will compel collaboration between the old Hatboro aristocracy, the new commercial class, and the summer people, all of whom have previously distrusted one another, while the opening of the union will obviously create new ties of interest and obligation between the workers and their benefactors.

These expectations, however, go awry. Instead of lessening tensions, the fund-raising increases them, and although money for the union is finally turned over to the workers, Annie is forced to realize that the union is not going to be a social bridge: "We people of leisure, or comparative leisure, have really nothing in common with you people who work with your hands for a living; and as we really can't be friends with you, we won't patronize you. We won't advise you, and we won't help you; but here's the money. If you fail, you fail; and if you succeed, you won't succeed by our aid and comfort." Distressed by the snobbery and the social irrelevance of the town's traditional families, repelled by the vulgarity of the newly rich merchants and by the superficiality of the summer crowd, and enjoying "really nothing in common" with the workers, Howells' heroine is truly a displaced person in her own home town. Her only meaningful relationship is with the jeering bystander, Dr. Morrell, whom she seems destined to marry.

Annie's predicament illuminates Howells' sense of his own situation at the close of the eighties. In the year of the novel's appearance, William Dean and Elinor Howells successively lived in New York, Boston, Cambridge, and Boston: wanderers between worlds, they belonged to none. Furthermore, the novelist's efforts to be a social healer had proved singularly unsuccessful. The more he had talked about social understanding, the more strikes and labor violence there had been, while his appeal for clemency for the anarchists had not moved the governor of Illinois one jot. Politically, he felt equally frustrated. On the one hand, he no longer considered the Republican party to be interested in the "safety and happiness" of the American people; on the other hand, he found that the Socialists, with whose sense of fair play he was now in sympathy, offered "nothing definite or practical to take hold of."

But it was on the philosophical and literary levels that he felt most confused and discouraged. Philosophically, Howells had believed all his life in the existence of a moral government of the universe and had even managed to accommodate Tolstoi's most tragic stories to the idea that morality is rewarded in this world and immorality punished because people have to live with the psychological consequences of their own actions. Tolstoi may have intended *Anna Karenina* as an illustration of the blind contingency of earthly life, but Howells in his review of the novel insisted that the story of Anna's adultery affirmed the existence of moral laws, for instead of finding happiness by taking a lover, Anna "destroys herself, step by step." And in all of Howells' own fiction of his early and middle periods, the faith which guides the Howellsian observer is the biblical belief in the connection between sowing and reaping. While the Reverend Mr. Sewell acknowledges to Silas Lapham that the operation of evil in the world is "often . . . very obscure . . . and often . . . seems to involve, so far as we can see, no penalty whatever," there is no question but that Sewell believes in the ultimate exaction of a penalty, well this side of the grave—which is why he is so "intensely interested in the moral spectacle which Lapham presented" after his expiation and why he invites us to believe at the end of the novel that Lapham's "rise" has left him financially poor but psychologically content. By the time, however, of *Annie Kilburn*, a chill of doubt had crept into Howells' philosophy, to the point where he could neither describe nor foresee a morally instructive fate for Mr. Gerrish, the dry-goods merchant, or for Mrs. Munger, the society leader, or for any other embodiment of social evil in Hatboro, Massachusetts. If a moral government exists in the universe of *Annie Kilburn*, it cannot be discerned.

Matching Howells' philosophical disenchantment at the end of the eighties was his literary disappointment. *The Minister's Charge* had been written too soon to reflect much of his Tolstoianism, but in its closing pages Howells had inserted a sermon on "complicity" by the Reverend Mr. Sewell that redefined the goals of the American

novel in terms of Tolstoian realism: "No man, he said, sinned or suffered to himself alone; his error and his pain darkened and afflicted
men who never heard of his name. If a community was corrupt, if an
age was immoral, it was not because of the vicious, but the virtuous
who fancied themselves indifferent spectators." But in the months
and years after composing the minister's sermon, Howells had found
himself unable to practice what Sewell had preached. Thus he later
told an interviewer that *April Hopes* (1888) was the first novel he
wrote "with the distinct consciousness that he was writing as a
realist", but consciousness of the realities of sin and suffering did
not, alas, have much effect on the book, which turned out to be a
charming but altogether familiar version of the Howellsian comedy
of manners. Nor did the essays and versions he included in *Modern
Italian Poets* (1887) fullfill the Sewellian prescription, nor did the
travel articles called "A Little Swiss Sojourn" which he wrote in
1888 for *Harper's Monthly*, nor did "Five O'Clock Tea" (1887), or
"A Likely Story" (1888), or any of the other farces he wrote in this
period. And when he at last confronted the challenge in *Annie Kilburn* of writing realistically about an entire community, he found
himself identifying his literary point of view with that of an upper-
middle-class observer who was very much interested in how the other
half lived but who lacked the imaginative resources to find out. As an
instrument for widening the bounds of sympathy between social
classes, the novel was a patent failure.

Thus as the eighties drew to a close, Howells was in full retreat
on all fronts from the manic optimism and self-confidence of 1885-
1887. Is it any wonder that Annie Kilburn should have felt homeless
in her own birthplace? Through the heroine of his last novel of the
decade, Howells registered the return of his helpless sense of alienation from American life.

IV

Howells opened the nineties—the most critical decade of his
career—with a novel that summed up, "at a moment of great psy-

chological import," both the kind of writer he had always been and the kind of writer he had tried to become. In the latter regard, *A Hazard of New Fortunes* is the supreme manifestation of Howells' Tolstoianism, a grand-scale fiction that dwarfs everything else he ever wrote. Before climaxing in a bloody outbreak of labor violence, *Hazard* encompasses the whole "frantic panorama" of New York City, from the swarming street life of the slums to high-society parties, introducing in the process one of the most varied casts of characters in all of American literature. Yet at the same time that Howells endeavored to write a serious, indeed a tragic, study of human suffering and class antagonism he also revived in full force all the devices of intellectual irony, anesthetizing wit, and comic perspective by which he had avoided the unpleasant implications of his urban material in *Silas Lapham*. Indeed, he reached even further back into his literary past and resuscitated the anagrammatically named, husband-and-wife team of Basil and Isabel March, whose end-man, straight-man badinage had established the whimsical frame of reference for Howells' superficial survey of the American scene in *Their Wedding Journey* (1872). Although Howells several times asserts in *A Hazard of New Fortunes* that the Marches have changed, that they no longer take a "purely aesthetic view" of New York, that their "whimsical, or alien, or critical attitude" has now been crossed with "a sense of complicity," he also asserts—in one instance, in the very same paragraph—that their "point of view was singularly unchanged, and their impressions of New York remained the same." The Marches' behavior in the novel proves the latter judgment to be correct. Despite their announced sympathy with the life of the metropolis, the Marches are forever holding the city at arm's length, exclaiming to one another in the outmoded and sterile aesthetic formulas of the 1870s how "incomparably picturesque" the elevated trains or the tenement houses are. In his supercilious way, Basil is "always amused" by "certain audacities of the prevailing hideousness," while Isabel's pertly condescending attitude toward New York's polyglot population is epitomized in her remarks about Negroes: "It's true. I *am* in love with the whole race. I never saw one of them that didn't have perfectly angelic manners. I think we shall all be black in heaven—that is, blacksouled.''

Caught between tragic theme and comic outlook, *Hazard* fails to come to grips with the meaning of the life it spreads before us. A tour of the East Side with Basil yields up detailed descriptions of "the small eyes, the high cheeks, the broad noses, the puff lips, the bare, cue-filleted skulls, of Russians, Poles, Czechs, Chinese," but although Basil wonders "what these poor people were thinking, hoping, fearing, enjoying, suffering," he never finds out, and neither do we. The only people whom the Marches are capable of getting to know are outsiders like themselves, so that while their acquaintance ranges from a midwestern oil millionaire to a German Socialist, they never see these people in a defining social context. Lindau, for instance, the German Socialist, is full of militant talk about the need for class war in the United States; yet this aging poet-scholar who makes his living by doing translations for Basil's magazine is no more a representative of the American labor movement than Bromfield Corey, sitting in his Beacon Hill dining room talking about dynamite. Similarly, the problems besetting harsh old Jacob Dryfoos, the oil millionaire, are—so far as the Marches know, at least—familial and philanthropic rather than entrepreneurial, with the result that we know him as a businessman in name only. Fulkerson, the breezy editor from beyond the Alleghenies, Margaret Vance, the society girl who likes to go slumming, and Angus Beaton, the selfish young illustrator from Syracuse, all live marginal lives which contribute nothing to the Marches' knowledge of the social structure of New York life. At the end of the novel, the Marches are as out of touch with the reality of the city as they were at the beginning.

In sum, the Marches are revealed in *A Hazard of New Fortunes* as understanding even less of modern American life than Annie Kilburn. For these Howellsian observers, New York is an impossible place, not only as a community to be joined, but even as a spectacle to be comprehended. Aesthetic clichés and attitudes of amusement are simply a cover-up for a loss of bearings, for a stunning inability to locate any meaning in the turbulence of events:

Accident and then exigency seemed the forces at work to
this extraordinary effect: the play of energies as free and
planless as those that force the forest from the soil and the
sky; and then the fierce struggle for survival, with the
stronger life persisting over the deformity, the mutilation,
the destruction, the decay of the weaker. The whole at moments seemed to him [Basil] lawless, godless; the absence
of intelligent, comprehensive purpose in the huge disorder,
and the violent struggle to subordinate the result to the
greatest good, penetrated with its dumb appeal the consciousness of a man who had always been too self-
enwrapped to perceive the chaos to which the individual
selfishness must always lead.

In such a world, the vaunted intelligence of Howellsian observers is
rendered helpless, while their traditional faith in a moral government
of the universe is torn to shreds. Deprived of intellectual authority
and robbed of moral reinforcement, the Marches become the novel's
best illustration of Howells' haunting remark that "there seems to be
some solvent in New York life that reduces all men to a common
level, that touches everybody . . . and brings to the surface the deeply
underlying nobody." Isabel, who is more given to wishful thinking
than her husband, tries to reaffirm the existence of a universal moral
government by suggesting at the end of the novel that Dryfoos, the
oil millionaire, has been punished for his selfishness by the death of
his son and in the wake of his punishment has "been changed—softened; and doesn't find money all in all any more." But Basil can no
longer find any evidence for such a faith. " 'Does anything from
without change us?' her husband mused aloud. 'We're brought up to
think so by the novelists, who really have charge of people's thinking,
nowadays. But I doubt it.' " Challenging the faith of Howells'
lifetime, Basil reluctantly suggests that if Dryfoos has changed—and
he is not at all sure that he has—it must be because of the inexplicable development within him of a different aspect of his character. Utterly unrelated to the death of his son or to any other external

event, such a development would have been foreordained "from the beginning of time." As Isabel says, in pained but ineffective protest, "Basil! Basil! . . . This is fatalism!"

Characteristically, Basil comes back at his wife with a joke; goes on more soberly; and ends the conversation with another joke. Mockery is, as always, his favorite stratagem for avoiding the pursuit of the darker implications of ideas. But whereas Howells had admired Basil's evasive humor in *Their Wedding Journey* as an indication of his superior intelligence, the novelist's appreciation of Basil's jokes in *A Hazard of New Fortunes* is tinged with contempt, even though the jokes are very much his own. For Howells' personality was marked, as is Basil's, by a "strain of . . . self-denunciation" which made it impossible for him to conceal the fact that after twenty years of writing satirical novels and farcical plays he had come to loathe his literary sense of humor. Despite his awareness of its charms, Howells came to view his mastery of the light touch as a means of avoiding all sorts of difficult confrontations.

That this painful self-judgment did not abate in the course of the nineties is attested to by *A Traveler from Altruria*, published four years after *Hazard*. A utopian romance, *Altruria* makes a number of telling criticisms of American culture, the most effective of which consists in the contrast between the nervous, insecure American writer, Mr. Twelvemough (that is, Duodecimo) and Mr. Homos, the traveler from Altruria, who is completely at ease at all times. As he shows the visitor about, Mr. Twelvemough tends more and more to give joking answers to the visitor's probing questions about American life. The jokes, though, go unappreciated, because, as the Altrurian says, "Our own humor is so very different." When Twelvemough presses him to tell what Altrurian humor is like, Homos replies, "I could hardly tell you, I'm afraid; I've never been much of a humorist myself"—at which point "a cold doubt of something ironical in the man" sweeps over Twelvemough. In the unstated but unmistakable opinion of the Altrurian, the American writer's humor is a disgusting defense mechanism.

Howells' remarkably critical attitude toward Basil March in *A Hazard of New Fortunes* stops well short, however, of outright rejection. In the course of the novel, the traditionally authoritative position of the observer in Howells' fiction is drastically undermined, in terms of perception, philosophy, and humor; yet at the end of the book Basil is still there, making judgments, cracking jokes, and attempting to reconcile the events of the story to his own way of thinking; quite literally, he has the last word. Despite his exposure of Basil's limitations, Howells clearly did not wish to give him up, or his wife either, for he not only clung to them in *Hazard*, he brought them back for encores in later novels of the nineties. If their old-fashioned viewpoint was out of date in 1890 and out of place in New York, it at least enabled them to function. In a time that was unreal, in a place that was an ugly exile, Howells found in the Marches a protective refuge from a world he did not wish to face.

## V

The novelist's sense of failure, though, raised obsessive autobiographical questions he could not ignore. In the same year that Basil March failed to enter into the slum life of New York's East Side, Howells began a historical exploration of his own boyhood in Ohio. The autobiographical effort that was launched with *A Boy's Town* in 1890 would persist for a quarter of a century, until Howells had surveyed half a century of his life in half a dozen full-length memoirs, a number of random essays, and a novel. At no point was the effort anything but difficult for him, emotionally speaking. In 1900, for instance, shortly after completing *Literary Friends and Acquaintance*, he expressed to Thomas Bailey Aldrich what a relief it was to finish the book: "In these days I seem to be all autobiography; but thank heaven I have done my reminiscences of literary Cambridge and Boston, and they are to be booked for oblivion next fall. How gladly I would never speak of myself again! But it's somehow always being tormented out of me, in spite of the small pleasure and pride the past gives me. 'It's so damned humiliating,' as Mark Twain once said of *his* past." Even more humiliating than the confrontation with his past was the autobiographer's knowledge that his memoirs did not tell the whole story about himself. Typically, Howells told only a part of the truth—and then scorned himself as a craven compromiser. Thus he confessed to Mark Twain that he would "like immensely to read your autobiography. You always rather bewildered me by your veracity, and I fancy you may tell the truth about yourself. But *all* of it? The black truth, which we all know of ourselves in our hearts, or only the whity-brown truth of the pericardium, or the nice, whitened truth of the shirtfront? Even *you* won't tell the black heart's-truth. The man who could do it would be famed to the last day the sun shone on." Henry Nash Smith and William M. Gibson have rightly observed that this paragraph is "in the diving mood of Hawthorne and Melville," but it also differentiates Howells' literary practice from his predecessors'. Although Howells had the courage to dive for the black heart's-truth, he was hesitant to describe to the world all he found.

Even so, *A Boy's Town* ranks as one of the most searching American autobiographies. Despite its reiterated and deliberately obscurantist thesis that boys are the same the wide world over, the book shows that Howells as a child was a very special case. At one and the same time, the boy's highly suggestible imagination was the willing servant of startlingly grandiose ambitions and devastating fears of inadequacy. On the one hand, when he precociously read Goldsmith's *History of Rome*, he promptly dreamed of himself as the heroic slayer of all tyrants from the time of Appius Claudius down to Domitian; and when he read and reread a little treatise his father gave him on Greek and Roman mythology, he transfigured himself in imagination into gods and demigods and heroes, "to the fancied admiration of all the other fellows." On the other hand, this fancier of "scenes and encounters of the greatest splendor, in which he bore a chief part," also dwelt "amid shadows." A remarkable compilation of recollected nightmares, *A Boy's Town* counts the goblins and other strange beings which were as vivid in Will Howells' youthful mind as anything that happened to him by day—which was not to say that the boy's daylight hours were not filled with imagined dangers, too. Thus the autobiographer remembered how his mother, attempting to cure her small son of the habit of talking to himself, said to him one day, in jest, "Don't you know that he who talks to himself has the devil for a listener?" Thereafter, the boy never dared to whisper above his breath when he was alone, even though both his Swedenborgian parents had taught him that there was no devil in the world save his own evil will.

Diving deeper into forgotten terrors, Howells recalled his shuddering reaction to the sound of a dog howling in the night because that was a sign that somebody was going to die, and how he used to keep his mouth tightly shut whenever he saw a lizard lest the lizard run down his throat. Will Howells also believed that if a blacksnake got the chance, it would run up his leg and tie itself round his body so that he could not breathe. Although he had never seen any, the boy accepted the existence of hairsnakes, which lurked in spring water and would grow in your stomach if you happened to swallow them. He had an abject fear of dying, too, and his fear was heightened by the fact that his grandfather Howells believed the end of the world was very near and went about talking of the need to prepare for the second coming of Christ. At home, the boy heard his father make jokes about this notion, but abroad, among boys who were predominantly Methodists, young Howells "took the tint of the prevailing gloom." One awful morning at school, the sky suddenly grew so dark that the students could not see to read their books. School was dismissed and Will walked home through the blackened air, convinced that the Judgment Day was upon him. After this apocalyptic crisis finally passed, other presentiments of death quickly took its place. The boy in fact tried very hard to will these presentiments because he was afraid of having them involuntarily. For the same reason, he attempted to fall into trances "in which he should know everything that was going on about him, all the preparations for his funeral, all the sorrow and lamentations, but should be unable to move or speak, and only be saved at the last moment by someone putting a mirror to his lips and finding a little blur of mist on it."

When he began to write stories and plays, this sort of imaginative projection also proved frightening to the boy, for as soon as he imagined the death of a character, he immediately became afraid that he was foreseeing his own fate. The climax of all these prophetic terrors was reached one night when he awoke and found the full moon shining into his room "in a very strange and phantasmal way." He sat up, looked at the moonlight washing the floor, and somehow it came into his mind that he was doomed to die when he was sixteen years old. Since he was only nine or ten years old at the time, the fear had ample time in which to wear itself out. But it did not. Instead, it became an increasingly severe torture to him with the turning of every year, until he passed his sixteenth birthday and entered upon the year of his doom. The agony became so great at this point that he could no longer bear it by himself, and so he confessed to his father what was going to happen. " 'Why,' his father said, 'you are in your seventeenth year now. It is too late for you to die at sixteen,' and all the long-gathering load of misery dropped from the boy's soul."

Sensing the spectral terrors in young Howells' mind, the other boys in town did their ingenious best to increase his torments. "Their invention," the autobiographer remembered, "supplied . . . any little lack of misery" that his own spectres and goblins had omitted. He frequently had narrow escapes from arrest and imprisonment—or so he thought—when the boys with whom he often built a fire in the street at night would suddenly kick the blaze and shout, "Run, run! The constable will catch you!" As the frightened Howells ran for his life down the street, he could hear the other boys laughing at him. The other boys were also fond of warning him that Solomon Whistler was bound to get him some day. The crazy man of the town, Whistler was a harmless creature who lived in the poorhouse, but he was sufficiently appalling in appearance and strange in manner to shrivel up Will Howells with terror whenever he saw him in actuality or in his dreams—and his terror increased under the other boys' mock-serious concern for his safety.

Given these cruelties, it is not surprising that although Howells in his youth knew "nearly a hundred boys," he "never had any particular friend among his schoolmates." He played and fought with them on "intimate terms," and he was a "good comrade" with any boy who wanted to go in swimming or out hunting. But there was no one in Boy's Town with whom he felt in total sympathy—save one, and he was an outcast from the group. This boy had never spent a willing day at school in his life. He had no more love of literature in him, or of learning of any sort, than the open fields. Yet it was precisely his kinship with nature that won Will Howells to him. In his company, Will felt able to rest his soul "from all its wild dreams and vain imaginings." Like a piece of the genial earth itself, the boy was "willing for anything, but passive, and without force or aim." No father was in evidence in the boy's life, but he seemed to have a mother, who smoked a corncob pipe, and two or three sisters, and they all lived in a log cabin that stood on the edge of a cornfield. How they survived was a mystery. The boy himself had no job, no plans, and no ambition, except to go swimming. He neither hunted nor foraged nor fished. He did not even care to play marbles. The contrast between him and the energetic, compulsively well-organized, future novelist could not have been greater. Nevertheless, Howells' reminiscence makes it clear that he had doted on this shiftless creature and had spent far more time with him than young Sam Clemens of Hannibal, Missouri, had with the ignorant, unwashed Tom Blankenship who later served Mark Twain as the model for Huckleberry Finn. On warm summer days, Will and his friend "soaked themselves in the river together, and then they lay on the sandy shore, or under some tree, and talked." What they talked about had nothing to do with the books Will was reading, or with the fume of dreams, both good and bad, that the books sent up in his mind. Instead, he simply "soothed" against the boy's "soft, caressing ignorance" the "ache" of his "fantastic spirit" and reposed his "intensity of purpose" in "that lax and easy aimlessness." Their friendship, Howells averred in *A Boy's Town*, was completely happy and completely innocent; "they loved each other, and that was all."

Perhaps the friendship could not have lasted in any event, and perhaps both boys knew it; yet the fact that Howells as autobiographer had to confront was that the breaking-up of the relationship was begun by his father and abetted by himself. Deeply committed to the Swedenborgian doctrine of selflessness, William Cooper Howells had taught his children to take the side of the lower whenever they were faced with a social choice. Practice, however, was somewhat different from theory, and he could not see "what good" his son would get from this "queer companion." As a result, the boy never once entered the Howellses' house and only seldom the yard; whenever he wanted to see Will, the boy stood outside the fence and waited patiently for him to appear, not even whistling to call attention to himself. Although the friendship persisted despite his father's disapproval, the young Howells eventually succumbed to parental objections in the sense that he attempted to reform the boy. He persuaded his friend to wash his hands and feet and face, don a new shirt, and come to school. As they had planned, Will escorted the boy to his seat, then turned around and owned his friendship with him before all the other students, who no more understood his fondness for the boy than had William Cooper Howells. He helped the boy to get his lessons, and stayed with him, "mentally and so cially," for the entire day, although he found it more difficult to do than he had expected. For some reason, there was a difference between being alone with the boy by the river and sitting beside him in the classroom, as if he "thought him just as good as any boy." Will was consequently much relieved when the boy dropped out of school a few days later, and neither of them seemed to care that they "never met again upon the old ground of perfect trust and affection." Only when he looked back on that event forty-five years later was Howells moved to declare that the death of this relationship was "somehow, a pity."

Why it was a pity, the author of *A Boy's Town* did not make explicit, but the meaning of his retrospective judgment was clear enough anyway. Through friendship with a shiftless boy (whose name he had apparently, in a Freudian lapse, forgotten), Will Howells had found psychic relief from the terrible tensions and loneliness of his early life. But in the end, his father's genteel values had reasserted their claim upon him and he had betrayed the friendship. In so doing he had betrayed himself. As a young man aspiring to success in Boston, Howells had learned how to hide his tensions behind a mask of unflappable urbanity—but would it not have been healthier if he had outgrown them in the course of a more relaxed and open childhood? As a novelist at the height of his powers, he had written *A Hazard of New Fortunes*, the most unsparing study of the middle-class, liberal mind in American literature—but would he not have written a more socially significant novel if he had been able to make the slum dwellers of New York the living, moving center of the story, as Tolstoi had made the Russian peasantry the ever-present protagonist of *The Cossacks* and *Anna Karenina*? In cutting himself off from circuits of American experience beyond the bounds of his father's approval, the child Howells had imposed both personal and artistic penalties upon the adult Howells. Beneath all of *A Boy's Town*'s diversionary rhetoric about how happy Howells was to have grown up where he did and how he did, and how certain he felt that whatever was "good in him now came from what was good in him then," there lurks the autobiographer's bitter consciousness that whatever was evil in him now had come from what was evil in him then.

In his understanding of the diseases of personality and of their tremendous staying power, the author of *A Boy's Town* was aided not only by the trained alertness of his literary intelligence but by the work of the French psychologist T. A. Ribot. A link in what Philip Rieff has called "the remarkable chain of reasoning about the relation between sickness and the past" that culminated in the investigations of Freud, Ribot's work so interested Howells that he wrote a novella based on his ideas. In the same *annus mirabilis* that produced *A Hazard of New Fortunes* and *A Boy's Town*, Howells published *The Shadow of a Dream*, in which he dramatized Ribot's contention that the evil we either forget or are oblivious of in our conscious minds nevertheless conditions our dreams, until finally we awake into full awareness of our illness. Like Ribot, Howells understood the past to be actively engaged in the present and constantly threatening to master it.

The dreams that Douglas Faulkner is tortured by in *The Shadow of a Dream* finally kill him; the autobiographical truths Howells uncovered in *A Boy's Town* markedly increased his pessimism in the years after 1890. As usual, he showed his "real face" most readily in his fiction. In *The Quality of Mercy* and *An Imperative Duty*, both published in 1892, a sense of entrapment is the predominating mood; for very different reasons, the most interesting character in each book feels himself to be caught in the mesh of old evils. Northwick in *The Quality of Mercy* steals money from the company of which he is the head, but although he vanishes into Canada and is rumored to be dead, he does not get away with the crime because he cannot escape his own memories. Rhoda Aldgate in *An Imperative Duty* has grown up thinking she is white, only to discover at the peak of her attractiveness to men that her mother was part Negro and that psychologically she herself cannot ignore her black "taint." Each book has a morally uplifting ending which illustrates the hoary Howellsian wisdom of as ye sow, so shall ye reap (in Northwick's case, the harvest is death; in Rhoda's, expatriate happiness in Italy), but the patent factitiousness of both illustrations only serves to intensify the impression created by these stories of an author who knew himself to be the prisoner of his past.

The essays Howells wrote in the nineties were also indicative of the darkness within him. "True, I Talk of Dreams," "Tribulations of a Cheerful Giver," and other magazine pieces that he collected in *Impressions and Experiences* (1896) puzzled and offended readers who had always counted on Howells' writings to entertain them. An anonymous critic who reviewed *Impressions* for the magazine *Critic* spoke for genteel Howellsians everywhere when he said that he found himself turning "away from Mr. Howells' impressions of our civilization, doubting their insight and sanity. They are too bad to be true, and have a certain malign, narcotic influence, difficult to describe and ill to feel."

A subtly malignant irony also undercuts the nostalgia of his literary reminiscences of New England that Howells began to publish in *Harper's Monthly* in the spring of 1894. When collected in *Literary Friends and Acquaintance* at the end of the decade, these essays brought Howells delighted letters from Annie Fields, Mrs. Francis J. Child, Thomas Bailey Aldrich, William James, and other New Englanders whose memories of Cambridge and Boston in the sixties and seventies had been rekindled by the novelist's deft evocations. New England egotism, however, prevented such readers from realizing that what Howells gave with one hand he took away with the other, in poetic repayment for the way that Boston had hemmed in an adventurer from Ohio and left him out at every turn. The portraits of Lowell and Holmes, for example, are graceful tributes to the wit and learning and hospitality of these men. But in the course of describing his first encounter with Hawthorne somewhat later on in his narrative, Howells took the occasion to reexamine Lowell and Holmes from a different perspective. First of all, he quoted Hawthorne's remark that the "apparent coldness" of the New England temperament was in fact a real coldness and that New England's "suppression of emotion for generations would extinguish it at last." Becoming more specific, Howells then affirmed that his memory of Nathaniel Hawthorne was

> one of the finest pleasures of my life. In my heart I paid him the same glad homage that I paid Lowell and Holmes, and he did nothing to make me think that I had overpaid him. This seems perhaps very little to say in his praise, but to my mind it is saying everything, for I have known but few great men, especially of those I met in early life, when I wished to lavish my admiration upon them, whom I have not the impression of having left in my debt. Then, a defect of the Puritan quality, which I have found in many New-Englanders, is that, unwittingly or wittingly, they propose themselves to you as an example, or if not quite this, that they surround themselves with a subtle ether of potential disapprobation, in which at the first sign of unworthiness in you, they helplessly suffer you to gasp and perish; they have good hearts, and they would probably come to your succor out of humanity, if they knew how, but they do not know how.

His later comments on Thoreau as abstract and air-drawn, on Whittier as "doubly cold to the touch of the stranger," on Parkman as possessing "those limitations which I nearly always found in the Boston men," and on Emerson as obtuse about Hawhorne, inaccurate about the West, contemptuous of Poe's verse in particular, insensitive to poetry in general, and "very gentle, like all those great New England men, but . . . cold, like many of them, to the new-comer, or to the old-comer who came newly," completed Howells' revised estimate of literary New England as he had known it.

Even Cambridge, which Howells at the time had preferred to Parkman's Boston or Emerson's Concord, and which loomed up in memory out of the materialistic frenzy of New York in the nineties as a kind of lost utopia of high thinking and plain living ("I do not believe," wrote Howells, "that since the capitalistic era began there was ever a community in which money counted for less"), was not permitted to escape from the memoirist's sweeping disgust with everything in his past that smacked of remoteness and not caring. Cambridge life, he said, may have been "refined," "intelligent," and "gracefully simple," but there was also a "good deal of contempt for the less lettered, and we liked to smile though we did not like to sneer." The democracy of James Russell Lowell, the literary Can-tabrigian to whom Howells had been closest, was a politics of the head, not the heart, and when Lowell blotted the line about America as the "Land of Broken Promise" he was "thinking of the shame of our municipal corruptions, the debased quality of our national statesmanship, the decadence of our whole civic tone, rather than of the increasing disabilities of the hardworking poor." In fine (albeit Howells did not say so in so many words), Cambridge had stood for a political, social, and intellectual elitism that had insulated Howells even more than had his genteel Ohio upbringing from the common run of American citizen who now concerned him, but whom he could not reach.

The only writer in *Literary Friends and Acquaintance* who fit-ted the Tolstoian ideals of the later Howells was not a New England-er. In August 1860, at the conclusion of his first literary pilgrimage to Boston and environs, Howells had proceeded south to New York, where he met Walt Whitman at Pfaff's on Broadway. The accidental encounter in the restaurant may very well have been awkward for the young Howells because his review—luckily unsigned—of the third edition of *Leaves of Grass* had just appeared in the New York *Satur-day Press*. While the reviewer had acknowledged that the book contained passages of "profound and subtle significance and of rare beauty," he had found others "gross and revolting." As for the verse, it was at once, "meterless, rhymeless, shaggy, coarse, sublime, disgusting, beautiful, tender, harsh, vile, elevated, foolish, wise, pure and nasty." Trying hard for sophistication, the twenty-three-year-old Howells had dissociated himself from "the Misses Nancy of criticism" who "hastened to scramble over the fence, and on the other side, stood shaking their fans and parasols . . . and shrieking, 'Beast! Beast!' " but then had revealed his own middle-class prudery by reproving Whitman for talking about "secrets of the body" which "should be decently hid." The embarrassed reader, the reviewer said, "goes through his book, like one in an ill-conditioned dream, perfectly nude, with his clothes over his arm." Thirty-five years later, however, the writer who recalled his "First Impressions of Literary New York" was not interested in reminding readers of his disagreements with Whitman. Instead of rehearsing his ancient objections to *Leaves of Grass*, the memoirist glided past them in a phrase: "The spiritual purity which I felt in him no less than the dignity is something that I will no more try to reconcile with what denies it in his page." John Burroughs in an article in *Critic* in 1892 had recently stressed the agreements between Howells and Whitman, and this is what Howells himself now wished to do. No moment in his memories of New England equals the emotional intensity of the recognition scene in Pfaff's. It was as if the author, in the process of recreating literary New York in 1860, had found again the lost and nameless friend of his Ohio boyhood:

> I remember how he leaned back in his chair, and reached out his great hand to me, as if he were going to give it me for good and all. He had a fine head, with a cloud of Jovian hair upon it, and a branching beard and mustache, and gentle eyes that looked most kindly into mine, and seemed to wish the liking which I instantly gave him, though we hardly passed a word, and our acquaintance was summed up in that glance and the grasp of his mighty fist upon my hand.

In these finely chosen and moving words, Howells announced his solidarity with the American writer who had most completely identified himself with the hopes and sufferings of all his countrymen. Yet there was also a quality of sadness in the announcement, which stemmed from Howells' awareness of how belated, how terribly belated, it was. As editor of the *Atlantic*, he had been mindful of Boston's prejudice against Whitman and had never printed a line of his work. Not until 1889, when he gave *November Boughs* a friendly review in the "Editor's Study" in *Harper's*, did Howells figuratively hold out his hand to the man who had stretched out his "for good and all" in the summer of 1860. Once again, an act of autobiography had reminded Howells of the betrayal of friendship and of self-betrayal.

## VI

Jonathan Sturges, the young Princetonian who cut a wide swath in London society in the nineties despite his being helplessly crippled by poliomyelitis, told his novelist friend Henry James in the fall of 1895 about an extraordinary conversation he had had with Howells the year before in the painter Whistler's garden in the Rue du Bac in Paris. Howells was leaving Paris, even though he had just arrived, called back to America by a cable saying that his father was dying. The novelist had been staggered by the news. As a child he had been much closer to his mother, loving her with "my child's heart," but in later years he had come to love his father with "my man's." Furthermore, his father's passing forcibly reminded Howells of his own mortality. As he would write to Charles Eliot Norton on October 25, 1894, "It has aged me as nothing else could have done. I am now of the generation next to death." When, therefore, Howells encountered young Sturges on the eve of his departure from Paris, he was feeling even more depressed than was his wont in the nineties. He had missed so much of life, he felt; he had turned his back on so many opportunities for spiritual enlargement; and now he was old, with iron-gray hair and an iron-gray mustache. Partly because Howells was upset and partly because Sturges was a cripple, handsome and vigorous above the waist, but terribly wasted below, the novelist spoke with utter frankness to a comparative stranger. In the midst of a garden party on a June afternoon in Paris, the grieving novelist revealed his rock-bottom despair. According to the record of his conversation with Sturges that James indefatigably set down in his notebooks, Sturges' first impression of Howells at the party had been that he felt somewhat "out of it," standing and watching the other guests in rather a "brooding, depressed, and uneasy way." At last, "under some determining impression, some accumulation of suggestions," Howells had laid his hand on Sturges' shoulder and made him a small speech:

Oh, *you're* young, you're blessedly young—be glad of it; be glad of it and *live*. Live all you can: it's a mistake not to. It doesn't so much matter what you do—but live. This place and these impressions, as well as many of those, for so many days, of So-and So's and So-and-So's life, that I've been receiving and that have had their abundant message, make it all come over me. I see it now. I haven't done so enough before—and now I'm old; I'm, at any rate, too old for what I see. Oh, I *do* see, at least—I see a lot. It's too late. It has gone past me. I've lost it. It couldn't, no doubt, have been different for me—for one's life takes a form and holds one; one lives as one can. But the point is that *you* have time. That's the great thing. You're, as I say, damn you, so luckily, so happily, so hatefully young. Don't be stupid. Of course I don't dream you *are*, or I shouldn't be saying these awful things to you. Don't, at any rate, make *my* mistake. Live.

Out of the materials of this speech (which he had already converted from the Howellsian to the Jamesian mode of discourse in the very act of recording it), James eventually created one of the most appealing of post-Civil War observers, Lambert Strether in *The Ambassadors*. Howells himself made a different use of his despair. In an act of ruthless creativity, he came home from Paris, buried his father, and wrote a novel in which he broke the observer's imaginative control of his fiction and permitted a new sort of ruling figure to come to the fore. *The Ambassadors* represented the culmination of a literary tradition; *The Landlord at Lion's Head* inaugurated another.

Howells started work on *The Landlord* in an apartment overlooking Central Park in the winter following the death of his father. The germ of the book had been working in his mind ever since the summer of 1890, when he and his wife had spent two weeks at the Green Mountain View House at Willsboro Point, New York, on the western shore of Lake Champlain. While there, Howells had written to his father that "the history of this house is a tragedy. The owner of the beautiful farm where it stands, an old soldier, began taking boarders, made money, became ambitious, built the hotel, and mortgaged everything to pay for it. Last year it was sold at auction; and the poor old fellow is living with his old wife in a second floor tenement in Rutland, picking up what jobs he can get." However, when Howells finally began to write the novel, he found that an anecdote of failure had somehow turned into a success story and that his attitude toward his material was unprecedentedly different from what it had been in all his other works.

Within a very short time, he started to have trouble writing the book. "I remember concerning it," he commented some years later, "a very becoming despair when, at a certain moment in it, I began to wonder what I was driving at." His only solution was to "keep working; keep beating harder and harder at the wall which seemed to close in me, till at last I broke through into the daylight beyond." Carrying the uncompleted manuscript with him to Magnolia, Massachusetts, and Long Beach, Long Island, he kept beating hard at the wall throughout the summer of 1895. By the time the Howellses returned to New York in the fall, the novelist had begun to see daylight. The manuscript was completed in the winter of 1896, approximately a year after it had been started. Yet Howells was still strangely uncertain about the worth of what he had created, so that when he took the manuscript to Henry Loomis Nelson, the editor of *Harper's Weekly*, to see if Nelson would be interested in serializing it, he did so "in more fear of his judgment than I cared to show." Upon hearing some weeks later that Nelson had accepted the novel, Howells could "scarcely gasp out my unfeigned relief." The first installment of the book appeared in the *Weekly* on July 4, 1896, a fitting date for a new beginning in American literature.

The stranger who comes up through the hill country of New England to paint a picture of the mountain that looks like a lion's head seems at first glance to be a particularly vigorous version of the Howellsian observer. A native of Wisconsin, Westover had "lived in the woods" until he was sixteen, when he began to "paint my way out." After a brief sojourn in New York, where "they made me think I was nobody," he had gone abroad, to Italy. Upon his return to the States he had decided to pursue his career in Boston. As he enters the yard of the Durgin family at the beginning of the story, Westover is still a young man, nattily dressed in a Norfolk jacket and aggressively self-confident in manner. Whereas the youthful Howells had been profoundly afraid of dogs and had fantasied that a bite he once received would probably cause him to die of hydrophobia, the young Westover expresses his opinion of the Durgins' dog by briskly kicking it in the jaw. Standing with "bold ease" in the farmhouse yard, Westover orders the Durgins' youngest boy, Jeff, to fetch his mother so that the painter may buy his dinner from her. Later in the day, when he has set up his easel and begun to paint the mountain, the boy returns and ventures the opinion that "I don't think that looks very much like it." Totally unruffled, Westover replies, "Perhaps you don't know." The boy rejoins, "I know what I see," to which Westover replies, "I doubt it." On the question of representing reality, the Howellsian observer thinks he knows best, and in fact Westover's relations with Jeff Durgin never cease to be marked by a sense of superiority, no matter what the question. During that first visit to Lion's Head, the painter does not hesitate to grab the boy by the scruff of the neck for playing a trick on young Cynthia Whitwell, and later in the story when Jeff grows up and goes to Harvard, Westover is there in Boston to rebuke the undergraduate for his cavalier treatment of debutantes.

For his part, Jeff Durgin is impressed by Westover in certain

ways; for example, he buys a Norfolk jacket, in imitation of the painter's sartorial mode, as soon as he is big enough to wear one and
can afford the price. Yet he is singularly unmoved by most of the advice he receives from the painter, while Westover's increasingly strin-
gent criticisms of his conduct do not deter him in the slightest. In
*The Adventures of Huckleberry Finn, The Portrait of a Lady, The
Rise of Silas Lapham*, and other major novels of the post-Civil War
generation, the protagonists had made moral choices, but Jeff Durgin
believes that human behavior is nonintentioned, that "most things in
this world" simply "happen," and are therefore not subject to moral
strictures. As for the idea that men pay for their sins with unhappiness, the rustic old Yankee named Whitwell, whose shrewdness is
indicated in his name, points out to Westover that even though Jeff
Durgin is a "bad feller," he has prospered "hand over hand."

Westover, on the other hand, argues that to deny the existence
of a moral government of the universe is to make a tragic mistake.
"A tree brings forth of its own kind. As a man sows he reaps. It's
dead sure, pitilessly sure." However, by the time he delivers himself
of this classic statement of observer-morality, the action of the novel
has revealed him to be not the sage he thinks he is but rather a pomp-
ous weakling whose didactic comments are colored by envy. Far
from fulfilling the artistic promise of his youth, this man from the
woods of the Midwest has achieved a rather frivolous success as the
teacher of an art class for select young ladies in Boston, while as a
painter in his own right he has found—to his disappointment—that
"painting pictures of the mountain . . . had . . . become his specialty."
The vigor of his personal manner has also faded in the course of
years. Among females old and young he has a considerable reputa-
tion for Christian goodness and cosmopolitan savoir faire; ladies as
different as the indomitable innkeeper, Mrs. Durgin, and the giddy
expatriate, Mrs. Vostrand, consult him constantly. But these
feminine relationships have the effect of revealing, indeed of foster-
ing, Westover's effeminate qualities. Despite his protestation that
"I'm not a woman in everything!" he very nearly is. A balding bachelor, he has lived a bohemian life not out of preference ("at
heart he was philistine and bourgeois"), but because he has lacked

the masculine assurance to propose marriage to Jeff Durgin's old girl friend, Cynthia Whitwell, whom he has loved for years. After a decade and a half of kissless frustration, he speaks his mind to her—only to add hastily that she "Take time. Don't hurry. Forget what I've said—or no, that's absurd!" Cynthia gravely indicates that she will probably accept him (Jeff Durgin having married someone else), but she is sufficiently constrained by the painter's Prufrockian rectitude as to feel sure that "I should always have to call you Mr. Westover"—to which arrangement he gives, in the last line of the novel, his assent.

Juxtaposed in the novel with this devastatingly ironic portrait of the artist as a middle-aged prig is the immensely vital characterization of Jeff Durgin. "A true rustic New England type in contact with urban life under entirely modern conditions," Jeff combines country-boy virility with Harvard-trained indifference. With his hard body and brutal insouciance, he fascinates a wide variety of women, from a simple girl like Cynthia Whitwell to a jaded post-debutante like Bessie Lynde. (When Jeff kisses Bessie, she realizes that "she had been kissed as once she had happened to see one of the maids kissed by the grocer's boy at the basement door. In an instant this man had abolished all her defenses of family, of society, of personality, and put himself on a level with her in the most sacred things of life.") Although his earlier philanderings are reported by Westover to Mrs. Vostrand, Jeff is not thereby prevented—as Westover was sure he would be—from marrying her daughter Genevieve, for Genevieve wants Jeff, no matter what his history. Taking what he likes and discarding what he does not, Jeff is rarely bothered by the damage he wreaks in the lives of others, and he justifies his recklessness by the biological fatalism that Basil March had merely "mused" about: "I didn't make myself, and I guess if the Almighty don't make me go right it's because He don't want me to." Such ruthless honesty does not, of course, sit well with Westover, but it did not prevent Howells in later years from saying that he had always liked Jeff "more than I have liked worthier men," and it definitely contributes to his appeal to the women in the novel. Like the mistresses of Frank Cowperwood, the superman-hero of Dreiser's *The*

*Financier* and *The Titan*, Jeff's girls are sexually responsive to a sham-smasher.

Womanizing, pleasure-oriented Jeff is also extremely practical. In contrast to Westover's sensitive quests for European beauty, Jeff goes abroad to pick up tips about hotel management. The Lion's Head that Westover paints and repaints is in Jeff's eyes just a real-estate asset which improves the value of the family property. At college, his wealthier classmates are "consumed with . . . melancholy . . . at the prospect of having to leave Harvard and go out into the hard, cold world," but Jeff can hardly wait to start earning money. When he finally is graduated from college and takes command at Lion's Head, he builds it into a far grander establishment than it had ever been before. Like another Dreiser hero, the saloon manager Hurstwood in *Sister Carrie*, Jeff likes the glamor and prestige of running a posh establishment. The genteel life of a Boston lawyer—his mother's dream for him—is a dead option in Jeff's imagination; the times he comes alive are on coaching parties with his rich clients, during which Jeff wears (so the old Yankee, Whitwell, tells us) "a reg'lar English coachman's rig, with boots outside his trouse's and a long coat and a fuzzy plug hat: I can tell you he looks *gay*!" In a brilliant review written in the spring of 1899, Howells would call Thorstein Veblen's *Theory of the Leisure Class* "an opportunity for American fiction," but he himself had already exploited the novelistic possibilities of conspicuous consumption and other Veblenian concepts in his account of the life and times of the luxury-hotel operator, Thomas Jefferson Durgin.

Even more remarkable, though, than Howells' satirization of Jeff is the extent to which he refrained from making fun of him. In *The Landlord at Lion's Head*, the shafts of Howellsian wit are primarily directed at Westover and his Boston society friends, while Jeff Durgin is placed in a social context that seriously explains rather than lightly derides his vulgar aspirations. The poverty of his childhood on a miserable, hard-scrabble farm; the deaths of four of his older brothers and sisters and the consumptive coughs of the remaining five; the appalling spectacle of his father, dragging himself "spectrally about the labors of the farm, with the same cough at sixty

which made his oldest son at twenty-nine look scarcely younger than
himself''; the extra efforts made by his massively strong mother
(whose good health only Jeff of all her children has inherited) to keep
the family alive, first by selling milk at five cents a glass and black
maple sugar at three cents a cake to the tourists who came to look at
the mountain, then by providing rooms and meals to Westover and
other visitors, and finally by opening an inn: these are the experiences which lie behind Jeff's savage conduct, and Howells tells us
about them with a sympathy that recalls Whitman and Tolstoi and a
pity that anticipates Dreiser. As Howells wrote to his sister Aurelia
immediately upon completing the novel, he had not made Jeff a
"determinate character," but rather a "mixture of good and bad." In
other words, instead of fixing him in a comic viewpoint, he had seen
him in the more complex perspective of American tragedy.

Neither the sales nor the reviews of *The Landlord* were particularly impressive. As Henry James told Owen Wister, only "six-
and-a-half Americans know how good it is" (when Wister said,
"Counting me?" James replied, "Yes, my dear Owen, you're the
half!"). Howells responded to these disappointments with a reflex action: he hauled out Basil and Isabel March once again and sent them
off on *Their Silver Wedding Journey*. The path-breaking achievement of *The Landlord* in putting aside the intermediary figure of the
observer and directly confronting American sordidness had largely
gone unnoticed, and Howells pessimistically returned to his tried-
and-true, sure-fire formulas. Convinced that his novelistic vision was
no longer relevant to modern readers, he continued writing because
he always had.

In May 1902, however, he received a letter from a young writer
telling him how much the work of William Dean Howells had meant
to him. In spite of his rapidly worsening despondency that spring
over the virtual suppression, two years before, of his first novel—a
despondency that was already making it difficult for him to proceed
with the writing of his second novel and that would shortly lead him
to the brink of suicide—Theodore Dreiser roused himself one day to
express to Howells

my spiritual affection for you—to offer my little tribute
and acknowledge the benefit I have received from your
work. . . . Thomas Hardy has provided some of this spiritual fellowship for me. Count Tolstoy yet some more. Of
you three however I should not be able to choose, the spirit
in each seeming to be the same, and the large, tender
kindliness of each covering all of the ills of life and voicing
the wonder and yearning of this fitful dream, in what, to
me, seems a perfect way. I may be wrong in my estimate of
life, but the mental attitude of you three seems best—the
richest, most appealing flowering-out of sympathy, ten-
derness, uncertainty, that I have as yet encountered.

The letter certainly must have cheered Howells, but with his com-
pulsive modesty he may have recognized it as an overstatement, as
certainly we must. For Howells found ''a perfect way'' of writing
about ''the ills of life'' on only two occasions, which makes his career
somewhat different from Hardy's and very different from Tolstoi's.
Yet each of those occasions was momentous. In the Haymarket letter
of 1887, he renewed the involvement of American writers in matters
of social and political consequence. In *The Landlord at Lion's Head*
he broke through the self-concern of the post-Civil War novelists to
the broader outlook of twentieth-century naturalism. The at-
tentiveness to human suffering that underlay both the letter and *The
Landlord* flowered out of the suffering of Howells himself.

# *5*

# The Octopus

Henry James criticized *War and Peace* for its looseness and bagginess; one wonders what he might have said about *The Octopus*. Sprawling and huge, crowded with characters, seething with events luridly outlined against the panoramic backdrop of an enormous western valley, Norris' most ambitious work extravagantly displays all the formal weaknesses to which James felt the epical novel was dangerously susceptible. Measured by any architectonic standard, *The Octopus* is a literary chaos. What gives the novel coherence, what focuses its terrific energies, is that for all its swirl and sweep and sprawl, the book is fundamentally a story of three young men. Through them, Norris' epic is bound together.

The three young men have only casual connections with one another. They are not related by family ties, as are the three brothers Karamazov; they do not remember a common loss, as do Hamlet, Laertes, and Fortinbras; in personality, they are miles apart—Annixter, with his explosive temper and nervous stomach, his ferocious energy and his curious fastidiousness, is as different from the neuras-

SOURCE: From "Introduction" in *The Octopus* by Frank Norris. Introduction by Kenneth S. Lynn. Reprinted by permission of the Houghton Mifflin Company.

thenic poet Presley as he is from the exalted, God-defying Vanamee. Nevertheless, they share certain extremely significant resemblances. All three are college graduates, widely read, conscious of their intelligence, what Europeans would call intellectuals—although Annixter would be the first to fling down the book he was reading and deny the charge. Above all, they are lonely, disaffiliated men. Vanamee's terrible self-exile in the desert makes his case the most dramatic, but Presley and Annixter both are acutely aware of what it is like to feel cut off from society. In the San Joaquin, Presley is completely out of place: "These uncouth brutes of farm-hands and petty ranchers, grimed with the soil they worked upon, were odious to him beyond words. Never could he feel in sympathy with them, nor with their lives, their ways, their marriages, deaths, bickerings, and all the monotonous round of their sordid existence." Annixter, boasting of how many men hate him, fearful of being trapped into marriage, who in a moment of rare self-revelation admits that he has never had a good time in his life, seems the loneliest of all. Finally, each is seeking, in the teeth of uncertainty and self-doubt, for a way out of his isolation.

In significant works of the imagination, a noted critic of modern literature has observed, the principal characters oftentimes represent unresolved aspects of the author's personality. Certainly this is true of Norris and the three young men of *The Octopus*. Through their seeking for a new relation to the world, he sought to resolve certain problems of his own. To appreciate the perils of their several quests—how big the game was that Norris and the three young men were hunting—it is necessary first of all to say something about the nature of the literary situation confronting Norris when, in the '90s, he decided to become a writer.

II

The sensation of loneliness, W. H. Auden has shrewdly observed, is the central quality of American writing. Whether one listens to the private confessions of the Puritan diarists, or to the screams of Davy Crockett in the southern wilderness; to the grotesques pouring out their dreams to George Willard in Winesburg, Ohio, or to one of Melville's word-drunk isolatoes, one hears a native accent imaging a vast loneliness. Sometimes the images have carried connotations of personal power and freedom, as in Emerson and Thoreau, or of momentary release, as in Emily Dickinson, but more often they have borne a darkly sinister freight of horror and despair. In particular has this been true of American writing of the nineteenth century—how often one encounters the ghastly specter of loneliness in Brockden Brown and Poe, in Irving and Hawthorne, in Melville, Mark Twain, and Henry James! Reappearing with increasing frequency across the century, the specter assumed two different guises.

In the first five or six decades, loneliness wore the mask of human pride; isolation was tied up with the mad temptations of the unbridled ego, with the fear of being overwhelmed from without or betrayed from within—in a word, with death. By the last twenty years of the century, however, the horror of death had given way, by and large, to the chilling despair at not having lived at all. Instead of associations with overweening ambition, loneliness now connoted powerlessness, emptiness, and futility. The characteristic heroes of American literature were still orphans and castaways, but Ahab and Natty Bumppo were succeeded by a collection of "bad" boys, fatally inexperienced young girls, and self-mocking middle-aged men who seem older than they are. Instead of Poe's M. Dupin, who sought to order the flux of life by a solitary effort of mind, who had no use for society's pathetic round, there emerged—for example—the disaffected little boy whom Henry James reminiscentially evoked in *A Small Boy and Others*. Overwhelmed with the sense of being an outsider, of being "other," to use James' poignant term, the boy stands wistfully gazing at the candy in the confectioner's window or at the children playing in the park—at the prizes of life which he cannot have; at the society in which he feels himself an alien. Somewhere, somehow, the terrors of self-sufficiency had metamorphosed into an aching sense of personal inadequacy and a yearning desire for human connection; the quest for the white whale had given way to the quest of Norris' three young men.

The point at which the first form of loneliness began to be replaced by the second can be located with some precision: the Civil War is the great divide. For what primarily the shift reflects is the bewilderingly swift social displacement suffered by the intellectual leadership in the United States between 1850 and 1870.

Well before the Civil War, it is true, Emerson had objected to the lack of a male principle in American literature, and "The American Scholar" had called with such passion and intensity on the bright young men of the country to stand up and assert their genius as to leave no doubt how deeply Emerson believed that the best lacked all conviction. But whatever their shortcomings, however often they timorously took popgun shots to be the crack of doom, intellectuals nevertheless retained a significant share in the control of American society down to the 1850s, when, as Henry Adams remembered in his *Education*, the violence of the slavery controversy made a mockery of the very concept of control.

Eighteen sixty-five did not restore the status quo ante. The unexampled rise to power of the new industrial elite effectively crushed all such hopes. In the age of Jackson, writers like Bancroft and Cooper had been influential voices in the community, but in the age of Grant, Henry Adams felt that nobody was listening any more, and Mark Twain found that no one would take his humor seriously. A "status revolution," as Professor Richard Hofstadter has called it, had eroded with stunning speed the prestige and authority of writers, editors, professors, and ministers. Anti-intellectualism, which had always fed on the tyranny of democratic conformism, now battened as well on the hero-worship of millionaires who boasted that they had never read a book. Unlike his European counterpart, who had also witnessed the triumph of the new industrial order, the American intellectual had no aristocracy to fall back upon as a refuge and a reinforcement against the Rockefellers and the Fisks, nor could he find any genuine reassurance within himself, because the greatest irony of all was that the potential American scholar in 1870 was sufficiently a child of his time that he could not help measuring himself by the very standards he deplored as vicious and vulgar, thereby lending his personal assent to the burgeoning myth of the essential irrelevance of his dreams and the impracticality of his ideas, of his inadequacy, even, as a man. By way of counterattack, attitudes of superiority—in education, in blood, in personal rectitude—were conscientiously cultivated, but they tended to be hollow at the center. Much of the intellectual humor of the day reveals this hollowness with particular clarity. Wendell Phillips' brilliantly sarcastic remark, in re American democracy, that as in chemistry the scum floats to the top, sprang not from serene condescension, but rather from an agonized awareness that the "best men"—as Lord Bryce termed them—were politically impotent. And was not Charles Francis Adams, Jr.'s witty confession that not one of the big financiers whom he had known would he care to meet again, "either in this world or the next," a product not only of his shame at having lent himself, for the better part of his mature life, to what he regarded as the coarseness of money-getting, but also of the disturbing fact that his railroad career had not even come close to matching the triumphs of a Vanderbilt or a Harriman?

For the most sensitive and revealing response to the fact that the intellectual had lost his role in American life, however, one must turn elsewhere than to the sour-grapes wit of a Phillips or an Adams; one must look to the writers of the period. Literary artists, to adapt Pound's famous phrase somewhat, are the antennae of the race, and it is in the work of Mark Twain, Henry James, and Henry Adams—the three greatest American writers of their day—that one finds the richest registration of what had happened.

Adults, Mark Twain said, were liars and cheats; his most memorable heroes are children. The magnetic pull backward to his childhood that Twain felt was, in part, a neurotic wish to retreat to a world of security and nonobligation—when one remembers the astounding proliferation of books about children that took place in this country after the Civil War, there can be little doubt that the wish to evade the psychological penalties which the American writer was forced to pay in the Gilded Age was always present in

Twain's imagination. But more than safety, Twain sought in his memories of the past to recapture a Wordsworthian freshness of experience, to taste again the delicious newness of first impressions. Joel Chandler Harris explained through one of his characters what quality of life it was that both he and his friend Twain were after in writing about children: "Folks ain't half as smart when they grow up as they is when they're little children. They shet their eyes to one whole side of life. Kin you fling your mind back to the time when your heart was soft, an' your eyes sharp enough for to see what grown people never seed?"

That a lustrous magic and mystery had been blotted out of the minds of adults was not so much because they were no longer young, but because of the business culture's drab insistence on the prosaic, its deification of the practical. Twain said of Franklin's *Poor Richard* that it was full of animosity toward boys—by which he meant that the self-help ethic was the deadly enemy of the imagination; and Harris said of the businessman that "his dreams remained so persistently on the hither side of concrete things, he was so completely invested with the cold and critical views that were the result of his education, that his mind never ventured much beyond his material interests, and he never tried to peep around the many corners that life presents. . . ." The same hunger—amidst the hog-swilling of the Great Barbecue—for a feast of the senses and imagination was what drew Henry Adams to the Middle Ages. Adams, to be sure, did not use the persona of the child on his journey into the medieval past—he preferred the mask of a rather exhausted avuncular figure. Nevertheless, as he wrote in his *Mont-Saint-Michel*, "the man who wanders into the twelfth century is lost, unless he can grow prematurely young." For what aged uncles were apt to encounter in the twelfth century was a world as keenly alive, and every bit as fantastic, as Tom Sawyer's Hannibal:

> The twelfth century had the child's love of sweets and spices and preserved fruits, and drinks sweetened or spiced, whether they were taken for supper or for poetry; the true knight's palate was fresh and his appetite excellent

either for sweets or verses or love; the world was young then; Robin Hoods lived in every forest, and Richard Coeur-de-Lion was not yet twenty years old. The pleasant adventures of Robin Hood were real, as you can read in the stories of a dozen outlaws, and men troubled themselves about pain and death much as healthy bears did, in the mountains. Life had miseries enough, but few shadows deeper than those of the imaginative lover, or the terrors of ghosts at night. Men's imaginations ran riot, but did not keep them awake; at least, neither the preserved fruits nor the mulberry wine nor the clear syrup nor the gingerbread nor the Holy Graal kept Perceval awake, but he slept the sound and healthy sleep of youth, and when he woke the next morning, he felt only a mild surprise to find that his host and household had disappeared, leaving him to ride away without farewell, breakfast, or Graal.

Shot through with color and light, havens of refuge for men who would be children, *Tom Sawyer* and *Huckleberry Finn*—and *Mont-Saint-Michel and Chartres*—are in a very real sense regressive fantasies. But on their journeys into the past, Twain and Adams were not "traveling light," in the manner of a Thomas Bailey Aldrich or a Booth Tarkington; they carried with them the burden of the present. Their mood of recaptured delight, as a result, constantly falters; suddenly, as darkness comes hugely down upon the light, child's play becomes a grim business. Havens of refuge turn out to be solitary confinement cells and sealed-off caves (no one can hear the anguished cries of the incarcerated victims); momentary interludes of feeling free and easy on a raft inexorably terminate in devastating loneliness. The beautiful equilibrium of a gothic cathedral is revealed, upon closer examination, to be "visibly delicate beyond the line of safety," and "danger lurks in every stone"; for all its skyward aspirations, the pathos of self-distrust and anguish are the cathedral's "last secret," buried in the earth by artists who once had stood at the very center of society, but who were already losing their place before Chartres was finished. (Gazing beyond the final disintegration of the medieval world, Adams bitterly challenged the twentieth century to read out of the cathedral "whatever else pleases your youth and confidence.") Inexperienced children and aging tourists that they are, the heroes of Twain and Adams are incapable of averting the tragedies of which they are the helpless witnesses; standing outside of history and society, they are strangers—strangers "in the extremest sense of the word," to borrow Melville's terrible phrase from *The Confidence-Man*—who are doomed to suffer because their understanding (which is the source of their heroism) is absurdly disproportionate to their ability to act. Like Miss Lonelyhearts or Tiresias, Quentin Compson or Nick Adams—who are their descendants—they can record their nightmares but not exorcise them.

For Henry James, holding tenaciously to his sense of the artist's glory, his inexhaustible sensibility, his power to turn the tables on all ghosts and send them fleeing, the despairing fun poked at a chaotic world by Twain and Adams, particularly in their later years, was an attitude he rejected to the end. Even in the black days at the end of the '80s when the interest in his work seemed to him to have been reduced to zero, and the even blacker days of 1895 when a five-year effort to become a successful playwright, to achieve honor and glory in what was to James not only the most glamorous of literary arenas but a "greater institution than the House of Commons," culminated in his being booed from the stage, one finds him in his notebooks rallying with amazing speed, and enjoining himself yet once again to meet the challenge of the life of the artist.

But the James who in 1895 rededicated himself anew to his art was nevertheless a changed man from the young writer who had once dreamed of being the secretary of modern society. He who had sought great audiences, only to be booed by the mob, now wrote, as one critic has put it, for an audience of one. The panoramic social novels he had attempted at the end of the '80s gave way to fairy stories and ghostly tales. The imagination once possessed, as Mr. Trilling has reminded us, by disaster, now became "the imagination of atrocity." Of the atrocities which engaged the later James, none fascinated him more than the morally innocent child who is corrupted or destroyed by society. In 1885, in "The Author of Beltraffio,'' James had written a story of a "Christian" woman who deliberately lets her child die of diphtheria, and in "The Pupil" (1892) he had again reverted to the child-atrocity theme, but only after the crushing disaster of his theatrical career—the point at which it might be said that James' personal experience of rejection became archetypical of the social experience of his whole literary generation in America—did the vision of the lonely child adrift in a monstrous world fully emerge in his imagination. *The Turn of the Screw* and *What Maisie Knew* are James' psychological equivalents of Twain's picaresques of childhood terror.

The Adamsian persona of the self-mocking middle-aged man who feels "out of it" also came to the fore in James' late work. Sometimes these men are artists or writers, who either "work in the dark," as the dying writer in "The Middle Years" exclaims, or who if recognized by a philistine society are suffocated to death in its embrace, like the hero of "The Death of the Lion." But more often they are men without métier, whose lives are all preparation and no fulfillment, all dilettante pleasure and no purpose. Afraid of women, unsure of their sanity, these men seem to be drowning—to use one of the most recurrent of James' late metaphors—in some dim waterworld in which they have never learned to swim until too late. Of all James' projections of this figure, Lambert Strether of *The Ambassadors* is, of course, the most subtly realized, and it is not surprising that Strether first came to the surface of James' consciousness in the months following the final fiasco of his career as a playwright. Nor is it a wonder that the conception of Strether should have germinated in an anecdote about William Dean Howells, the apostolic successor to the Brahmins of Boston culture and the most influential American writer of his day. For while James purposely did not make Strether a writer, in order to heighten the ineffectuality of his hero's career, Strether's inferiority complex nevertheless mirrors the personal uncertainty which in a world of robber barons haunted even a writer as beloved and honored as Howells. Ashamed of the fact that he has never "succeeded" in the conventional American way, a failure as a husband and a failure as a father, who in his youth had had high hopes of literary achievement, but who is now the aging, disappointed editor of a little magazine that publishes articles on subjects in which he has no interest, who is obsessed with the idea that he has missed out on life, Strether is a forlornly comic, Quixotic figure, incapable of acting positively; he can reach heroism only through renunciation. If the later James left open the possibility of salvation, as Twain and Adams did not, salvation is nevertheless to be won only through a total surrender and abnegation. James' maturest vision of the American intellectual's relation to his society is that if the latter were to be saved from the consequences of its success, then the former must be prepared to stick to his career of failure, write for an audience of one, gain nothing—in any of the accepted American senses—for himself.


### III

The virtues of renunciation and solitary dedication, however, were not what Strether—and James—preached to Norris' generation. Little Bilham, the young artist whom the hero of *The Ambassadors* encounters in Paris, is enjoined by Strether to make the connection with life that he has missed, is urged, in the most vitally important scene in the novel, to live all he can. For many of the bright young men of America who came of age in the '80s and '90s, something like Strether's recommendation became the motto of their lives. Like Little Bilham, they had witnessed the older intellectual generation's agony of being "out of it" and were determined, for their part, to make a plunge into life. With the futility of the mugwumps in mind, Theodore Roosevelt determined to succeed in politics by coming up through the wards (the bosses—he was almost fanatical about this—would never scornfully refer to *him* as a eunuch or a "Miss Nancy" figure, as they had to George William Curtis and other postwar reformers). John Jay Chapman, descendant of abolitionists, took Emerson as his hero and restated "The American Scholar" as a turn-of-the-century credo. The novelist Henry Blake Fuller, torn between expatriatism and the South Side of Chicago, between realism and what he called idealism as fictional modes, chose Chicago and realism; by an act of will, he turned his back on the culture of Latin Europe, to which he was instinctively drawn, because he wished to ally himself—to make a connection—with democracy and the bright norm of commonplace American life.

The attempt by so many of the younger intellectuals of the '90s to reestablish vital contact with the mainstream of life in the United States was emotional in the extreme, produced as it was by a revulsion against the crippling isolation of their elders. The emotion is most clearly discernible in the striking fact of their terrific energy and their inordinate admiration of strenuousness. Like Stephen Crane, they were prepared to go to the ends of the earth at the drop of a hat; like Theodore Dreiser, they were intoxicated by the drive and pace of metropolitan life; like the muckraker David Graham Phillips, they worked prodigious hours (or fantasied that they did). The classic example of the type was T. R., the neurasthenic young man who joined the Harvard boxing squad and broke horses in the West. (Roosevelt's self-conscious athleticism has had a continuing vogue—one thinks of how hard Fitzgerald took his failure to make the football squad at Princeton or of Hemingway's insistence on talking about life and literature in metaphors derived from the prize ring and the baseball diamond.)

But the strenuous life could not cloak, for all its swift movement and titanic energy, a fundamental indecisiveness and unsureness. For the decision to plunge into life was more easily taken than happily carried out—as Frank Norris' best novel would demonstrate. The urgent desire to escape the dilemma of the older generation did not make that dilemma any easier to resolve—indeed, the problem of effective action by the intellectuals had become even more severe in the era of financial trusts and social plutocracies, of enormous urban concentrations and the "new immigration" that sprang into being at the close of the century. "Too lateness," as "The Snows of Kilimanjaro" testifies, has continued to haunt the minds of even the most muscular American authors.

More distinguished by their energy than by their ideas, many of the young intellectuals were an easy prey to dubious notions; in avoiding the sickness of "otherness," they became the victims of more virulent fevers. A little war with Spain, the novelist Robert Herrick felt, might be just the "tonic" that a sick nation needed. John Jay Chapman honored the spirit of Emerson when he urged young Americans to trust the voice of inner conscience, but he also desecrated it with his rantings against the Catholics and Jews in the *Ku Klux Kourier*. The cult of violence, with roots deep in the frontier experience, underwent a new and savage flowering in the fiction of the period; the preference expressed by William James for the tough-minded as opposed to the tender-minded was given an interpretation by certain Little Bilhams that alarmed James, for it seemed not to involve mind at all.

Assuredly, the plunge into life was fraught with peril.


## IV


The idea that he had been born too late was one of Frank Norris' strongest convictions. Like Edwin Arlington Robinson, Norris was a student for a time at Harvard; while in Cambridge, both Robinson and Norris were encouraged by their teachers in their attraction to the Middle Ages—for the revival of interest in the medieval period which Henry Adams had helped to stimulate at Harvard had widened by the middle and late '90s to include philosophers, classicists, and specialists in the fine arts, as well as historians. Robinson, as his poem "Miniver Cheevy" suggests, was capable of a satiric detachment about the Middle Ages and the idea of having been born too late; yet his long narrative poems centering on various figures of Arthurian romance indicate how powerfully his imagination was drawn backward in time from the world in which he had been born. Norris' attraction was equally strong but less discriminating. From the time he was a teen-age boy who produced (with lead soldiers as actors) a dramatic version of *Ivanhoe* and wrote and illustrated chivalric stories of his own, through his Paris period when he discovered Froissart's *Chronicles* and painted a canvas of the battle of Crécy, to the literary essays written toward the end of his life in which he praised modern-day steel executives by comparing them to Richard the Lion-Hearted, Norris was enchanted by the medieval world. Unlike Robinson, however, who followed in the tradition of Henry Adams, Norris exploited the Middle Ages as an escape route from the problems of the present, not as a symbolic means of confronting them. An adolescent desire to evade rather than confront difficult situations would remain for Norris a lifelong temptation.

The problems from which Norris fled into the past began at home. His parents' marriage was not a happy one and eventually culminated in divorce. One of their battle grounds was the question of what Benjamin Franklin Norris, Jr., was to be permitted to do. Indomitably energetic, a self-made millionaire, Norris' father wanted his son trained for a business career, but his mother, a thwarted actress, cherished the dream that her son would have the artistic career which marriage had prevented her from enjoying. That Norris did as badly at the Atelier Julien in Paris as he did in commercial arithmetic at the Boys' High School in San Francisco suggests how completely he was immobilized by the crossfire of quarrels. His situation was further complicated by his conflicting attitudes toward both parents. As the titanic, indomitable figures of Curtis Jadwin, the grain speculator in *The Pit*, and Shelgrim, the railroad magnate of *The Octopus*, imply, Norris deeply responded to the physically powerful, financially successful man who was his father. He seems, too, to have shared his father's aversion to the literary teas, poetry readings and pursuit of artistic lions so dear to the heart of Mrs. Norris. Again and again in his books, Norris attacks the literary and artistic culture of the upper middle classes, and always it is the moonily "sensitive" female or the gushingly inane lady sponsor of art (one thinks in *The Octopus*, of Mrs. Derrick and Mrs. Cedarquist), who is viewed most hostilely. But if Norris tended to hero worship his father, they were not close. In the years when the senior Norrises were still married, relations between father and son seem to have been formally polite, but nothing more. Possibly this was due in part to the father's business commitments, which were both numerous and transcontinental, but the fact remains that after the divorce of his parents Norris never saw his father again. Conversely, Norris' relationship to his mother was as warm as his literary portraits of women who strikingly resemble her were cold. She took up residence in Cambridge during Norris' year at Harvard; she was her son's literary and religious confidante, his nurse during bouts of ill health that plagued him in his twenties, his constant correspondent. Not until late in his short life did Norris marry, and the intense closeness of the writer and the "artistic" mother persisted well into his maturity.

Given the tangled web of feeling as regards his parents—which Norris would eventually attempt to unravel in his portrayal of the Jadwins' troubled marriage in *The Pit*, his last novel—it is not surprising that Norris found the task of deciding on a career difficult. His personal unsureness as to who he was or what he was destined to become persisted during four frivolous (and, as it proved, degreeless) years at the University of California; his one whole-hearted undergraduate enthusiasm was football. Just as wars in the Caribbean or South Africa would do for him later on, football permitted Norris to make a total commitment of his loyalties, to let himself go with the cheering crowd, to identify with the concentrated and violent activity of the heroes on the field below. Two years after Norris left Berkeley, he went to work for *The Wave*, a West Coast magazine, for which he conducted a department called "The Week's Football." The release from mental anguish experienced by Norris in giving over his intelligence to the worship of power can be sensed again and again in his rhapsodic columns: "He is so big [wrote Norris of a star player] that he ceases to be broad and tall—you feel like speaking of him as wide and high, as though he were the steeple of a clock tower—and he has an enormous bell-toned voice and a fist that your hand loses itself inside."

Yet if Norris responded all his life to the appeals of violence and medieval escapism, he could not finally depend on these appeals as a permanent substitute for tough decisions. As vividly as Henry James imagined what horrors indecisiveness could bring down upon a man, there is no nightmare in the canon of James' work that matches the frightful penalties for a life of sensation-hunting dilettantism that descend upon the hero of Norris' first novel *Vandover and the Brute*. Educated at Harvard and possessed of real artistic talent,

Vandover fritters away his youth until finally, his rich father dead, his fortune dissipated, his painterly ability gone, he falls victim to lycanthropy. Groveling on the floor, howling like a wolf, Vandover has degenerated at the end into a filthy, hideous animal. Awkward and melodramatic, *Vandover and the Brute* nevertheless has moments of great force, a force which derives from its author's horrified belief in what the failure to make a connection with life could mean. In his first novel Norris symbolized his fear of what might become of him if he persisted in his dilettante ways.

As much as Fuller or Chapman, then, as much as Roosevelt or indeed any other member of the new generation, Norris came to believe that his salvation depended upon a plunge into the American stream. The writer in the United States, Norris decided, had somehow to recover his moral authority in the community. To do this, the writer had to acquaint himself more fully with the true nature of reality in America and to come to understand the dreams of a democratic people. Norris' program, in short, was to become a writer, as his mother wished, but a writer who would deal not with the fabulous voyages of outcast children or of despairing old men, but with the "real world" of modern business—that pulsing, vital universe inhabited by men like Benjamin Franklin Norris, Sr.

Norris set down the ideas embodying his decision on what sort of career he wanted for himself in a series of essays (later collected in a book called—the title is significant—*The Responsibilities of the Novelist*). The essays assert a bold conception of the place of the literary artist in modern society. They maintain that of all the arts literature is the most democratic and that therefore in a democracy the novelist had a great opportunity. Occupying a position of greater potential moral authority than the minister or the Sunday-school teacher (to appreciate the magnitude of this boast, it is perhaps necessary to know that Norris' father conducted one of the most famous Sunday-school classes in the country), the novelist could if he willed stand at the very center of his time. Without qualification, Norris envisioned the novel as "the great influence of modern life"—if it would deal with the right subjects. The highest form of the novel, what Norris called in a phrase which again reveals both the scope and the nature of his ambition "the preaching novel," would confront the problems of modern capitalism. The growth of business enterprise, the enthralling competition between agriculture and industry, the romance of imperialism, were the subjects of which the novelist would treat if he were to assume his responsibilities. For only by seeking to understand his society could the American novelist hope to become its spokesman.

With the notable exception of *McTeague*, the novels that Norris wrote in the years immediately following *Vandover* are quest stories, sagas of young men in search of effective self-realization. There is in these books, in *Blix* and *Moran of the Lady Letty* and *A Man's Woman*, an enormous emphasis on physical and mental health. Over-refinement, dilettantism, exhaustion, disease, are the blights against which Norris' well-born, neurasthenic heroes struggle. But instead of giving way to their weaknesses, thus dooming themselves to act out once again the blasted career of Vandover, they triumph, like Theodore Roosevelt, by an act of will. At the conclusion of these stories, Norris' heroes stand exultantly poised on the threshold of new careers.

While, however, this group of novels is directly related to Norris' tremendous concern with the artist's relation to society—indeed, it could be said that they represent a working-out on an imaginative level of the doctrines he would later enunciate in *The Responsibilities of the Novelist*—they deal with lonely young men and their personal problems, not with the great issues of contemporary politics and economics. In March 1899, however, as he was completing *A Man's Woman*, the third and last of the group, Norris wrote to William Dean Howells that he had finally found a theme worthy of the "preaching novel"—an epic trilogy on the production, distribution, and consumption of wheat.

Norris would die, of peritonitis, with the novel of consumption unwritten. *The Pit*, the second novel in the epic and the product of his last years, is the weakest of all his books, weakly designed and poorly executed. The weakness which all of Norris' fiction is heir to is that its inflated, imitation-epic tone can suddenly go ludicrously flat, and in *The Pit* this happens again and again, a fact which Norris might have realized, for the novel finally pays more attention to Curtis Jadwin's home life than to his Napoleonic career on the floor of the grain market. But *The Octopus*, the novel of production, is a fine achievement; nothing else Norris ever wrote comes close to matching its quality. One of the most significant novels in our literature, *The Octopus* penetrates to the heart of the American consciousness at a crucial moment in our history.

V

The three young men who are the main characters in *The Octopus*—to come back without further delay to the point of a long departure  are ridden by self-doubt. The Spanish name of Annixter's ranch, Quien Sabe—perhaps, who knows?—is conveniently symbolic of the tentativeness and unsureness they all feel. Presley, the poet, should by now seem rather a familiar literary representative of the post-Civil War American intellectual: "One guessed that Presley's refinement had been gained only by a certain loss of strength. One expected to find him nervous, introspective, to discover that his mental life was not at all the result of impressions and sensations that came to him from without, but rather of thoughts and reflections germinating from within. Though morbidly sensitive to changes in his physical surroundings, he would be slow to act upon such sensations, would not prove impulsive, not because he was sluggish, but because he was merely irresolute. It could be foreseen that morally he was of that sort who avoid evil through good taste, lack of decision, and want of opportunity." Annixter, for all his driving energy and hard, brusque manner, his insolently direct speech and bullying disposition, is as unsure of himself as the poet; indeed, his energy and directness are but the masks imposed upon a terrible inner turmoil. His rapid switching from civil engineering to law to bonanza agriculture betrays a part of his irresolution, but the brilliant scene in which he expresses an exaggerated dislike for a female cat, and then explodes in hysterical rage when he finds that someone as a practical joke has placed a sticky pudding in his bed, makes clear that what he fears above all else is sex, because sex involves the abhorrent notion of someone touching him. Presley has come to the San Joaquin suffering from consumption, but Annixter, savagely dosing his nervous stomach with prunes, is also sick; in both cases, the physical illness serves Norris as a metaphor for portraying a psychological disability. Vanamee, the third of the young men, appears to Presley's imagination to belong to the company of "half-inspired shepherds of the Hebraic legends, the younger prophets of Israel, dwellers in the wilderness, beholders of visions, having their existence in a continual dream, talkers with God, gifted with strange powers." But Vanamee is a desert prophet without a faith, a talker with God who does not know God. After the rape of Angéle, he had roamed the countryside like a wolf, knife and revolver in hand; after her death, there were rumors that he had killed himself. Even after years of wandering, his grief has not abated. It has "become a part of him." If, in the darkness, he sometimes prays, his prayers incoherently ask " 'Why?' of the night and of the stars."

Out of their loneliness and sickness, the three young men seek a way back to life and human connection. Presley strives for "the diapason, the great song that should embrace in itself a whole epoch, a complete era, the voice of an entire people, wherein all people should be included"; Annixter, tentatively, blunderingly, fearfully, seeks an end to his outcast bachelordom through his courtship of Hilma; Vanamee listens for an answer to his cosmic questions. Through their strivings, a whole world is fitted together by bits and pieces and exposed to view; through their collective consciousness, a "true and fearless setting forth of a passing phase of history"—to quote Presley's epical ambition—is accomplished.

At first glance, this assessment of the novel's accomplishment seems an overstatement. When, for example, the masterpieces of Zola, whom Norris idolized, are compared to *The Octopus*; more specifically, when one sets the second chapter of Part 3 of *Germinal* beside the sixth chapter of Book 1 of *The Octopus*, one immediately notices not only how closely Norris attempted to model his work on Zola's, but how inexact is the imitation. The scene from *Germinal* cited above, which depicts a midsummer festival day in the coal-mining region of northern France, has been singled out by Professor Erich Auerbach as one of the great representations of reality in modern literature. While portraying, in grotesque and sensory detail, an orgy of drinking and dancing, the scene is nevertheless not a farce. Zola's style, Professor Auerbach shows, is not exuberant, but dry and clear, almost inhuman; the details of the orgy that Zola gives point up not merely its emotional extravagance—its colorfulness—but the awful poverty, both economic and spiritual, of the miners and their women. Zola's comic festival is presented with a high moral seriousness; its final aim is not to amuse and entertain the reader with the simple and antic pleasures of the poor, but to shock him into an awareness of the power of industrialism to break human beings down into such work-drugged automatons that they can only snatch at fleeting and momentary leisure with the furious unrestraint of animals.

Norris' festival seems at first a cheap and gaudy thing by comparison, a kind of western movie version of *Germinal*. Obsessed with bigness, Norris had a passion for portraying gigantic men and women, and reveled in the epic details of Homeric eatings and drinkings; the scene of the barn-dance at Annixter's ranch gave him a golden opportunity to let his imagination run riot. Zola's miners drank only beer, but Norris' ranchers drink champagne, brandy, and whiskey; Annixter's barn is "colossal," its floor shines magnificently, its walls are hung with expensive decorations. Musicians have been hired to play until dawn; the women are beautifully gowned; the air of the summer night is superb (in *Germinal* it had been humid). To give the extravaganza its final Hollywood touch, the gaiety is suddenly interrupted by the melodramatic entrance of the cowpuncher Delaney, crazy drunk and bent on humiliating Annixter:

> He came with the suddenness of an explosion. There was a commotion by the doorway, a rolling burst of oaths, a furious stamping of hoofs, a wild scramble of the dancers to either side of the room, and there he was. He had ridden the buckskin at a gallop straight through the doorway and out into the middle of the floor of the barn.

Once well inside, Delaney hauled up on the cruel spadebit, at the same time driving home the spurs, and the buckskin, without halting her gait, rose into the air upon her hind feet, and coming down again with a thunder of iron hoofs upon the hollow floor, lashed out with both heels simultaneously, her back arched, her head between her knees. It was the running buck, and had not Delaney been the hardest buster in the county, would have flung him headlong like a sack of sand. But he eased off the bit, gripping the mare's flanks with his knees, and the buckskin, having long since known her master, came to hand quivering, the blood spume dripping from the bit upon the slippery floor.

But to quote this passage is to see at once that Norris was a far abler craftsman and a more serious artist than any sensationalizing scriptwriter. The sentences are charged with kinetic energy; the whole passage produces an overwhelming effect of anarchic power. Yet the style does not go out of control. Norris' vision never wavers in his steady regard of the violence. If his festival does not duplicate the one in *Germinal*, this is not because he was unable or unwilling to do an exact imitation. Rather it was because he had a different reality to portray.

The opulent scale of life in the San Joaquin, the richness of the empire over which the railroad and bonanza farmers are contending, is not a Hollywood dream. Norris' sensory details are lavish rather than mean because the master of ten thousand California acres in fact had a standard of living almost unimaginable to the mind of the European peasant or miner; his problems flowed out of the phenomenon of abundance, not, as was the case with Zola's miserable people, out of want. Norris' style is highly charged and kinetic because he sought to convey not the necessity for social reform (to which task Zola's dryness was remorselessly appropriate) but the existence of certain conditions of life in America that engendered violence. In northern France, a man might be hungry, but he knew who he was. The class lines between bourgeois and workers are sharply drawn in *Germinal*; political awareness defines and explains the world. But in the hot California sunshine, political and class lines have dissolved; in this chaos of abundance, men have only the anxiety that they are not getting their share of the loot to guide their behavior. As Norris brilliantly reveals, the embattled ranchers of the San Joaquin are not revolutionaries, but frontier freebooters, *redivivus*. Recklessly raping the fertility of their land, extravagant in the purchase of machines and equipment, ready to gamble for a quick fortune now and contemptuous of the future, they have no program except violence with which to meet the railroad's exploitation. Ideologically, they have no quarrel with the railroad; both sides believe in the frontier ethos that the individual has the God-given right to grab all he can. Consequently, the ranchers meet the railroad's threat to their livelihood not with the strategy of revolution nor with the tactics of reform but with a facsimile of the railroad's corrupt practices. When their attempt to bribe the commissioners fails, their only recourse is to get out their rifles, frontier-fashion.

But the dynamics of American violence are so centrifugal that even men who face a common enemy cannot unite. The ranchers constantly quarrel with one another, hide secrets from their fellows, heap recriminations on their chosen leaders; when the bloody showdown comes at the Derricks' ranch—ominously named Los Muertos ("The corpses")—only a handful of ranchers honor their sworn oaths to be there. The unforgettable image of resistance that emerges from the novel is the solitary one of Dyke in the cab of the train engine, fleeing alone, gun in hand, across the valley floor.

At once suspicious of everyone and naively gullible, the ranchers are driven back upon their individual resources at the very moment that they begin to realize the overwhelming power of the economic forces which grip them. In their confusion and bewilderment at being defeated on every side by the irresponsible power of free enterprise—the very doctrine in which they all believe—the ranchers turn violently to doctrines of hate as a way of discharging their aggressive feelings. Perhaps only George Washington Cable, among American novelists before 1920, matched Norris' understanding of the way in which the spark of race hatred could be kindled to a flame when the breath of economic and political discontent blew upon it. To the enraged ranchers, S. Behrman, the fat man with the great stomach, the thick neck, and the blue-gray, tremulous jowl, comes to seem the cause of all their troubles. When Harran Derrick mutters, "I wonder I keep my hands off the man," he expresses that peculiar combination of murderous impulse and yet impotent frustration that characterized the flare-up of anti-Semitism in the United States at the turn of the century. Only in the bloody massacre of the jackrabbits can the ranchers find the intoxicating release of indiscriminate violence. This, then, is the society of the San Joaquin in which Annixter, Presley and Vanamee seek an end to their disaffiliation.

Annixter's attempt to subjoin his prickly individualism to the collective good of the community is a tragedy. Achieving with Hilma for a few fleeting months the only happiness and serenity he has ever known, Annixter ends as one of the corpses at Los Muertos. The affiliation he ultimately finds is the ironic comradeship of the dead.

If Annixter's story is tragic, Presley's is pathetic. As Annixter had sought to be a good citizen, so Presley attempts to become the voice of the people. He writes a lengthy poem that is full of political implication; he addresses a mass meeting with an inflammatory speech urging the ranchers to revolt; suiting action to his words, he throws a bomb at S. Behrman's house. But just as the bomb does not hurt the fat man, so the speech, as Presley himself has to admit, is shrill and unconvincing. Presley as an agitator is farcical. If his quest for affiliation has discovered anything, it is that political activity of any sort, whether employing the bomb or the ballot box, is even more of a farce. With his world collapsing like a house of cards, Presley suffers a nervous breakdown. A doctor diagnoses his ailment as a case of "overcerebration" and recommends a long sea voyage.

Only Vanamee finds a way in which the isolated man of intelligence can redeem himself from loneliness and reestablish a connection with life. Through the mind of this wanderer, one is led in the novel into contact with the "Spanish earth" of California. The priest, Father Sarria, cannot satisfy Vanamee's questions with his Catholic answers, but walking past the crumbling sun dial and the moss-rimed fountain of the Mission in the company of this cigar-smoking, fighting cock-fancier of a priest, Vanamee nevertheless moves toward an apprehension of the mystery to which he can give over his lonely spirit. In the perfume-clogged atmosphere of the beautiful Seed Ranch he moves even closer. But it is not until he hires himself out in ploughing season at the ranch named Quien Sabe that he unconsciously absorbs the lesson of his life:

The ploughing, now in full swing, enveloped him in a vague, slow-moving whirl of things. Underneath him was the jarring, jolting, trembling machine: not a clod was turned, not an obstacle encountered, that he did not receive the swift impression of it through all his body, the very friction of the damp soil, sliding incessantly from the shiny surface of the shears, seemed to reproduce itself in his finger-tips and along the back of his head. He heard the horse-hoofs by the myriads crushing down easily, deeply, into the loam, the prolonged clinking of tracechains, the working of the smooth brown flanks in the harness, the clatter of wooden hames, the champing of bits, the click of iron shoes against pebbles, the brittle stubble of the surface ground crackling and snapping as the furrows turned, the sonorous, steady breaths wrenched from the deep, labouring chests, strap-bound, shining with sweat, and all along the line the voices of the men talking to the horses. Everywhere there were visions of glossy brown backs, straining, heaving, swollen with muscle; harness streaked with specks of froth, broad, cup-shaped hoofs, heavy with brown loam, men's faces red with tan, blue overalls spotted with axle-grease; muscled hands, the knuckles whitened in their grip on the reins, and through it all the ammoniacal smell of the horses, the bitter reek of perspiration of beasts and men, the aroma of warm leather, the scent of dead stubble—and stronger and more penetrating than everything else, the heavy, enervating odour of the upturned, living earth.

In the worship of the mystical, unassailable, eternal power of the wheat-giving earth, Vanamee finds the way to accept the universe and achieve a solidarity with mankind.

The romantic vitalism of the exalted Vanamee at first means nothing to the doubt-ridden Presley. But at the very end of the novel, as Presley is bound for the Orient, the words of the shepherd come back to him—"*But the* WHEAT *remained.*" They comfort the poet, and clearly Norris intended to conclude his book on a buoyant note of vitalistic faith. But what is taking place undercuts what is being said, for Presley, like Ishmael, has taken to the ship as a desperate last resort. Although Presley summons up, in the very last words of the book, the vision of a communality of all things working "together for good," one cannot but note that as he stands there on the deck in the darkness Norris' intellectual is utterly alone.

## *6*

# Sister Carrie

Attending a party in New York in the early 1880s, Henry James encountered a young lady whose presence seemed to him "perceptibly
unsupported and unguaranteed" by any sponsor or other connections. James inquired about her and learned that she was a representative of a new social phenomenon: the feminine and polite-society
counterpart of that emergent hero of post-Civil War American life,
the self-made man. Having left her family behind, the audacious
young lady had sailed out into society on her own, depending solely
on personal appeal to enable her to work out her social salvation.
Struck by the drama of the situation, James wrote a story about such
a girl, called "Pandora," thus bringing to the center of the stage a
heroine who theretofore in American fiction had only been glimpsed
in the kind of supporting role in which Henry Adams had cast the
aptly named Victoria Dare in his novel *Democracy* (1880). In the
course of the next twenty-five years, a great many American authors,
perhaps most notably Edith Wharton in *The House of Mirth* (1905),
focused their full attention on the unsponsored young girl as she

Source: From "Introduction" in *Sister Carrie* by Theodore Dreiser.
Introduction by Kenneth S. Lynn. Copyright © 1957 by Kenneth S. Lynn.
Reprinted by permission of Holt, Rinehart and Winston, Inc.

made her independent way into drawing rooms and salons in New York and Washington and Chicago. As James himself admitted in 1909, "the Pandora Days can no longer, I fear, pass for quaint or fresh."

Yet only two years before James' admission, there had finally reappeared in the United States a novel about a freewheeling, unconnected American girl that was so explosively fresh that the original publisher of the novel had virtually suppressed it for seven years. In 1900, on the recommendation of Frank Norris, the house of Doubleday had contracted to bring out a first novel by Theodore Dreiser. But at the last moment, when the book was in page proofs, it was read by the publisher's wife, Mrs. Frank Doubleday. She was horrified by the novel and convinced her husband that it should be withdrawn. Obliged to fulfill the letter of the contract, the firm published one thousand copies of the book, but saw to it that very few would be sold by refusing to advertise or promote it in any way. Not until 1907 did another American publisher have the nerve to publish *Sister Carrie*.

The central plot of the novel is a variation on James' theme, the success story of an independent American girl, but Dresier's heroine operates in a far less polite society than that in which Pandora Day had moved. The fact that Carrie begins her career in a factory rather than a drawing room is a significant difference, yet is hardly the source of the novel's disturbing freshness. Howells and Crane and Norris had, after all, dealt with the sordidness of the metropolis and the dreams of the poor before Dreiser, and in *Maggie: A Girl of the Streets* (1893) Crane had presented the American girl in the vilest of environments and occupations. These authors had, however, approached metropolitan low life in a radically different way than Dreiser did. Howells, for all his sympathy with human misery, had viewed the poor from the standpoint of an interested onlooker and was never able imaginatively to enter into their lives, with the result that his account of "An East-Side Ramble" in *Impressions and Experiences* (1896) is an externally observed report on how the other half lives, while *A Hazard of New Fortunes* (1890), his most vital novel of city life, lapses into melodrama as soon as it moves away from the middle-class world with which Howells was so familiar and attempts to deal with the underprivileged. Norris' *McTeague* (1899), for all of the local color and flavor of lower-class San Francisco life that it conveys, is far more flawed by melodrama than any work of Howells. The one implausible scene of mob violence that occurs in *A Hazard of New Fortunes* is capped in Norris' novel by a bloody reign of torture and murder. A millionaire's son with a yen for violence, Norris felt that the seamier city life was, the more lurid it was bound to be, and he wrote *McTeague* in the spirit of a rich boy seeking thrills in the slums. As for Crane, he was interested in the urban jungle in the same way that he was to be interested in the battlefield, as an arena of fear (he once observed that "the root of Bowery life is a sort of cowardice"). Although he penetrated Maggie's world to a far greater degree than Howells or Norris ever did the milieu of their down-and-out characters, Crane's self-conscious rebellion against both respectable New Jersey life and his own distinguished ancestry caused him to romanticize his prostitute as an almost perfect girl whom circumstances alone had degraded. For all the honesty of Crane's art, the heroine of *Maggie* is a stereotype; like Howells and Norris, Crane in the Bowery was an outsider looking in.

But *Sister Carrie* is the work of an insider writing out of the heart of his own experience. The son of an impoverished German immigrant, Dreiser had torn away from the misery of life in his native Indiana while still in his teens and had gone to Chicago to seek his fortune. He wandered the streets, drunk with their glittering spectacle, and dreamed of the mansions and the beautiful women that might someday be his; he experienced the terror of not being able to find work, and of having it discovered that he had stolen twenty-five dollars in order to buy himself a winter coat; later in New York he felt the excitement of being known as a prominent magazine writer and the thrill of dining in expensive restaurants where the headwaiters nodded to him in recognition. He poured so many of these personal memories into his first novel that Dreiser might well have said of the principal characters, "I am Carrie; I am Drouet; I am Hurstwood."

Drouet is exactly the kind of flashily dressed, skirt-chasing

Lothario that Dreiser fancied himself in the early nineties when he was an up-and-coming young newspaperman in Chicago and St. Louis, and the idea of Hurstwood's tragedy was born one wintry day in New York when Dreiser, out of money and haunted by failure, sat among the bums in City Hall Park and gazed up at the tall office buildings he had once dreamed of taking by storm. In working out Carrie's story, Dreiser drew not only on the memory of his own initial response to Chicago but also on his knowledge of what had happened to one of his sisters, who had been the mistress of a Chicago architect and had subsequently become involved with the manager of a fashionable saloon. Although a married man, the latter persuaded her to elope to Toronto, explaining that he was forced to leave town because he had stolen fifteen thousand dollars from his employers. The scandal was grist for the mill of the yellow press, and the owners of the saloon for a time threatened to press charges, agreeing finally to withdraw them on condition that the money be returned.

Dreiser himself recognized how close to home *Sister Carrie* was in his account of its composition. He declared that one day he simply wrote the words of the title on a sheet of paper without any notion of what the book was to be about. Suddenly, he started to write "as if I were being used, like a medium." It would be a mistake to take this reminiscence too literally, for Dreiser's novel is a conscious work of the imagination, not a passive, mediumistic transcription. Like most fiction of importance, *Sister Carrie* is controlled by its creator's objective understanding of, and detachment from, his material. Yet the reminiscence is important in that it emphasizes how Dreiser triumphed over prevailing literary attitudes toward his material by ignoring what other writers had done and writing simply of what he knew.

In thus breaking new ground, Dreiser was working in the characteristic American vein, which has always been empirical, innovative, and exploratory: the abandonment of tradition is our tradition. If the perpetual fresh start has its glories, it has its weaknesses as well, and in *Sister Carrie* the danger of paying no attention to the past is made manifest in a diction that is characterized by a vast vulgarity. It is the vulgarity not of the four-letter word and the GI profanity of the latter-day naturalistic novel, but of the women's magazines and the popular fiction trash of the nineties. *Sister Carrie* is full of clichés, outworn literary tags, fine writing in the worst sense of the word—when Dreiser describes two carriage horses he calls them a "prancing pair of bays," and Carrie is referred to as "a half-equipped little knight" or as "the little toiler." Dreiser does not use this stilted, bookish diction out of any self-conscious awareness that it is the language his lower-class version of Pandora Day would admire; Carrie does admire it, of course, but when Dreiser once explained his quantitative interest in women by saying that in his "affectional relations" he was a "varietist" he betrayed the fact that he shared his heroine's linguistic taste. Occasionally the language in *Sister Carrie* displays a certain slangy freshness, but whenever he strives for an effect, Dreiser abandons the colloquial for a pretentious, confectionery prose that is, if anything, more saccharine than that employed in such a contemporary bonbon as Charles Major's *When Knighthood Was in Flower* (1898). Completely lacking James' awareness of the great tradition of English prose, Dreiser was the helpless (because unwitting) prisoner of a trite and obvious language.

Dreiser's characters are as vulgar as his diction, but once again the novelist seems only partially aware of the fact because he had no traditional standard against which to measure the limitations of their taste. There is, for example, nothing ironic, no amused awareness, in Dreiser's lovingly detailed descriptions of Drouet's get-up as we meet him for the first time, because throughout his career Dreiser affected the same kind of blatantly showy finery. (In the 1920s, for instance, Broadway bystanders were startled by the apparition of Dreiser strolling downtown, dressed to the eyes and with a Russian wolfhound in leash. George Jean Nathan noted that his wardrobe heavily emphasized "Caribbean blue shirts, vanilla ice-cream socks, and pea-green bow ties.") When Carrie, riding the wave of her success as an actress, thrills to the decor of her new hotel-apartment, Dreiser is describing his own reaction as well, for in his magazine career he often exuded admiration for just such ornate and showy interiors. But it is in his portrait of Hurstwood that Dreiser's unexamined, unselfconscious enthusiasm for the meretricious emerges most clearly, for

Hurstwood, the manager of "a gorgeous saloon . . . with rich screens, fancy wines, and a line of bar-goods unsurpassed in the country," ranks higher in the social scale than Carrie or Drouet. To the reader, Hurstwood appears an unctuous and cunning man of limited culture, but Dreiser admiringly describes him as "altogether a very acceptable individual of our great American upper class—the first grade below the luxuriously rich." Both in the language and the attitude of that judgment, as well as in the fact that Dreiser makes the saloon manager wealthier than he would have been in reality, are contained all the naive aspirations of a second-generation American from the wrong side of the tracks who had broken free from hicktown Indiana and gone to Chicago to make good.

The loose moral habits of the characters in *Sister Carrie* are also depicted forthrightly and directly, without apology and without shame. So alien to Dreiser were the going moral standards of the America of his day that not only did he blithely violate the ironclad literary convention that the wages of sin are death, he did not even believe that Carrie had sinned. Yet this was not a flaw but one of the triumphs of the novel; if Dreiser's "immorality" scandalized Mrs. Doubleday, it also revolutionized American social fiction. For no other American novelist who had dealt with the urban masses had ever presented them with such ruthless honesty; no previous author had been able to free his imagination of all moral preconceptions and confront the culture of the modern American city for what it was. Hence the resistance to the book, even after Dreiser had won the battle for publication. Howells, who was enthusiastic about both *McTeague* and *Maggie*, thoroughly disliked *Sister Carrie*—although Crane and Norris had dealt with tawdrier themes than Howells ever permitted himself, they both approached their material from a point of view that he could understand, whereas Dreiser did not. (For his part, the author of *Sister Carrie* regarded the author of *A Hazard of New Fortunes* as simply "uninformed.") But the main attack on Dreiser was mounted by the critic Stuart Sherman in a notable essay in the *Nation* in 1915. Appalled by the fact that Dreiser did not share the traditional moral ideas of America, Sherman blasted Dreiser for his portrayal of a world from which "the obligations of parenthood, marriage, chivalry and citizenship have been quite withdrawn." And he concluded, "hence Mr. Dreiser's field seems curiously outside American society." Yet in drawing on his sister's and his own experience for *Sister Carrie*, Dreiser had, if anything, made fiction less harsh than truth.

Dreiser's handling of sex was not the only thing that troubled many of his contemporaries. His attitude toward reform bothered them almost as much. Mrs. Doubleday was a social worker and Howells was a socialist; like Jane Addams and Jacob Riis and many other middle-class reformers, they were disturbed by conditions in slum homes and factories and wanted to ameliorate them. But Dreiser had absolutely no interest in political or social reform. His attitude toward the poor varied between scorn for the class he had successfully struggled to escape and a sympathy for human suffering that was based directly on his fear that he might someday slide back into the poverty he had known in his youth. Dreiser conceived of the world he wrote about in *Sister Carrie* not as the subject for a sermon or a muck-raking exposé, but as the given. He looked upon life "as a fierce grim struggle in which no quarter was either given or taken," but he had no notion of changing it, because to him fighting and suffering were fundamental to existence—to eliminate them was impossible.

The only point at which Dreiser agreed with Howells was in the paradoxical opinion that, although city life was infinitely preferable to the grossness of country life, the city was also artificial, it's ambitions false, its love of light and show and finery somehow diseased. By contrast with "the serene light of the eternal stars," Dreiser writes in *Sister Carrie*, the lights of a city saloon were "a strange, glittering night-flower, an odour-yielding, insect-drawing, insect-infested rose of pleasure." But, unlike the older novelist, Dreiser felt that the artificiality was irresistible, the disease fatal; Howells' Silas Lapham retains through thick and thin a natural, rural integrity that in the end proves impervious to the wiles of Boston, but Dreiser believed that once the mind had been exposed to the magnificent residences, the gilded shops, the splendid restaurants, "the flowers, the silks, the wines . . . the glances which gleam like light from defiant spears," nothing could save it. Remembering the overwhelming effect the daz-zling spectacle of the city had had on him when he first arrived in Chicago, Dreiser could not help feeling that the "opium" of Chicago and New York inevitably corrupted "the unsophisticated and natural mind," that to spend even one day in the artificial city "will so affect and discolour the views, the aims, the desire of the mind, that it will thereafter remain forever dyed." The greatness of *Sister Carrie* lies primarily in its portrayal of the blinding impact of the modern city on the human personality.

Because Dreiser was supremely aware of the hypnotic effect of the artificial city, much of *Sister Carrie* takes place at night, when the city is most artificial and most fascinating. The opening chapter, showing Carrie en route to Chicago, climaxes with the train's arrival in the city just at evening, that "mystic period" when the lamps are beginning to shine out their "promise of the night." Carrie is mysteriously moved by the nighttime metropolis; she can hardly get enough of it. When at first she is boarding with her sister, she stands for hours at the foot of the stairs or sits alone in the front room "looking out upon the street, where the lights were reflected on the wet pavements, thinking." After she has become Drouet's mistress, and then later when she is living with Hurstwood, Carrie is depicted again and again sitting in a rocking chair by a window, gazing out at the city as the darkness gathers. For Dreiser's characters, the night is full of mystery and terror: it is in the night that Hurstwood tricks Carrie into fleeing from Chicago with him; it is "in that kindness which is night" that Hurstwood turns on the gas and lies down to die. But the night is also the source of a glittering enchantment; it is the time when the restaurants and great hotels kindle into life, and above all, when the marquees of the theaters blaze with "incandescent fire."

Dreiser himself, from the time of his arrival in Chicago, had been excited by the theater, and in St. Louis he had worked for a time as a drama critic and had dreamed of becoming a playwright. With its beautiful actresses and suave, well-dressed actors, its glitter and its thousand make-believe excitements, the theatrical world was to Dreiser a microcosm of the glamorous city, a quintessence of its ar-tificial splendors, and the theater magnetizes his characters as well.

No other urban institution fascinates them nearly so much. The first thing that Carrie wants to see in Chicago is H. R. Jacob's theater; before his seduction of Carrie, Drouet takes her to a performance of the *Mikado*; the affair between Hurstwood and Carrie is developed in the course of several evenings at the theater; Carrie begins to be dissatisfied with Hurstwood after seeing a matinee with her friend Mrs. Vance; the desperate Hurstwood begs for money from Carrie at a stage entrance. Although it would be an exaggeration to say that *Sister Carrie* is a novel about the theater, it is nevertheless the story of a young girl who gets a part in a neighborhood lodge production of Augustin Daly's melodrama *Under the Gaslight*, rises to the head of the chorus line in a New York revue, and ends as a famous actress. Much of the conversation in the novel is about the theater and about Carrie's career: just as Drouet early in the novel gives her advice on her acting, so at the end Ames tells her that her destiny lies not in comedy, but in more serious drama.

Yet there is a more profound level than the simple story line on which *Sister Carrie* is theatrical. For if the hypnotic influence of the city claims everyone who comes within its orbit as its victim, then natural personality assumes an artificial dye and all the world's a stage. The characters in *Sister Carrie* are all actors; their personalities are not expressions of themselves, but of the roles they are playing. Drouet not only gives Carrie tips about how to become an actress, but personal advice on how to walk, how to hold herself, how to dress, how, in sum, to disguise her own personality and "act like a lady." As for Drouet he is not *a* salesman, he is *the* salesman, not an individual at all, but simply and appallingly "an order of individual." Without his flashy clothes that instantly typify him, Drouet has no reality; take away the salesman's clothes, Dreiser says, and "he was nothing." Hurstwood, too, is a type, so that after having forsaken the job that defines his character he is described by Dreiser as a man who has become "nothing," a fact which Hurstwood finally recognizes when, during the streetcar strike, he is asked if he is a motorman and he replies, "No, I'm not anything." Becoming a motorman, Hurstwood tries to behave like one, just as in Chicago he had lived his role of saloon manager to the hilt, but unable to sustain the part, he becomes an unshaven cipher who sits at home all day long, reading the newspapers; when he is no longer able to play a part, there is absolutely nothing of Hurstwood left. Even people's names—that vestige of autonomous personality—change with their status: Carrie Meeber is known by another name when she is Drouet's mistress and her stage name is Carrie Madenda; the successful saloon manager is named George Hurstwood, but the same man becomes, in the years of his degradation, George Wheeler.

Without real personality, these people have almost no real feelings. Beneath the masquerade of saloon manager or gracious lady or happy-go-lucky salesman, there is a terrible coldness. Hurstwood is a consummate actor, whose "eyes of cold make-believe" fill with warmth and friendliness when he most wishes to deceive and who smoothly manipulates his personality to suit the social status of the company he is in. Drouet, although capable of random gestures of generosity, is, like Happy Loman in *Death of a Salesman*, a shallow Don Juan who cannot conceive of relations with women in any terms other than sexual conquest; it is only because he sees that other people think highly of Carrie that he considers marrying her. But it is Carrie who is the coldest of all. She cuts herself off from her family with a finality unmatched by any other Pandora Day in American fiction; not once in the novel does she write a letter to her parents or to her sister. Although she is seduced by two men, these experiences, beyond certain perfunctory guilt feelings, seemingly have no effect upon her and at no time is she in love with either man. After she and Drouet have separated, she never thinks of him, and as soon as she walks out on Hurstwood at the end of their long relationship, she completely shuts him out of her mind. Carrie spends long hours brooding, but introspection produces only one emotion in her—the mood of longing, of yearning for something that she does not have. In moments of crisis, she never knows how she feels, because with the exception of a craving for pleasure which is "the one stay of her nature," she has no genuine emotions or attitudes about life. When Ames tells Carrie that she has it in her to be a great actress, he says that the look on her face catches "something which represented the world's longing"—not its grief, or its happiness, or any of the other emotions which have distinguished great actors in the past, only its desire.

Desire, indeed, is the one emotion that exists for Dreiser, once the mind has been exposed to the opium of the city, and the lives of his characters are as narrowly focused as those of so many drug addicts. His descriptions of their longings for material objects have a unique animation; not even Scott Fitzgerald ever talked about money the way Dreiser does. When Drouet forces money upon Carrie, Dreiser says that "the money she had accepted was two soft, green, handsome ten-dollar bills," and later he writes that "the twenty dollars seemed a wonderful and delightful thing. Ah, money, money, money." Expensive clothes and jewels are hungered after by Dreiser's characters with such an intensity that their desire actually seems to breathe life into what they seek: "As he cut the meat his rings almost spoke." Or again, "Fine clothes to her were a vast persuasion; they spoke tenderly and Jesuitically for themselves. When she came within earshot of their pleading, desire in her bent a willing ear. . . . 'My dear,' said the lace collar she secured from Partridge's, 'I fit you beautifully; don't give me up.' 'Ah, such little feet,' said the leather of the soft new shoes; 'how effectively I cover them.' "

Materialistic desire is not only powerful but unquenchable, for possession only momentarily slakes the thirst for "things"; everything in *Sister Carrie* is in the optative mood; all passion is spent on what is just beyond the horizon. The world that Dreiser portrays is a ceaseless flux, a fluid, wide-open universe in which people are constantly rising and falling—a quality which he seeks to suggest by the cluster of water images he employs in the novel, his countless descriptions of Carrie as "drifting with the tide," his summation of Hurstwood in New York as "an inconspicuous drop in the ocean," and his various comparisons of the city to the sea. In such a world, the only reality is movement, the only good is upward movement, the only objects worth having are those one can't afford. There is, therefore, no letup on the emotional commitment to material possessions, no possibility for the development of any feeling other than longing for the ever more expensive. Indeed, the only change that rising in the world can bring is diminishment of the number of things to be yearned for, so that Carrie's personality is not only defined by the pleasure principle but doomed by her success to expend itself on fewer and fewer dreams. As she sits in her opulent suite in the Waldorf at the end of the novel, in possession of all the "things" her heart has ever desired, she is immensely bored.

The people in *Sister Carrie* are vulgar, sometimes vicious; their dreams are paltry, and they do not even know it. But because they do not know it, their commitment to those dreams is total, and they long for what they are sure is happiness with an energy and an intensity that invests their careers with an importance that transcends their intrinsic meaning. There is nothing wholehearted about these people except their worship of money and luxury; they are as dehumanized as the artificial city, and their hearts are as cold as the glittering lights that hypnotize them, but like Fitzgerald's Jay Gatsby, they believe that they have found the symbols commensurate with their capacity for wonder, and they stake everything on attaining them. There is an important irony in the fact that Carrie's success brings her only boredom, but Hurstwood's confrontation of the fact that he has bet and lost pierces through the paltriness of his career to an even deeper meaning. Success means everything to Hurstwood, and when he loses all, he is faced with a situation that calls for a degree of courage worthy of a more significant life than he has ever dreamed of. In the slow, measured manner of Hurstwood's preparation for suicide, Dreiser reveals to us the essential dignity, as well as the tragedy, of man.

# *7*

# Living My Life

Emma Goldman began writing *Living My Life* in an "enchanting little cottage" in Saint-Tropez in 1928. But the peaceful loveliness of the setting had no chastening effect on the autobiographer's recollections of anger and ugliness, and she at once told the story of her startling outburst of temper in Rochester, New York, on the evening of November 11, 1887.

Unnerved by a news bulletin from Chicago which stated that four of the anarchists who had previously been found guilty of the Haymarket bombing had been hanged early that morning, the eighteen-year-old Emma made her way to her father's house after dark, where she found a crowd of people excitedly discussing the executions. The coarse laugh and sneering voice of a woman suddenly rose above the din: "What's all this lament about? The men were murderers. It is well they were hanged." With one leap, Emma was at the woman's throat. Someone pulled her away, but Emma wrenched herself free, grabbed a pitcher of water from a table, and threw it with all her force into the woman's face. "Out, out," Emma cried, "or I will kill you!" The terrified woman ran out of the house and Emma

SOURCE: *The New Republic* (CLXV, November 27, 1971). Reprinted by permission of *The New Republic*, © 1962 (71), Harrison-Blaine of New Jersey, Inc.

collapsed in a spasm of crying. "The child has gone crazy," someone remarked.

"By what destiny or virtue," Ignazio Silone asks in *The God That Failed*, "does one, at a certain age, make the important choice, and become an 'accomplice' or 'rebel'? From what source do some people derive their spontaneous intolerance of injustice, even though the injustice affects only others?" A generation before Silone gave these haunting questions their classic statement, the author of *Living My Life* addressed very similar inquiries to herself, for she often was as surprised and shaken by the vehemence with which she expressed her beliefs as were the unlucky people who got in the way of her intolerance. Why, indeed, did she become so violently angry about injustices done to others? In the thousand pages of her remarkable autobiography, she was never quite able to formulate an answer. Yet the raw evidence she presents is so detailed and so brutally candid as to make it unmistakably clear that her political militancy was not only a response to objective injustices but also a subjective response to sexual exploitation. Through her defiance of the dominating and/or deceiving men whom she encountered in her childhood and young womanhood, she was psychologically prepared for participation in other rebellions.

In Königsberg, where her lower-middle-class parents sent her to live with her grandmother for a time, Emma came under the discipline of an uncle, who refused to allow the child to go to school and made her instead his personal servant; whenever she protested about the work, he kicked her. At the insistence of the grandmother, Emma was finally permitted to become a student—only to discover that one of her instructors was a sadist who delighted in beating her hands and that another was a seducer whom she had to fend off by pulling his beard.

But the most titanic battles of her childhood were fought with her father. Many years later, she came to realize that his "violence and hardness had only been symptoms of an intensely sexual nature that had failed to find adequate expression," mainly because of his wife's adamant refusal to risk further pregnancies after four childbirths had all but destroyed her health. In the years, however, when she was growing up, in the Baltic town of Popelan, in Königsberg, and in St. Petersburg, all Emma knew was that her handsome, dashing, vital father, whom she could have adored if she had not been so afraid of him, had made her life a living hell with his violence and cruelty. "The whip and the little stool were always at hand," she remembered, and on one occasion when she received low marks in school because of intransigent behavior, he beat her with his fists until finally he fainted from the exertion. Yet unlike her two older half-sisters, both of whom quailed before him, Emma resisted his tyranny. When he arranged to have her make an advantageous marriage at fifteen, she protested that she be allowed to continue her studies. By way of reply, he threw her French grammar into the fire. The marriage, however, was canceled. And when he refused to allow her to accompany her half-sister Helena to America, she threatened to jump into the Neva—and probably would have, if he had not hastily reversed his position.

In addition to enduring private torments, she also witnessed, throughout her formative years, the authoritarian cruelties of the czar—with whose victims she identified, even though they were, more often than not, despised goyim. One day in Popelan, she came upon a half-naked peasant being lashed with knouts. The scene, she relates, "threw me into hysterics, and for days I was haunted by the horrible picture . . . : the bleeding body, the piercing shrieks, the distorted faces of the *gendarmes*, the knouts whistling in the air and coming down with a sharp hissing upon the half-naked man." The plight of the peasant in the terrible grip of the czarist police was the plight of the embattled Emma in her father's household, and she gave way to hysteria because she felt his wounds as her own. Is it any wonder that this precocious child also read as many nihilist tracts and novels as she could get her hands on? Dreams of subverting and destroying authoritarianism flooded her mind.

America, too, was a dream of freedom, but in fact it proved not to be, as Father Goldman quickly followed his emigrating daughters. In Rochester, he once again established a home which was no better than "a prison." "Every time I tried to escape," runs a particularly bitter sentence in *Living My Life*, "I was caught and put back in the chains forged for me by Father.'' More out of desperation than of love, Emma at seventeen married a hapless young man named Jacob Kershner. At least he could give her a home of her own, as well as satisfy her mounting sexual needs. On the wedding night, however, ''ardent anticipation'' gave way to ''utter bewilderment'' as she learned the trembling Jacob's well-kept secret: he was sexually impotent.

Again she had been victimized by a man—and again she saw her personal grievance mirrored in a larger injustice. The wedding occurred in February 1887; in the months that followed she became excitedly, then obsessively, interested in the legal lynching of the Chicago anarchists on the basis of no hard evidence other than their philosophical belief in violence. Her indignation at their imprisonment was tremendously intensified by her own sense of entrapment, and when she ''went crazy'' in her father's house on the evening following the executions, she served notice to the world that her life was now irrevocably committed to the dead men's cause.

The first step she took, in the days following the hangings, was to separate from Kershner, and when in early 1888 he finally consented to a divorce, she also broke free of her father—who was constantly screaming at her to settle down and behave like a good Jewish daughter—by going to work in a corset factory in New Haven, Connecticut. A year later, in a café on Suffolk Street in New York City, twenty-year-old Emma was introduced to a boy of eighteen, Alexander Berkman, who had the forehead of a scholar and the neck and chest of a giant. Berkman at once invited her to go with him to hear a lecture by Johann Most in denunciation of the execution of the Chicago anarchists. The following November, on the second anniversary of the Haymarket executions, she and Sasha Berkman again heard one of Most's tirades on the subject, at the conclusion of which the speaker called for individual acts of vengeance. Most's passionate oratory had such an intense sexual effect upon Emma that by the time Berkman had escorted her to her doorway her whole body was shaking ''as in a fever.'' Previously she had repelled Berkman's sexual overtures, but now ''an overpowering yearning possessed me, an unutterable desire to give myself to Sasha, to find relief in his arms from the fearful tension of the evening." In time, of course, Sasha and Emma would attempt a spectacular act of political vengeance, but her bedding-down with a disreputable anarchist on the Haymarket anniversary night may also be counted as an act of vengeance in which a bad Jewish daughter made a further mockery of her father's bourgeois ambitions for her. That she soon was sleeping with "Fedya" as well as "Sasha," that she went on to love affairs with Ben Reitman, Ed Brady, Hippolyte Havel, and Arthur Swenson, and that she finally had to admit that "my own sex life had always left me dissatisfied," suggest, however, that her need to retaliate against her father never eventuated in final victory but only in endless compulsion.

The eager promise of cooperation that she made to Berkman in 1892 when he proposed to intervene in the Homestead steel strike by blowing up Henry Clay Frick was, beyond a doubt, the craziest gesture of her life. Like the blast in the brownstone on West Tenth Street and other explosions of our own time, the story of the Frick caper is a tragicomic tale in which the reader's laughter—at the conspirators' feverish efforts to follow the recipe for bomb-making in Most's *Science of Revolutionary Warfare*, at their nervous apprehension that the bombs would go off prematurely and kill all the tenants in their apartment building, and at their "aw-shucks" disappointment when the test bomb failed to work because of dampness in the dynamite—is limited only by the sober realization that human lives hung on the outcome of their child's play. So completely out of touch were they with the realities of American life that when Sasha wounded Frick with a pistol, he and Emma were stunned to discover that the Homestead strikers were embittered by what they had done. In fact, many of the strikers were convinced that Berkman was a capitalistic provocateur who had been hired to kill Frick as a means of turning public opinion against organized labor.

Yet the Frick case catapulted Emma into celebrity and the effort to reduce Sasha's sentence of twenty-two years in prison gave her a cause. By the end of the 1890s, the speech-making of Emma Goldman was being hailed by friend and foe alike as one of the great oratorical performances of American history. She was intellectual, she was witty, and she was well organized. But what was truly stunning about her speeches was that she brought to the podium and translated to her audiences at full blast the emotional violence of her screaming, fist-swinging family combats. Speaking often without notes, her eyes in fact closed at the peaks of passion, she achieved an intensity of feeling that no other speaker of the day could match and that endowed oratory with the same sort of excitement that the highly-charged temperament of Sarah Bernhardt was currently bringing to the theater. There were still times, to be sure, when the famous Goldman temper exploded in overt acts of violence. For example, when she decided that Most had become a traitor to the cause of Sasha's freedom, she showed up at his next public lecture with a horsewhip and jumped him at the first opportunity: "Repeatedly I lashed him across the face and neck, then broke the whip over my knee and threw the pieces at him." But for the most part, she channeled her aggressiveness into unforgettable displays of oratorical fervor.

At first, she spoke only in German or Yiddish to immigrant audiences. However, when she came out of Blackwell's Island in 1894—where she had been confined for inciting a crowd in Union Square to riot—she began to attract some native-born sympathizers who were also disaffected by middle-class American life, including such writers as James Gibbons Huneker, Ambrose Bierce, and the radical journalist John Swinton, as well as a number of social workers, notably Lavinia Dock and Lillian Wald. These friendships persuaded her that the message she had to convey would not fall on deaf ears if she changed over to English. In having the courage and the imagination to make the switch, she brought her considerable intelligence and her enormous passion into the mainstream of American history and readied herself for the key role that she would play in the cultural upheaval of the early twentieth century.

If she had stuck to agitating for Berkman's release or to calling for vengeance against the capitalist executioners of the Haymarket anarchists, her impact on American life would have been slight, no matter how pyrotechnical her oratory was. Very quickly, though, she began to expand her repertoire, until Berkman's imprisonment became not so much a subject as a metaphor of man's fate (especially woman's), and anticapitalism became only one item on an agenda, which included Ibsenism, feminism, free speech, and birth control. Through her contributions to the latter three causes, she affected the lives of every modern American.

Although she failed to acknowledge it in her self-mythologizing autobiographies, Margaret Sanger came to the birth-control movement via her political association and personal friendship with Emma Goldman, who had become aware of the social need for freely available contraceptives while working as a midwife and nurse in the slums of New York in the 1890s. And when Margaret Sanger started to publish *Woman Rebel* in the early teens as a propaganda sheet for her ideas, she modeled its polemical style on an anarchist magazine, *Mother Earth*, which Emma Goldman had been publishing since 1906. Emma Goldman's arrest in 1916 for delivering a public lecture on the use of contraceptives also helped Margaret Sanger to advertise the fight against Comstockery, as Emma Goldman was immediately saluted by George Bellows, John Sloan, Robert Henri, and other Greenwich Village friends at a well-publicized dinner in her honor at the Brevoort. At the trial, she again seized the initiative by belting out one of her most impassioned paeans to human freedom. When the judge sentenced her to fifteen days in Queens County Jail, her public-relations triumph was complete.

As a feminist, she differed from other leaders of the struggle in her refusal to believe that constitutional guarantees of equal suffrage would do very much for either the quality of politics or the happiness of women. While the attention of the other leaders was focused almost exclusively on winning independence from external tyrannies, Emma Goldman felt that internal tyrannies, sexual prudishness above all, were the most important problems facing American women. Militant feminists like Charlotte Perkins Gilman regarded excessive sexual indulgence as a threat to womanly health, but Emma Goldman insisted that the "tragedy of the self-supporting or economically free woman does not lie in too many, but in too few experiences." Inasmuch as her own love affairs never seemed to dampen her energy or damage her morale, Emma Goldman therefore became a heroine to many of the restless girls who came to Greenwich Village in the teens and who in turn inspired the flappers of the 1920s to cast loose from all bonds and assumptions and "try things out." No Americans, however, were more grateful to her for her attacks on emotional inhibition than homosexuals. Crowding up to talk with her after her unprecedented lectures in denunciation of American society's ostracism of the sexual invert, men and women across the nation confessed their anguish, their isolation, and their appreciation to her for giving them back their self-respect.

Wherever she went on her lecture tours, she was apt to be hounded by the police, threatened with physical harm by vigilantes, or at the very least denied on some pretext a permit to speak. Partly for her own self-defense, therefore, she encouraged the founding of the Free Speech League in 1903. Eight years later, she struck another blow for liberty when a speech she gave in St. Louis aroused a young Harvardman to a sense of what he might do with his life. Throughout his long career as a defender of civil liberties, Roger Baldwin has never forgotten how much that speech in St. Louis and his subsequent friendship with Emma Goldman meant to his moral imagination.

Yet at the very time that Baldwin was organizing the National Civil Liberties Bureau to combat the red scare of 1919-1920, the political hysteria of the period brought the American career of Emma Goldman to a close. As her biographer, Richard Drinnon, points out, she had denounced the Spanish-American War without incident; but when she opposed the draft and other aspects of United States involvement in World War I, the government deported her. (No one worked more tirelessly toward her deportation than a former George Washington University student who had been recently named head of the Justice Department's General Intelligence Division, J. Edgar Hoover.) In the course of her long exile, though, she recaptured her American life in one of the most revealing autobiographies of modern times, and when she died, she came back to her adopted land for good. On May 18, 1940, the Immigration and Naturalization Service permitted her corpse to be transported from Toronto, Canada, to a grave in the Waldheim Cemetery in Chicago, where the Haymarket anarchists are also buried.

# *8*

# Trumpets of Jubilee

*Thronging.* It was one of Constance Rourke's favorite words. She loved, as Whitman did, the sense of being a part of the American crowd, and the best of her books make us feel the throb of a collective excitement. While her literary attention centered on individuals—in whose personal eccentricities she clearly rejoiced—the one was always taken to be the symbol of the many. As she wrote in the foreword to *Trumpets of Jubilee*, her first book, popular leaders like Lyman Beecher, Harriet Beecher Stowe, Henry Ward Beecher, Horace Greeley, and P. T. Barnum were "nothing less than the vicarious crowd, registering much that is essential and otherwise obscure in social history, hopes and joys and conflicts and aspirations which may be crude and transitory, but none the less are the stuff out of which the foundations of social life are made"; even when she went on to deal with writers like Nathaniel Hawthorne and Emily Dickinson—who could scarcely be described as having the popular touch of a Barnum or a Beecher—she nevertheless conceived of them in a social way: as interpreters of a people's quest for national identity.

SOURCE: © 1963 by Harcourt Brace Jovanovich, Inc. Reprinted by permission of the publisher from *Trumpets of Jubilee* by Constance Rourke.

When *Trumpets of Jubilee* appeared in 1927, Constance Rourke's insistence on the vital connection between the American artist and his society was a lonely position indeed; as for dealing sympathetically with popular leaders, "it is a habit in these days to scorn popularity." Ever since the Civil War, so she was to acknowledge in *American Humor* (1931), American critics had been carrying on what one of Henry James' characters had called the "wretched business" of quarreling with their country. The masterworks of post-Civil War writing had all voiced in their various ways the alienation of their authors from the accepted values of the Gilded Age. In the artistic generation to which Constance Rourke belonged—that truly remarkable group of poets, painters, literary critics, and social commentators who were born between the end of the 1870s and the mid-1890s and who came of age in the first decade and a half of the twentieth century (Miss Rourke was twenty-one in 1906)—the attitude of the American artist toward his society became even more intransigent. Where Henry Adams, Henry James, and Mark Twain had been deeply troubled by their inability to feel at home in their society, the iconoclasts of the new generation gloried in their separateness. The word of the day was *new*, and contempt for the conventional was vast. Gaily vying with one another as to how best to offend American proprieties, the young image-smashers adopted cubism, Nietzscheanism, Freudianism, Bergsonism, and Marxism. At Mabel Dodge Luhan's fabulous salon on Fifth Avenue in New York, representatives of these rebellions gathered together and discussed even more outrageous schemes for upsetting "the old order of things." Recalling the period 1911-1916, Malcolm Cowley has suggested that subversive conspiracies were everywhere in these years: "Everywhere new institutions were being founded—magazines, clubs, little theatres, art or free-love or single-tax colonies, experimental schools, picture galleries. Everywhere was a sense of secret comradeship and immense potentialities for change." A group of young radicals, among them Walter Lippmann, dreamed of a "new republic" and founded a magazine with that name. Harriet Monroe's new magazine, *Poetry*, spoke for a new poetry. Joel Spingarn called for a new criticism. Ezra Pound's critical exhortation was "make it new," and Pound further foresaw an "American Risorgimento" that would "make the Italian Renaissance look like a tempest in a teapot." For scores of young painters, the famous New York Armory Show of 1913 represented the dawn of a Renaissance in American painting. That reincarnation of the Renaissance woman, Isadora Duncan, cast off conventional dance patterns and conventional sex morality with equal abandon; Amy Lowell wrote free verse and smoked Havana cigars; and neither woman cared when the editorial writers of America screamed in pietistic protest. Alfred Stieglitz, the famous photographer, expressed the contempt that the young iconoclasts in all the arts felt for the middle class's disapproval of their activities when he placed on a framed picture of the rear view of a horse the title, "Spiritual America."

In literary criticism, the focal point of the new generation's quarrel with their society was "puritanism." Different as they were from one another in some respects, Randolph Bourne, H. L. Mencken, Van Wyck Brooks, Waldo Frank, and Lewis Mumford were united in their belief that the cultural legacy of Massachusetts Bay had proved to be a first-class disaster to a later America. Although Brooks derived a certain number of ideas on the subject from Bourne's striking essays and his even more striking conversation ("I shall never forget my first meeting with him," Brooks later wrote in tribute to Bourne's unforgettable personality, "that odd little apparition with his vibrant eyes, his quick, bird-like steps and the long black student's cape he had brought back with him from Paris"), Brooks' own essays constituted the most formidable case against the Puritan tradition put forward by any critic of his time; certainly this was Constance Rourke's view. (Mencken may have had more readers, but in her opinion his scoffing humor was a narrow and "methodical hilarity"—whereas she honored Brooks' opinions as important, even when she disagreed with them.) In *The Wine of the Puritans* (1908), Brooks contended that the Puritans had disapproved of the desire for beauty and pleasure and had saddled upon our society a worship of "things." The result was moral blindness as well as aesthetic stupidity. America was not without ideals, he went on to say in his famous manifesto, *America's Coming-of-Age*

(1915), but these ideals were formless and juiceless and bore little relation to life. Constantly in danger of being ground to a powder between the upper and nether millstones of a vapid idealism and a "catchpenny opportunism," was it any wonder that American culture was thin?

"Attracted to failure"—a phrase that almost surely was resounding in Constance Rourke's mind when she wrote in her first book that "in the expectancy of considerable rewards we shall fix our gaze upon success"—Brooks next turned his attention to the lives of Mark Twain and Henry James, both of whom he depicted as victims of American life. Thus in *The Ordeal of Mark Twain*, which next to *Main Street* was the literary sensation of 1920 (and which makes some of the same assumptions about American small towns as does Lewis' novel), Brooks described the post-Civil War era as "a horde-life, a herd-life, an epoch without sun or stars, the twilight of a human spirit that had nothing upon which to feed but the living waters of Camden and the dried manna of Concord." "There is no denying," Brooks wrote the following year, "that for half a century the American writer as a type has gone down to defeat." The reasons advanced for this defeat were not only sociological but psychological, for like his friend Sherwood Anderson and many of their contemporaries Brooks had been deeply influenced by Freud. "Puritanism," as the intellectuals of the teens and twenties used the term, was not only the symbol of a suffocating environment; it pointed to an inner repression as well. *Winesburg, Ohio* (1918) had painted a nightmare picture of sexual guilt, frustration, and fear, and Brooks' version of Mark Twain's Hannibal was only slightly less chimerical. The religious intensity of puritanism had once proved a mighty weapon in the battle to subdue the wilderness, as Brooks freely admitted, but in 1920 it was three hundred years since the landing at Plymouth. What had once been grand had long since become debased. The traditional Protestant culture of the country was not just a corrupter of institutions, not merely the font of a crass materialism; it was a form of psychic cancer that was rotting the American personality from within. Clearly, if modern American culture was to have a chance for significance, it would have to make a break with its past.

Yet at the same time that the young iconoclasts were endeavoring to make a fresh start, they became keenly conscious of the need for continuity. "I can connect/Nothing with nothing" was the piteous cry of the young woman on Margate Sands in *The Waste Land*, a poem published in the same year—1922—that Willa Cather said the whole world "broke in two" for her; the comments of both women were expressive of a hunger for connection with some external order that was felt by an entire generation. If Freud reinforced rebellions against repressive customs, the "Cambridge School" of anthropology lent support to the idea that individual artists derived both reassurance and inspiration from collective myths. Jane Harrison, whose work meant a great deal to Constance Rourke—and whose ideas T. S. Eliot encountered via Jessie Weston's *From Ritual to Romance*—had uncovered, along with F. M. Cornford, A. B. Cook, and Gilbert Murray of Oxford, the ritualistic basis underlying the art, religion, and philosophy of ancient Greece. To Constance Rourke, their findings confirmed Herder's theories about the connection between folk art and the fine arts. To T. S. Eliot, they gave a resonance to his own thinking about the relationship between the individual talent and the Western cultural tradition. To Van Wyck Brooks, they underscored the necessity for linking the modern American artist to a "usable past." To artists like Scott Fitzgerald and Eugene O'Neill, who had read little or no cultural anthropology but who felt with particular sensitivity the needs of their generation, the quest for the Holy Grail of belief in some self-transcendent myth of the past became the subject of their most compelling works. The lonely and depressed professor in Willa Cather's *The Professor's House* (1925), whose imagination is uplifted by the vision of a primitive but culturally harmonious Indian village in the American Southwest, was the intellectual symbol of an era.

Eliot, however, an expatriate living in London, was more interested in establishing a bridge between himself and the poets and dramatists of Elizabethan and Jacobean England than he was in aligning himself with a specifically American tradition. And Brooks, despite his acknowledgment that the regeneration of American literature could be accomplished only by writers who had a proud sense of who their predecessors were and what their achievements had been, was too busily engaged in demolition work to say anything very affirmative about the American past. (Even his portrait of Emerson in *Emerson and Others* (1927), while it lacked the devastating irony of his assessments of Twain and James, nevertheless had the effect of diminishing Emerson's claim on our admiration.) Lewis Mumford and Waldo Frank also delved into our cultural past, but their primary purpose in doing so was to enlist history on their side in the battle against their bêtes noirs, the American megalopolis and the American business culture. Like Vernon Louis Parrington, whose monumental *Main Currents in American Thought* appeared in the same year as did Constance Rourke's *Trumpets of Jubilee*, Mumford and Frank were myth-makers who recreated the American heritage in the image of their own preoccupations.

The unique achievement of Constance Rourke's first book is that she alone, among all the other members of her generation who were bent on exploring the cultural resources of the country, was willing to honor the spokesmen of an older America for their own sake as well as for the sake of present and future American artists. Yet she was no more a pious antiquarian, who approached the past hat in hand, so to speak, than she was a debunker or a myth-maker. At once sympathetic and objective, she was a superb cultural historian; by her quiet but compelling example, she has had a continuing influence on writers concerned with the American past for more than thirty-five years.

## II

Born in Cleveland, Ohio, in 1885, a graduate of Vassar in 1907, a student at the Sorbonne for a brief period, she began her career as a teacher. For several years, beginning in 1910, she was an instructor in literature at Vassar. Then in 1915—the year of Brooks' famous announcement that America had at last reached an age when it could begin properly to evaluate its past—she resigned from her alma mater in order to devote more time to research and writing. Whether consciously or coincidentally, she had answered Brooks' call to the intellectuals to regenerate America by rediscovering it, and her later career continued to be curiously intertwined with his. 1927 not only witnessed the publication of *Trumpets of Jubilee,* but it was the year that Brooks gave personal illustration to his thesis that the American writer was the victim of a morbid psychology by suffering a severe mental breakdown, an event which decisively terminated the first phase of his literary life. When he emerged from the darkness in 1932, he began to publish a series of books that revealed a drastic change in emphasis. Under the impact of Constance Rourke's and Bernard DeVoto's scholarship, he recanted his assertion in *The Ordeal of Mark Twain* that America had no indigenous folk art, and his own illustrations of our native folk tradition drew heavily on their work. It was altogether fitting, then, that in 1942, a year after Constance Rourke's untimely death, Van Wyck Brooks should have written the preface to *The Roots of American Culture,* a collection of her essays which were to have been part of a three-volume history of American culture that she had been planning and preparing to write for thirty years.

Yet if Brooks' *Makers and Finders* series was a massive accomplishment in cultural rediscovery, it did not supersede Constance Rourke's more slender achievement. Brooks changed his ideas about American folk art and about the literary importance of Mark Twain's humor, but he never really freed himself from the false notion that Henry James' stories were not in the American grain—even though Constance Rourke's brilliant chapter on James in *American Humor* had demonstrated otherwise. Brooks persisted, too, in the animus against the Puritans that was typical of his generation. (Significantly, the *Makers and Finders* series begins the story of the writer in America in the year 1800, whereas *Trumpets of Jubilee* opens with a brief sketch of Calvinism in Connecticut in the eighteenth century and then pursues, via the lives of Lyman Beecher and his remarkable children, the Calvinist tradition in nineteenth-century America.) But the main point of comparison lies in the blandness of the later Brooks. When he finally turned to an affirmation of the national past, he saw everything through an Indian-summer haze that softened and rounded the harsh outlines of many an American tragedy. Constance Rourke, by contrast, was never tempted into lobotomizing our cultural history, for she had never exaggerated its more dismal aspects and therefore had no need to compensate. First and last, she took a balanced view; as she wrote in the foreword to *Trumpets of Jubilee*, her aim was to let "a little of the singular life of the . . . [past] . . . crowd through, with its constricted spaciousness, its stirring trouble, and loud laughter." Except for Barnum, all the major figures in *Trumpets of Jubilee* endure a public trial and humiliation in one form or another: Lyman Beecher was tried for heresy by the Presbyterian General Assembly; his daughter Harriet Beecher Stowe's attack on Lord Byron's sexual mores brought down on her head the vilification of thousands of readers who had once worshipped her as the author of *Uncle Tom's Cabin*; his son Henry Ward Beecher, in one of the most sensational legal battles of American history, was tried for adultery with the wife of one of his parishioners; Horace Greeley's presidential ambitions led him to a downfall that was literally mortifying.

Laughter, however, as well as trouble, is given its due. Constance Rourke's appreciation of Yankee wit, which is more fully manifested in *American Humor*, seasons her treatment of Lyman Beecher and immensely humanizes him; in a decade when the term *Puritan* became a synonym, in Charles Beard's phrase, for anything that interfered with "the new freedom, free verse, psychoanalysis, or even the double entendre," Constance Rourke insisted on the sly humor, the homely ways, and the boisterous passion of Lyman Beecher. With her folk-detective's instinct for finding older forms beneath newer ones, she conceived of Beecher's sermons—and those of his son Henry even more so—as a kind of theatrical performance that ranged from high tragedy to low comedy. Indeed, she conceived of all the dramatis personae of *Trumpets of Jubilee* as theatrical performers, for she adored the theater, as Whitman did, as the most social of all the arts—the place where the one and the many confronted one another most directly. The theater had the "constricted spaciousness" that she felt was the key to American culture and therefore all things theatrical became a primary source of her metaphors. The very title, *Trumpets of Jubilee*, leads us to anticipate a circus—with cosmic overtones. In her second book, *Troupers of the Gold Coast, or The Rise of Lotta Crabtree* (1928), she indulged her delight in theatricality in less oblique terms,[1] but whomever she wrote about, whether *Davy Crockett* (1934) or *Audubon* (1936), the gaudy theatricality of her subject's imagination was the quality that most stirred her own. In her own way she was Barnumesque, and the reader comes away from her studies of American life with the feeling that he has just witnessed the Greatest Show on Earth.

Which is not to say that she was not discriminating or that she lacked standards—quite the contrary. Unlike many students of the popular arts, Constance Rourke was equally at home in discussing the fine arts. If her study of *Charles Sheeler: Artist in the American Tradition* (1938) is valuable for the connections it establishes between an individual artist's practice and the aesthetic expression of a communal group (in this case the Shakers), the book is also important for what it says about the intrinsic merits of Sheeler's work. To state the case in literary terms, Constance Rourke was a critic of texts as well as of contexts, and when she undertook to defend some of the masterpieces of an earlier America against the jeering sophisticates of the 1920s, she did so with an authority that only those who have read the best of what has been thought and said can command.

Writing with that combination of descriptive specificity and visionary sweep which constituted her personal signature, Constance Rourke helped bring us to an awareness of a tradition that, as she wrote in *American Humor*, was "various, subtle, sinewy, scant at times but not poor."

---

[1] Constance Rourke was also drawn to Lotta Crabtree's career because of the touching, lifelong intimacy between an artistic daughter who never married and her mother, a relationship that bears a strong similarity to Constance Rourke's relationship with her mother. Both *Trumpets of Jubilee* and *American Humor* are dedicated to the author's mother, to whom Constance Rourke was utterly devoted. When she wrote that "the bond between Lotta and her mother was close—too close, too confining, even mysterious, some observers said—but there was no sign that it chafed," she might have been describing her own situation.

# *9*

# Patriotic Gore

The American Civil War has been on Edmund Wilson's mind for a far longer time than the fifteen years which went into the making of *Patriotic Gore, Studies in the Literature of the American Civil War*. As his other writings reveal, he has been brooding about the subject for most of his life.

Over the years, Wilson has been almost obsessed by the proposition first advanced by Henry Adams in his *Education* that the Civil War destroyed the eighteenth century in America—the century in which Wilson, no less than Adams, has always felt most at home. Although he concedes that the first seventy years of our national life did not exactly bring into being the reign of reason envisaged by Jefferson, Wilson nevertheless believes that the general scrimmage for money in Jacksonian America was restrained by ideals of republican responsibility deriving from the Enlightenment and shared by influential citizens in all sections of the country. The Civil War, however, broke up what Wilson refers to in *A Piece of My Mind* as the "common cause" between the enlightened patriots of the North

SOURCE: "The Right to Secede from History," *The New Republic* (CXLVI, June 25, 1962). Reprinted by permission of *The New Republic*, © 1962 (71), Harrison-Blaine of New Jersey, Inc.

168        VISIONS OF AMERICA

and the South, and fostered "the wild and overwhelming growth," as
he phrases it in *Europe Without Baedeker*, of "impulses to self-
aggrandizement and appetites for material success." Ever since, the
"children of serious republicans" have been—to a greater or lesser
extent, depending on the decade—displaced persons.

The three decades following Appomattox—"banal in a
bourgeois way and fantastic with gigantic fortunes"—were the most
difficult of all for "Americans brought up in the old tradition," and
as Wilson has made clear in an extraordinarily candid memoir of his
father, for no one of the postwar generation was life more trying than
for Edmund Wilson, Sr. Educated at "18th Century Princeton," the
senior Wilson became by the early 1890s a highly successful lawyer,
although he seems not to have cared about building up a fortune;
what he really wanted was to become a public servant so that he
could help to further that special destiny of American society in
which, as an inheritor of eighteenth-century utopianism, he was
strongly inclined to believe. The sordidness of politics at the turn of
the century so appalled him, however, that he refused to run for office. Ridden by a sense of unfulfillment, he became subject, by the
time he was thirty-five, to "neurotic eclipses, which came to last
longer and longer and prove more and more difficult to cope with."
Beginning in 1908, he served for a time as attorney general of New
Jersey, and when Woodrow Wilson entered the White House he had
hopes of being appointed to the Supreme Court—but in this expectation as in so many others, he was doomed to disappointment. In his
"later and darker years," he withdrew more and more from the practice of his profession, preferring to spend his time at Talcottville,
New York, in the eighteenth-century house which actually had been
in his wife's family, but which in its drastic isolation and enchanting
evocation of an older America was truly his home. When he died in
1923, he was sixty.

Edmund Wilson Jr.'s relationship to his father has been a complicated one. "As a child," he has written, "I imagined that a permanent antagonism existed between my father and me, that I was always, in tastes and opinions, on the opposite side from him." His
father was dogmatic and overbearing—"not an easy man to talk to."

Yet the child was startled one day to discover that his penmanship was an uncannily exact imitation of his father's elegant handwriting, and in his young manhood Wilson came to realize—while going through his father's papers, after his death—that the literary style he was endeavoring to perfect was an emulation of the senior Wilson's silvery-clear prose. Furthermore, Wilson notes, when he suffered a nervous breakdown in his middle thirties, he was the same age as his father had been at the time of his first "eclipse." And when Wilson set down his reminiscences of his father, he had reached the age at which his father had died. The memoir—need it be added?—was written at Talcottville.

At the heart of this complex relationship stands the figure of Abraham Lincoln. The senior Wilson admired Lincoln enormously. He had a whole library of Lincolniana, and he was fond of giving a speech called "Lincoln the Great Commoner." His son automatically made a point of knowing as little about Lincoln as possible and considered his father's interest in the subject to be nothing but a pose which "verged upon demagoguery." For while the elder Edmund Wilson wished to serve the American people, he was no commoner himself, and he lacked the common touch; he dealt with political crowds, as well as with the clients who came to his office, *de haut en bas*. Only after his father's death did the author of *Patriotic Gore* come to understand his parent's kinship with Lincoln. For he now read Herndon's life of Lincoln, which his father had always told him was the least sentimental of all the biographies, and at last realized that here was "a great lawyer who was deeply neurotic, who had to struggle through spells of depression, and who . . . had managed, in spite of this handicap, to bring through his own nightmares and the crisis of society—somewhat battered—the American Republic." Wilson has been fascinated by Lincoln ever since, and he figures most importantly in his most recent book. Wilson's Lincoln is Herndon's all over again, except that he is more neurotic and more aloof: a cold aristocrat who deals with the people *de haut en bas*.

The same constellation of qualities that Wilson finds in Lincoln he also discerns in Lenin. Both the Springfield station and the

Finland station stand in Wilson's imagination for a superior man who had a lucid, skeptical, toughly realistic intelligence, yet who was also possessed by a mystical vision of human destiny; who was curiously indifferent to the world around him, yet who committed all his intellectual strength to a worldly career; and who was lucky enough to catch the express train of history at the right time. As he observed a few years ago, Wilson has a "special susceptibility" to this man, but it is a susceptibility which has always involved as much distrust as it has admiration. We can see these contradictory feelings at work wherever we turn in Wilson's writings, in his fiction as well as his criticism, but nowhere are they more vividly displayed than in the description he wrote in 1935 of Lenin's death-mask:

> We are struck by the aggressive intellect of the boxlike skull which seems always to be tilted forward; here the nose and lips are still rather thick, the eyebrows sharply bristling. . . . But the head in the tomb, with its high forehead, its straight nose, its pointed beard, . . . its sensitive nostrils and eyelids, gives an impression in some ways strangely similar to that one gets from the supposed death-mask of Shakespeare. It is a beautiful face, of exquisite fineness; and—what surely proves its authenticity—it is profoundly aristocratic. Yet if this is an aristocrat, it is an aristocrat who has not specialized as one; and it is a poet who has not specialized as a poet. . . . Nor is it in the least the face of a saint.

Analyzing this passage twenty-one years after it was written, Wilson remarked that it is suffused with "a yearning for 'Holy Places,' " but it is a yearning that is deeply crossed by a sense of danger. Well before Wilson fell out of sympathy with the Soviet Union, he betrayed an uneasiness in the presence of the dead Lenin that reflected the personal tensions of a lifetime.

The most violent denunciation Wilson has ever written of the ruthlessness of superior men—and nations—occurs in the introductory chapter to *Patriotic Gore*. Lincoln and Lenin are mentioned in the same breath—but only in order to set up a comparison between the crushing of the Confederacy by the Union armies and the Russians' descent upon Budapest in the mid-1950s. In a series of scorching paragraphs which are as bitter and disillusioned as anything to be found in the later essays of Mark Twain (to mention another child of the Enlightenment with extremely ambivalent views of politics and politicians), Wilson asserts that wars are not fought for ideals, but for the voracious reasons that prompt sea slugs to attempt to ingurgitate one another (again like Mark Twain, Wilson has always been fond of relating human behavior to zoological phenomena), and he dismisses the anti-slavery speeches of northern leaders, as well as the wartime slogans of Woodrow Wilson and Franklin Roosevelt, as mere propaganda designed to justify aggression. In Wilson's view, the United States of the 1960s is the greatest sea slug of them all, and our fine talk about the "free world" and the "Iron Curtain" is nothing but an inky excretion behind which we stalk our prey. To halt this murderous—and suicidal—quest, Wilson offers us his massive study of the literature of the Civil War, corrosively entitled *Patriotic Gore*. For it is Wilson's hope that by "objectively" examining the northern and southern "myths" in the name of which Americans fought and killed one another a hundred years ago, we will be able to recognize "the kind of role that our . . . country is playing" in the dangerous drama of contemporary world politics.

After such an urgent beginning, it is indeed strange to find that *Patriotic Gore* makes almost no effort to expose the humanitarian idealism of the North as propagandistic; on the contrary, the book honors the northern "myth" in almost all its manifestations. When Wilson writes of *Uncle Tom's Cabin* that it shows how the character of the white South had been weakened "through the luxury and the irresponsibility that the institution of slavery breeds," he is praising the brilliance of Mrs. Stowe's moral insights, not damning her as a warmonger; when he cites an 1841 letter of Lincoln's in which Lincoln refers to the sight of ten or a dozen slaves shackled together with irons as "a continual torment to me," he is paying tribute, as Herndon did, to the compassion that resided side by side with the coldness in Lincoln's character; and when he quotes from Francis

Grierson's poetical remembrance of the 1850s as a decade in which "things came about not so much by preconceived methods as by an impelling impulse," he does not undercut Grierson's mysticism by subsequent references to an economic, let alone a sea-slug interpretation of the period. In the presence of these inspired individuals—and of General Grant and General Sherman and the other northerners he considers—Wilson is at Lenin's tomb all over again: despite all his reservations about the harsh singlemindedness, or the emotional aridity, or the animalistic savagery of these history makers, he cannot help registering, in a language that is often deeply moving, his yearning to believe in the honor of their cause. In his chapter on Grierson, Wilson quotes Dr. Paul Tillich to the effect that "the cultural vocation of the United States was to realize the Kingdom of Heaven on earth, that the motive behind the American Dream . . . was primarily a religious one," and in the mildness of Wilson's demurrer—"It is somewhat surprising to hear that this expectation still survives as a phenomenon sufficiently general to be noticeable to a foreign theologian"—one can hear the voice of an eighteenth-century idealist who has never given up his utopian dreams, no matter how biological his historical metaphors have become.

These contradictions make for chaos in the logical structure of *Patriotic Gore*, but they also make for interest, and in the chapter on Justice Holmes they are actually essential to a striking literary portrait. Inasmuch as Holmes was also a Junior, as well as a post-Civil War lawyer who made it to the Supreme Court, it is perhaps not surprising that Wilson has for years had a special interest in the Justice. But Wilson has felt even closer to Holmes than these details suggest, for reasons which have to do with Holmes' ambivalent attitude toward the Civil War and toward American society in general. Although Holmes had accepted the call to arms as a holy crusade, the experience of fighting cured him for life, Wilson says, of "apocalyptic social illusions." Yet the "paradox," as Wilson rightly calls it, of Holmes' mind is that in the midst of his disenchantment with all idealisms (a disenchantment that became the cornerstone of his achievement as a legal philosopher), Holmes retained what he called in one of his most famous speeches "The Soldier's Faith"—

I do not know what is true. I do not know the meaning of the universe. But in the midst of doubt, in the collapse of creeds, there is one thing I do not doubt, that no man who lives in the same world with most of us can doubt, and that is that the faith is true and adorable which leads a soldier to throw away his life in obedience to a blindly accepted duty, in a cause which he little understands, in a plan of campaign of which he has no notion, under tactics of which he does not see the use.

Similarly, Holmes' ability to remain "aloof and detached from the life of the United States was a phenomenon of a very uncommon kind," at the same time that he was intensely patriotic. Holmes, in sum, was a "rare survival of the type of the republican Roman," perhaps, indeed, "the last Roman in American life," a "man of the old America" who was somehow miraculously unbroken by the new—who carried forward into the twentieth century the old ideals of "independence and fair-dealing," of "rectitude and courage," as well as the ancient conviction that "the United States had a special meaning and mission to devote one's whole life to which was a sufficient dedication for the highest gifts." If by now this list of Augustan virtues is as familiar as are the grounds for Wilson's reservations about Holmes (his bleakness, his ambition), it is nevertheless true that in this instance Wilson's penchant for projecting personal preoccupations into historical and literary studies increases our understanding of the subject as well as of the author. *Patriotic Gore* begins by asking the sneering question, "why should we pay taxes to a government that spends our money on biological warfare research?" —and closes with a celebration of a Supreme Court Justice who had no interest in seeing America, or in reading the newspapers, or in otherwise feeling the "pulse," as Holmes wrote to Pollock, "of the machine," but who bequeathed his entire fortune to the government of the United States: in the agony of his own love-hate affair with modern America, Wilson has correctly sensed in Justice Holmes a spiritual kin.

Again contrary to the expectations set up by the introduction, *Patriotic Gore* deals as gently with the southern "myth" as with the northern; for it, too, represents a set of values in which Wilson finds much to admire (as well as much to disapprove of). The two "myths" are, of course, very different from one another, as Wilson conceives them (they have, indeed, been contending in his imagination from the very beginning of his career—long before he thought to call them northern and southern, or to refer to their struggle as a Civil War); one stands for history, its symbol is a railroad station, its protagonists are men of affairs; the other stands for art, its symbol is a medieval castle, its characters are dreamers. The key to the former is Edmund Wilson, Sr.; to the latter, the man whom Wilson says had more influence on his formative years than anyone except his father, Christian Gauss.

Gauss was also "a part of that good eighteenth-century Princeton," but the ideal he served was a "certain conception of art," not a dedication to public duty. In *The Shores of Light*, Wilson has tried to define what that ideal was. Although Gauss had a sense of the world and of the scope of art that was much bigger than was common among the aesthetes and symbolists of the end of the nineteenth century, he had a fundamental loyalty to the aestheticism of the late nineties which he had first encountered as a foreign correspondent in Paris. He had known Oscar Wilde, and admired him, "and Christian used to tell me, with evident respect," Wilson writes, "that Wilde in his last days had kept only three volumes: a copy of Walter Pater's *The Renaissance* . . . Flaubert's *La Tentation de Saint Antoine* and Swinburne's *Atalanta in Calydon*." Gauss' own literary pantheon also centered on Flaubert (and Dante), and he adhered to a Flaubertian conception of the artist's morality "as something that expressed itself in different terms than the churchgoer's or the citizen's morality; the fidelity to a kind of truth that is rendered by the discipline of aesthetic form. . . ."

Wilson's international renown as a literary critic began with the book that most overtly expressed his response to the fin-de-siècle tastes of Christian Gauss, *Axel's Castle*. In a sense, the book was not a response but a reaction, for it appeared at the height of Wilson's enthusiasm for the Soviet Union; as Wilson himself observed many years later, the imaginary medieval castle of Villiers de L'Isle Adam's *Axel* was intended as a decadent contrast to the "very shabby little railroad station" where Lenin, returning from exile, had got off the train, and which had thus become "the scene of a climax in man's moral and political life." Yet hard-core communist critics were far from satisfied with *Axel's Castle*; they detected a softness in Wilson's treatment of the aesthetic credo that raw life can never be as satisfactory as one's exquisite and intense imaginings—and they were dead right. In spite of his being under the spell of Lenin, Christian Gauss' most brilliant student was as faithful as his teacher to the doctrine that art has its own kind of truth that history knows not of.

Wilson's sympathy with the people of the Old South proceeds directly out of his "aesthetic" belief that people have the right to secede from history if they so desire (as for living, the fin-de-siècle hero of *Axel* remarks, "our servants can do that for us"). Wilson is convinced that if the imaginative life of mankind is to survive, then the private enjoyment of one's own dreams must be defended against onslaughts on the mind from outside—a doctrine that was first enunciated by the greatest southern writer of the antebellum period before being taken up by Baudelaire. Thus *Patriotic Gore* pays tribute to Alexander H. Stephens, the Vice President of the Confederacy, whose concern for individual rights was so intense that he even resisted Jefferson Davis' efforts to bind the seceded states into some semblance of a union; to Mrs. Mary Chesnut, the cultivated and aristocratic diarist whose family reminds Wilson of the Bolkonskys of *War and Peace* (just as Lincoln and the Army of the Potomac remind him of Lenin and the Soviet Army); and to all writers of the Civil War period, whether of northern or of southern origin, who preferred to be observers of life, rather than participants. "They also serve," Wilson says, "who only stand and watch. The men of action make history, but the spectators make most of the histories, and these histories may influence the action."

# *10*

# The Achievement of John Dos Passos

Like Thorstein Veblen, "Fighting Bob" La Follette, and the other lonely men whom he honors in *U.S.A.* for their "constitutional inability to say yes" to the dominant doctrines of the American mind, John Dos Passos has never been afraid to be different. In the era of laissez-faire capitalism his fictional spokesmen drank champagne toasts to "Revolution, to Anarchy, to the Socialist State"; with the dawn of the welfare economy they switched to the individualistic insistence that "if we want to straighten the people out we've got to start with number one"; future social changes will doubtless engender further disagreements between Mr. Dos Passos' voices and the vox populi. Yet to illustrate the intransigence of this Ishmaelite by examples of his political waywardness is merely to scratch the surface of his prickly genius. At heart, his formidable independence is a literary matter and always has been. Alone of all our modern novelists, and in the face of a critical wisdom which has endlessly reiterated that American writers should stick to telling us about the particular cornpatch in which they were raised, Dos Passos has per-

SOURCE: From the "Introduction" to *World in a Glass* by John Dos Passos. Introduction by Kenneth S. Lynn. Reprinted by permission of the Houghton Mifflin Company.

sisted for almost fifty years in his determination to catch both a con-
tinent and a century in the camera eye of his fiction—to project upon
a panoramic screen so many varieties of American experience that
they would constitute, when taken together, a comprehensive record
of life in the United States since 1900. Like Whitman, whose *Leaves*
he read and loved "as a kid," Dos Passos has endeavored to enfold
an entire democracy within his vision—sailors and salesmen, bums
and bankers, mechanics and mannequins, prostitutes and poets; and
like Gibbon, whose *Decline and Fall* he came to admire in his college
days, he has tried to trace time's corruption of the world's most
powerful empire. He has wished, in sum, to "tell all." If he has not
quite succeeded in doing so (one finds, for example, next to nothing
about Negro life in Dos Passos), his failures merely point up the unprecedented magnitude of the task he long ago set himself—and the
unclassifiable grandeur of what he has now achieved.

The first real evidence of the largeness of Dos Passos' vision
was *Three Soldiers* (1921). In a brilliant act of synthesis, he combined the Stephen Crane kind of war story, in which the horrors of
the battlefield are set in ironic contrast against the manufactured
romanticism of patriotic slogans, with the Jamesian story of young
Americans abroad whose New World innocence is tested and shaken
by the confrontation with Old World sophistication—and thereby
established the form that the American war novel has followed ever
since. Not only Faulkner's apprentice novel, *Soldier's Pay* (1926),
which was written in naked imitation, and Hemingway's *A Farewell
to Arms* (1929), whose account of how Frederic Henry makes his
separate peace was obviously indebted to Dos Passos' story of John
Andrews' disastrous defection, but all the World War II novels which
show American soldiers emerging from their baptism in fire to encounter further initiations in the arms of Neapolitan street girls and
Japanese geishas hark back to *Three Soldiers*. Dos Passos' pioneer-
ing book was also the first to emphasize the polyglot makeup of the
modern American army and the first to acknowledge the intramural
tensions between the conscripted sons of the old and new immigra-
tions (an acknowledgment which Dos Passos was peculiarly fitted to
make, for his mother was the descendant of a distinguished

Maryland family and his father the offspring of a Portuguese immigrant), while the technical device he employed to accomplish these things—i.e., dividing the narrative focus among three soldiers of widely differing geographical and social backgrounds—has not merely received the flattery of frequent imitation, it has become one of the most resounding clichés of contemporary fiction.

The imaginative freshness and trailblazing originality of *Three Soldiers* have been manifested again and again in the course of Dos Passos' career. For in addition to goading him into a ceaseless productivity, his ambition to tell the entire story of twentieth-century America has inspired him to remain a continuously inventive author, forever anxious to extend the lines of literary inquiry into new areas of the national experience. In *Number One* (1943), for example, he portrayed a demagogue who was not only a savage reincarnation of the late Huey Long, but a symbol, of the widest general significance, of the suspicions and the resentments which have always smoldered at the secret heart of the populist personality. No serious American writer had previously had the wit—or the courage—to depict the irrational behavior to which such feelings could lead (except Frank Norris, and Norris had reveled in the xenophobia he uncovered), and when Robert Penn Warren took up the "case" of the Louisiana Kingfish a few years after Dos Passos, he was more interested in its metaphysical than its political implications. Finally, in the 1950s, a number of historians and sociologists undertook to study the psychology of populism as a means of explaining McCarthyism; but while these left-liberal social scientists never suggested that they were indebted to a Taft-Republican novelist, the fact remains that their analyses did little more than retrace the behavioral pattern Dos Passos had delineated a decade before. (The only original element in the social scientists' argument was their apparent belief that city folk never hate as vehemently as their country cousins; further study of Dos Passos could have taught them differently.)

By the time other students of the American scene were concerning themselves with the dynamics of American fascism, Dos Passos had moved on to the even more tricky and painful subject of home-grown communism. *Most Likely to Succeed* (1954) is probably the bitterest book Dos Passos ever wrote, but it is as illuminating as it is excoriating. Whereas other writers with left-wing memories have spent most of their energies on summoning up remembrances of the 1930s, Dos Passos' novel shows that the depression years tell only half the story. With his characteristically wide-angled perspective on the past, Dos Passos conceived of the whole interwar period as a continuity, and *Most Likely to Succeed* is a devastating demonstration of how the ferocious leftist infighting in the off-Broadway theatrical world of the 1920s was the perfect sort of training for later survival in the lawless jungle of the Hollywood studios; of how the irresponsible bohemianism of private lives in Greenwich Village easily led to the deer-park ambiance of the Pacific slopes; of how communism could initially appeal to a conceited young man as the political expression of his contemptuously antibourgeois aesthetic—and then become a desperate guarantee against guilt feelings after artistic honor has been sold for a mess of movie dollars. By connecting the sickness of the thirties with the infections of the twenties, by understanding the inhumanities of communism as the consequence of the decay of traditional American values, Dos Passos' bitter book opens up the meaning of a dark and baffling period in American history as no other novel, historical analysis, or ex-radical "confessional" has ever done.

Impressive, however, as such special studies as *Number One* and *Most Likely to Succeed* may be, and as poignant as are the autobiographical recollections in *Chosen Country* (1951) and *The Great Days* (1958), the core of the Dos Passos canon, and the basis of his claim to greatness, consists of the five books which move across the entire range of the American social spectrum, the generous, inclusive books which recall Whitman's relish of variety and Gibbon's sensitivity to social change: *Manhattan Transfer* (1925), the three volumes of *U.S.A.* (1930-1936), and *Midcentury* (1960).

Thematically, *Manhattan Transfer* falls squarely in the center of an important literary succession: on the one hand, it looks back to William Dean Howells' panoramic survey of the New York scene in

*A Hazard of New Fortunes* (1890); on the other hand, it anticipates
Thomas Wolfe's gargantuan evocations of Brooklyn and Manhattan
in *Of Time and the River* (1935) and *You Can't Go Home Again*
(1940). But stylistically *Manhattan Transfer* is utterly unlike these
novels. Dos Passos' prose lacks the density, the marvelous piling-up
of detail, that makes the reader of Howells and Wolfe feel that his
senses are all but directly in contact with the sights, sounds, and
smells of the metropolis. The style of *Manhattan Transfer* has altogether different qualities, which are as special with Dos Passos as
his signature, and which lend to the book an excitement equaled by
no other New York novel ever written. With a jagged, broken rhythm
that Dos Passos apparently absorbed from his fascination with the
movies, the camera eye of the novel ranges restlessly across the city,
swooping in for a "shot" and then moving out again, cutting abruptly
from the barge captain who is exasperated at having to fish Bud Kor-
penning's lifeless body out of the river, to the bizarre inhabitants of
the theatrical boardinghouse where the unhappy young actress Ellen
Thatcher lives, to the ruined "Wizard of Wall Street" cadging
whiskey money on the Bowery; from the sound of a newborn baby
squalling in a hospital, to the unctuous patter of a real estate agent,
to a quarrel between an overwrought Jewish girl and her immigrant
mother ("But Rosie, married life ain't all beer and skittles. A vife
must submit and work for her husband." ". . . But I ain't a Jew no
more," screeched the young girl. "This ain't Russia; it's little old
New York."). In these strange, hurried scenarios there are no por-
traits-in-depth, no leisurely evocations of atmosphere, only a split-
second responsiveness to the sensuous details of a fleeting image, a
beautiful alertness to the nuances of all voices, whether heard or
overheard ("the mind of a generation," Dos Passos once wrote, "is
its speech"), and an instinct for the jugular in every human situation,
no matter how briefly described—while over all the fragments of
frenzied lives of which the novel is composed there presides a
historical consciousness of a more haunting, more implacable movement: the blind tumbling-forward of everyone and everything down
the stream of time. Thus Dos Passos' camera eye is not only constantly switching focus in any given day, it is also forever scanning

forward from today to tomorrow—from the era when there were still empty lots on Broadway ("where tin cans glittered among grass and sumach bushes and ragweed, between ranks of billboards and Bull Durham signs") to the time when a line of cheap hotels has filled up the street (such as the tawdry place where Anna the dressmaker gives the out-of-town buyer "a good time"); from the period when George Baldwin was an ambulance-chasing lawyer to his emergence as a "reform" politician; from Congo Jake the hard-up sailor to Congo Jake the affluent bootlegger. The fire engines that are recurrently heard or seen racing through the crowded streets were intended by Dos Passos to be his leading symbol of the fast-moving, exhilaratingly beautiful, and stupefyingly frightening city that owns them, but in fact the most meaningful emblem of Manhattan in *Manhattan Transfer*, and the quality that makes the book the most original work of American fiction of the 1920s, is the darting, hectic, haunted mode of the narration. The style of the novel *is* New York—or as close to it, at any rate, as any writer has ever come.

In *U.S.A.* Dos Passos raised his sights from a city to a nation, and much later in *Midcentury* he repeated the effort. Unlike *Manhattan Transfer*, these books cannot be compared to any purpose with the work of other writers. Novelistically, they are *sui generis*; indeed, in their dazzling mixture of biography and fiction, of poetry and social documentary, of autobiographical reminiscence and mass-cult pastiche, they at least partially transcend the novel form, creating a kind of literature so radically new that it is still unnamed and that may very well have had more of a technical influence on the way American history is now written (Oscar Handlin's *The Americans* is a recent example of the Dos Passos methodology) than it has on the literary practice of even the most experimental of younger novelists. But if it is difficult to pin an appropriate label on these incomparable books—to decide, once and for all, whether we should call them epics or novels or "contemporary chronicles"—there is no doubt that they cover the ground of our twentieth-century experience as more orthodox storytelling could never have done.

The first and foremost purpose of Dos Passos' experimentation in *U.S.A.* was to record a language. As the author observes at the very outset of the trilogy, "mostly U.S.A. is the speech of the people." The literary ambition implicit in that statement represents the ultimate extension of the prefatory note to *Huckleberry Finn*, wherein Mark Twain lays claim to the linguistic accuracy of the various dialects employed in the book, and of all subsequent attempts by Hamlin Garland, Mary Wilkins Freeman, Stephen Crane, Ernest Hemingway, Sinclair Lewis, and a host of other writers to make American literary expression a registration of the American language. While not blessed with as perfect pitch as some of his colleagues (one recalls, for example, Ring Lardner's unbeatable renditions of "Midwestern Mastoid"), Dos Passos has been willing to listen in more places than they have. *U.S.A.* is, consequently, a veritable anthology of the American idiom—of Texas drawl, Harvard broad "a," and immigrant pidgin; of middle-class female twaddle and proletarian male coarseness; of popular songs, advertising slogans, and fragments from the yellow press. Furthermore, the time span of the trilogy covers the thirty years from Admiral Dewey's invasion of the Philippines to the stock-market crash of 1929, and the texture of Dos Passos' prose continually adapts to the thousands of alterations, some of them subtle, some of them blatant, which American expression underwent during this period. When we meet Doc Bingham at the beginning of the first volume, the extraordinarily versatile and florid lingo which he brings to his salesmanship of dirty books and religious tracts makes him sound like the last of the old-time confidence men—like the younger brother, perhaps, of the fraudulent King who made life hell for Huck Finn and Nigger Jim; but when we encounter Bingham again, toward the end of the third volume, he is pushing a health-fad "philosophy" which sounds remarkably like the pseudoscientific nutritional pitch that lifted Bernarr Macfadden to fame and wealth in the 1920s. The permutations in political oratory, from the grandiloquent imperialism of Albert J. Beveridge to the highfalutin idealism of Woodrow Wilson to the crassly provincial realism of Calvin Coolidge, offer equally rich contrasts, as do the changing manners of sexual invitation—especially as exemplified by the disingenuous chatter of Annabelle Marie Strang in the summer of 1909 and the flippancies favored by Margo Dowling twenty years later. Out of his sensitivity to linguistic changes, Dos Passos created in *U.S.A.* not only an anthology but a morphology of modern American speech. Out of his awareness that such changes were the sounds made by a culture in the process of a profound upheaval, he wrote an anatomy of money, of power, and of sex—of the great American themes which Henry Adams found so fascinating and wished someone would write about (characteristically, Adams was doomed to disappointment, for he died just as Dos Passos' career was getting underway). If, in Dos Passos' own words, the writer who gets "the words and phrases . . . straight . . . is the architect of history," then the author of *U.S.A.* is the grand designer of our twentieth-century past.

*Midcentury* is in its own right a fascinating book. By a similar diversification of narrative techniques, it evokes the period 1945-1960 as effectively as *U.S.A.* summons forth an earlier era. But *Midcentury* becomes even more fascinating when it is read in conjunction with the trilogy it so closely resembles—when it is listened to as if it were the coda to a great American symphony. For in doing so we gain a unique understanding of what has happened to us as a people in the course of a fantastic century. *U.S.A.*, for example, unfolds saga after saga of how poor boys made their way from rags to riches:

> Samuel Insull landed in America on a raw March day in eightyone. Immediately he was taken out to Menlo Park, shown about the little group of laboratories, saw the strings of electriclightbulbs shining at intervals across the snowy lots, all lit from the world's first central electric station. Edison put him right to work and he wasn't through till midnight. Next morning at six he was on the job; Edison had no use for any nonsense about hours or vacations. Insull worked from that time on until he was seventy without a break; no nonsense about hours or vacations. Electric power turned the ladder into an elevator.[1]

[1] Copyright by H. Marston Smith and Elizabeth H. Dos Passos, co-executors of the estate of John R. Dos Passos.

But *Midcentury* introduces us to a new kind of American success story, in which self-indulgence has replaced ruthlessness as the golden key:

> In the drab summer desert of New York, James Dean lacked friends; he lacked girls, he lacked dough;
> but when the chance came he knew how to grab it: a young director took an interest, invited him out sailing on a sloop on the Sound—farmboy turned deckhand—gave him a part in a show which immediately flopped;
> but he'd been seen on the stage. Next he played the blackmailing Arab in a dramatization of André Gide's *The Immoraliste*. He walked out on the part, the play closed, but he'd been seen by people who knew show business: rave writeups: he was an actor.
> They took him on to study at the Actor's Studio. The Actor's Studio was celebrity's lobby in those days. That year Marlon Brando was the artistic idol of the screen. Directors saw a young Brando in Dean (the hepcat school, sideburns and a rat's nest for hair, leather jackets, jackboots and a motorcycle at the curb. These are tough guys, delinquents; but sensitive: Great God how they're sensitive). Elia Kazan hired him to play a sinister adolescent: "Live the part," Stanislavski told his actors.
> Dean did just that. He was obstreperous as hell. "I can't divert into being a social human being," he snarled at the reporters through the butt that dangled from his lip, "when I'm working on a hero who's essentially demonic."
> Demonic, but lovable under it all.
> The sinister adolescent was box office. Long before the picture was released he was besieged by Hollywood agents, promoters, feature writers, photographers.

As late as the 1920s, the world of science had been comprehensible to the mind of the layman:

NEWLY DESIGNED GEARS AFFORDING NOT
ONLY GREATER STRENGTH AND LONGER
LIFE BUT INCREASED SMOOTHNESS

NEW CLUTCH—AN ENGINEERING
ACHIEVEMENT THAT ADDS WONDERFUL
POSITIVENESS TO POWER TRANSMISSION
THAT MAKES GEARSHIFTING EASY AND
NOISELESS

But by the end of the Second World War, scientific talk had become disturbingly, even frighteningly, strange:

*at a few degrees above absolute zero the application even of a small electric field to a sample of germanium will grossly affect equilibrium of the conduction of electrons and increase their average energy by a factor of twenty five or more*

The lines of connection (and contrast) can be endlessly projected: from the Cape Cod cottage to the split-level ranch; from the anodyne of bootleg booze to the tranquilization of the Miltown; from the naive enthusiasms of advertising's infancy ("WE FEEL VERY FRIENDLY TOWARDS THE TYPEWRITER USERS OF NEW YORK CITY") to the hidden-persuader techniques of Madison Avenue ("IF YOU KNOW THE WOMAN WHO SHOULD HAVE THIS CAR . . . you must admire her very much. She never tries to impress . . . it isn't necessary. She never 'makes an entrance,' yet, somehow, people turn when she comes into a room. If she's impatient, it's only with pretension. If she's proud, it's mostly of being a woman. She's gentle, durable . . . and intensely feminine . . ."); from a solitary, penniless young man named Vag, walking down a road in quest of the just America of his dreams, to that merciless parody of Holden Caulfield named Stan Goodspeed, who loads up with his uncle's credit cards and takes off in search of kicks and chicks. Time, in Dos Passos, is a tissue of ironies.

The ironies are by no means restricted to what the observer has observed these many years, for time has also had its effect upon Dos Passos—thereby lending a further fascination to his best books. *U.S.A.* was informed by the idea that big business was the chief threat to individual freedom in America, whereas *Midcentury* insists that big labor is the power which threatens our liberties. (For all his admiration of Veblen, it took Dos Passos many years to learn the master's bitter lesson that the workers, too, are corruptible.) Yet for all the antiunion indignation that *Midcentury* generates, the book is not nearly as dogmatic in its conservatism as the trilogy was in its radicalism, because Dos Passos is today a humbler and a more troubled man than he was thirty years ago. In the early novels, Dos Passos' typical hero was a young man full of passionate intensities—like Martin Howe in *One Man's Initiation* (1920) or the Harvardman, Wendell, in *Streets of Night*—a young man who was avantgarde in his art and radical in his politics and who believed that if we could but escape from the past, wipe the slate clean, we could build a better world. This burning belief, which is significantly protected against the acid of the author's otherwise pervasive scorn, towers into a pillar of fire in the three volumes of *U.S.A.* Evil institutions, these books proclaim, must be brought to judgment; Walt Whitman's "storybook democracy" will arise again only by a total reconstitution of society; history, in a word, must go. Thus Dos Passos entered the labyrinth of our twentieth-century past in order to prepare the way for the demolition teams. But the act of recapturing time had an unexpected effect upon him. Critics who have written about Dos Passos' journey to Spain during the Civil War, and who point to his shocking discovery while there of how ruthlessly the Communists were undercutting their supposed allies within the Popular Front as the operative cause of his disillusionment with radicalism, miss the point; the central experience in Dos Passos' political education in the early 1930s was the titanic labor of creating *U.S.A.* The trilogy changed the man who wrote it, inducing in him a new respect for "the ground we stand on," a new awareness of historical continuity, a new appreciation of the complexities of human motivation. History was not escapable, after all, nor was it as simple as it had seemed.

In the novels after *U.S.A.* we no longer look at American life through the eyes of a fervent and iconoclastic young man; we view men and events through the bloodshot vision of Tyler Spotswood in *Number One* or Ro Lancaster in *The Great Days*. There are no passionate intensities in these men's lives, unless it be the nauseating memory of earlier mistakes: last night's drunk is over, and now the morning after is full upon them, with all its physical and mental punishments. Their hangovers are the symbols of Dos Passos' troubled consciousness, his anguished appreciation of how difficult it is to understand the times we live in. The battlecry of *U.S.A.*—"all right we are two nations"—evokes the certainty of the younger author's mind, while the title Dos Passos gives to his *Midcentury* sketch of J. Robert Oppenheimer—"The Uncertainty Principle"—indicates the older writer's state of mind. Dos Passos in the 1960s is less sure about everything in his "chosen country," but his power to communicate his doubts is the source of our undiminished interest in an amazing career.

# *11*

# Violence in American Literature and Folklore

Recurring themes of violence in American literature and folklore bear witness to the continuing violence of American life. The cruel practical jokes and bloodthirsty tall tales of frontier humorists tell us a good deal about what it was like to live on the cutting edge of a wilderness. The burning cities of Ignatius Donnelly's *Caesar's Column*, Jack London's *The Iron Heel*, and other social novels of the turn of the century reflect in their flames the revolutionary discontent of farmers and industrial workers in the 1890s. Mark Twain's *Pudd'nhead Wilson*, Melville's "Benito Cereno," and Richard Wright's *Native Son* measure the racial animosities with which black and white Americans have been struggling since the seventeenth century. The war novels of Stephen Crane, and of Hemingway and Dos Passos, register the central experience of life "in our time."

American literature and folklore have great significance, therefore, for all those who are interested in the violent realities of our society. The trouble, however, with the way in which these

SOURCE: *Violence in America. Historical and Comparative Perspectives.* A Report to the National Commission on the Causes and Prevention of Violence, June 1969. Prepared under the direction and authorship of Hugh Davis Graham and Ted Robert Gurr for the President's Commission.

materials have been used by historians, sociologists, anthropologists, and psychiatrists is that literature has been assumed to be nothing less (or more) than a mirror image of life. The effects of fictional conventions on representations of reality have been ignored, as have the needs of authors and audiences alike for the pleasures of hyperbolic exaggeration. Furthermore, by extrapolating violent incidents out of their literary contexts, social scientists have not taken into account either the mitigating dreams of peace which are threaded through the very bloodiest of our novels and stories, or the comic juxtapositions which take the curse off many of the most unpleasant episodes that the American imagination has ever recorded.

The false impressions created by social scientists have been reinforced by certain literary critics who have used their judgments of American literature as a basis for making larger judgments about American society. The errors of these critics have not proceeded out of any lack of literary subtlety, but rather out of their wish to be recognized as cultural messiahs. The messianic strain in modern literary criticism has been in any case very strong, embracing such diverse commentators as T. S. Eliot, Northrop Frye, F. R. Leavis, and Marshall McLuhan, but it has been particularly strong among commentators on American literature. From D. H. Lawrence in the 1920s to Leslie Fiedler in the 1960s, the desire of literary critics to lead a revolution in American values has been continuing and powerful, and this desire has led them to insist that violence is the dominant theme of American literature, that American literature is more violent than other literatures, and that the violence of our literature has become more deadly with the passage of time. For the first stage in a revolution is to prove its necessity, and what better evidence could be offered as proof of the sickness of historic American values than the unique and obsessive concern of our literary artists with themes of blood and pain? To the messianic critics, the indictment of American books has opened the way to the conviction of American society.

The question of American literary violence thus needs reexamination. By looking closely at certain representative examples, from the humor of the Old Southwest to the tragic novels of our own time, we may be able to measure more accurately than heretofore both the extent and the significance of violence in American literature and folklore.

When we consider the humorists of the region between the Alleghenies and the Mississippi River, which in the 1830s and 1840s was known as the American Southwest, we are immediately struck by the theoretical possibility that the literature of violence in America has been written by losers—by citizens who have found their political, social, or cultural position threatened by the upward surge of another, and very different, group of Americans. The southwestern humorists were professional men—doctors, lawyers, and newspapermen, for the most part—who were allied on the local level with the big plantation owners and who supported on the national level the banker-oriented Whig party of Daniel Webster and Henry Clay; and what bound these writers together as a literary movement, what furnished the primary animus behind their violently aggressive humor, was their fear and hatred of Jacksonian democracy. Longstreet, Thompson, Kennedy, Noland, Pike, Cobb, Thorpe, Baldwin, Hooper—all the best-known humorists of the Old Southwest—were agreed that Andrew Jacksonism stood for a tyrannical nationalism which threatened to obliterate states' rights; for a revolutionary politics which by 1860 would democratize the constitution of every southern state except South Carolina; and for a new spirit of economic competitiveness which everywhere enabled poor white entrepreneurs to challenge the financial supremacy of the bankers and the planters, even as Faulkner's Snopes clan would crawl out of the woodwork after the Civil War and take over the leadership of the biggest bank in Yoknapatawpha County.

Augustus Baldwin Longstreet's *Georgia Scenes* (1835) established the basic literary strategy of southwestern humor, which was to define the difference between the emotionally controlled, impeccably mannered, and beautifully educated gentleman who sets the scene and tells the tale and the oafish frontiersmen who are the characters within the tale. By keeping his narrators outside and above the barbaric actions they described, Longstreet (and his successors) drove home the point that southern gentlemen stood for law and order, whereas Jacksonian louts represented an all-encompassing anarchy. However hot-tempered the author might be in private life (and Judge Longstreet was only one of many Southwestern humorists who had a notoriously bad temper); however much the hideously cruel, eyeball-popping fights they described gave vent to their own sadistic sense of fun; whatever the political satisfaction that they secretly derived from the spectacle of Jacksonians clawing and tearing at one another; the literary mask of the southwestern humorists was that of a cool and collected personality whose thoughts and conduct were infallibly above reproach. Politically and socially, the humorists had a vested interest in maintaining that mask.

They also had a vested interest in enlarging upon the violence of backwoods bully boys, riverboat toughs, and other representatives of the new democracy. The more inhuman his Jacksonian characters were made to appear, the severer the gentleman-narrator's judgment of them could become. No matter how much lip service they paid to realism as a literary ideal, there was a built-in, political temptation to exaggerate the truth, which Whig humorists found impossible to resist. One and all, they wrote comic fantasies, which the historian of American violence will cite at his own risk.

Even those social scientists who are aware that the purported reality described by a story must always be understood as a projection of the storyteller's mind generally distort the meaning of southwestern humor by taking its violence out of context. Doubtless, as I have already suggested, the humorists' fascination with scenes of violence tells us a good deal about the frustrations and fears of the southern Whig mind. Yet if we set out to calculate the total imaginative effect of, say, Longstreet's *Georgia Scenes*, we find that the "frame" devices which encapsulate the stories within a gentleman's viewpoint and the balanced, rational, Addisonian language of the gentleman-narrator's style remove a good deal of the horror from the stories. As in Henry Fielding's *Tom Jones*, a novel of which Judge Longstreet was very fond, violence becomes funny rather than frightening, sanative rather than maddening, when it is seen from a certain elevation, when it is understood by the audience to be a kind of marionette show that is controlled by, but does not morally implicate, the master of ceremonies.

In the years after 1850, when relationships between the sections steadily deteriorated and the South gave way to a kind of collective paranoia, southwestern humor finally lost its cool. Instead of speaking through the mask of a self-controlled gentleman, the humorist of the new era told his sadistic tale in the vernacular voice of the sadist himself. Whereas Judge Longstreet had been at pains to keep his distance, imaginatively speaking, from the clowns he wrote about, George Washington Harris gleefully identified himself with the prankster-hero of *Sut Lovingood's Yarns* (1867)—for in a world ringed by enemies, the only hope of survival which a paranoid imagination could summon up was to strike first, an ungentlemanly act of which Longstreet's narrator would have been manifestly incapable. Just as the Whig party disappeared after the mid-1850s, so did the literary persona who had incarnated Whiggery's conservative ideals. In his place there arose a grotesque child-hero who was the literary equivalent of the fire-eating, secessionist spirit which increasingly dominated southern politics after 1855. The vernacular narration of young Sut Lovingood is not intended to remind us of the virtues of moderate behavior—indeed, just the reverse. For Sut's humor blocks intellectual awareness in order to release a tremendous burst of vindictive emotion; he is concerned not to instruct society, but to revenge himself upon it. A rebel without a cause, Sut tells us much about the rebels of the lost cause of 1861-1865.

Yet in the overall picture of southwestern humor, *Sut Lovingood* is the exception, not the rule, a rare instance of the sadistic humor of the frontier being expressed in a manner unqualified by any kind of stylistic or formal restraint. For the most part, the humorists of the Old Southwest had a more ambivalent attitude toward violence. Clearly, they were fascinated by it, no matter what they said to the contrary. The way in which the narrators of their stories linger over the details of physical punishment indicates that there was a lurking hypocrisy in the law-and-order stance of the humorists. However, in dealing with southwestern humor, the historian of the Whig mind must be as careful about leaping to exaggerated conclusions as the historian of Jacksonian reality. If the humorists were hypocrites to a degree, they were also sincere to a degree. If they secretly delighted in the human cockfights they pretended to deplore, they also were genuinely committed to a social standard of moderation in all things. This commitment was expressed in the literary qualities of their writing. In southwestern humor, the style was, in a very real sense, the man.

Another striking outburst of violent stories in American literature occurred in the social fiction of the turn of the century. Thus Ignatius Donnelly's widely read novel, *Caesar's Column* (1891), projects a dystopian vision of American society in 1988. At first glance, New York City is a smokeless, noiseless, dream city, with glass-roofed streets, glittering shops, and roof-garden restaurants. But beneath the surface, the narrator of the novel (a white visitor from Uganda) discovers that the city, like the nation at large, is engaged in a deadly social struggle between a ruling oligarchy, which maintains itself in power with a dirigible fleet armed with gas bombs, and a brutalized populace, made up for the most part of a sullen-tempered, urban proletariat, but also supported by a degraded peasantry. The story climaxes in a lurid account of the definitive breakdown of the social order, which occurs when the looting and burning of the city by a revolutionary organization called the Brotherhood of Destruction rages beyond the control of the oligarchy's troops. The number of corpses littering the streets finally becomes so great that an immense pyramid of dead bodies is stacked up and covered with cement, partly as a sanitary precaution and partly as a memorial to the violence. In the end, the entire city is put to the torch, and except for a small band of Christian socialists who escape to Africa, the entire population is consumed in the holocaust.

The apocalyptic fury of the novel relates very directly to the political hysteria of the 1880s and to the agricultural and industrial unrest of the 1890s—to the fears of an anarchist takeover, for example, that swept the nation after the Haymarket riot in Chicago in 1886, and to the bitter, bloody strikes at Homestead, Pennsylvania, and Pullman, Illinois, in the mid-1890s. The novel is also a startling prophecy of the events of the summer of 1967 in Newark and Detroit. Yet in the very act of calling attention to these resemblances between literature and life, we are also confronted with the important difference, which is that the novel is much more extreme than the reality. As in the case of the southwestern humorists, Ignatius Donnelly was not a mere seismograph, passively recording social shocks or even forecasting them; rather, he was a man who had been driven to become a writer by the experience of political loss, and the apocalyptic darkness of his novelistic vision tells us more about Donnelly's state of mind than it does about American society, past or present.

A political reformer from Minnesota, Donnelly had been deeply upset in 1889 by the overtly corrupt practices of the legislature in his state. In addition to his commitment to good government, Donnelly was a Populist who combined a concern for the deteriorating economic position of the midwestern farmer with a political and moral concern that American life was coming to be dominated by its big cities. If the demographic trends of his time continued, Donnelly realized, they would reduce the importance of the farm vote and would spread the spirit of corruption that had so appalled him in the Minnesota legislature. In equating the spread of urbanism with the spread of corruption, and in envisioning damnation and destruction as the ultimate penalty of city life, Donnelly revealed himself, in the judgment of Richard Hofstadter, as a sadist and a nihilist. *Caesar's Column* is "a childish book," so Hofstadter has written, "but in the middle of the twentieth century it seems anything but laughable: it affords a frightening glimpse into the ugly potential of frustrated popular revolt." Donnelly's novel is thus for Hofstadter a key to the provincial spirit of midwestern America, a spirit ruled by suspicions of the East, distrust of intellectuals, and hatred of Jews, and given to raging fantasies of Babylonian destruction. The violence depicted in *Caesar's Column* may never have been matched by the social data of American history, but Hofstadter would contend that the sado-nihilism of the American hick is very much a part of the emotional actuality of our civilization and that Donnelly's novel is expressive of a profoundly dangerous phenomenon.

Yet Donnelly's ambivalent view of the city—a place on the one hand of glittering amusements and technological marvels and on the other hand of social exploitation and spiritual degradation—is a view he shares with a vast number of American writers from all centuries of our history, all sections of the country, and all ranges of literary excellence from the least memorable to the most distinguished, the most intellectual, and the most cosmopolitan. The urban imagery summoned up by Hawthorne and Melville in the 1850s is characterized by starkly symbolic contrasts of blazing light and sinister darkness, as is the imagery of *New York By Gaslight* and other trashy books of the period. E. P. Roe's bestselling novel, *Barriers Burned Away* (1872), which depicts the great Chicago fire as a judgment upon a wicked city, is part of an incendiary tradition which not only includes Donnelly's mediocre novel, but Part IV of T. S. Eliot's *The Waste Land* (1922). Clearly, what Donnelly was expressing in his novel was a frustration which fed into a familiar American concern, at heart, a religious concern, with the question of whether honor, charity, and other traditional values of western civilization were capable of surviving in the modern city. That Donnelly gave a gloomy answer does not necessarily prove that his political frustration contained an "ugly potential" of violence. It is, indeed, more likely that the ending of his novel was a religious strategy that went back through Hawthorne and Melville to the Puritans. By issuing a jeremiad which warned of the terrible consequences of abandoning the Christian life, he hoped to bring an urban America back to the faith of its fathers.

Jack London's *The Iron Heel* (1905) also ends cataclysmically. Although the plot of the socialists to overthrow capitalism in America has been led by the dynamic Ernest Everhard (whose medium size, bulging muscles, and omnivorous reading habits recall Jack London himself), the awesome power of the ruling oligarchy— the so-called Iron Heel—is too much for the outnumbered revolutionaries. At the climax of the book, the slum classes—for whom Everhard and his fellow socialists feel nothing but contempt—go pillaging through the city. However, this act is the self-indulgent gesture of a degenerate, racially mongrelized mob which does nothing to benefit the military position of the gallant elitists of socialism. According to the novel's twenty-seventh-century editor, three hundred years of bloodletting were to pass before the Iron Heel is finally overthrown and the brotherhood of man established.

The question at once arises as to why London, after building up his hero as a superman, should have permitted him to be defeated, especially since he was an exponent of the same revolutionary cause as Everhard was. The answer has seemed unavoidable to some readers that London was interested in violence for violence's sake, even if it meant denying himself the pleasure of a socialistically happy ending. However, the confusion which London displayed in his ideological writings suggests another explanation for the ending of *The Iron Heel*. For these ideological writings reveal that London was as committed to a belief in the competitive ethic of American success as he was to socialism and that he was hagridden by the conviction that the victory of socialist principles would lead to social rot because it would terminate competition between individuals; consequently he found it imaginatively impossible to write a novel depicting the triumph of the socialist revolution. To portray Everhard and company in charge of a socialist America would have meant that London would have been forced to show his autobiographical hero presiding over a society characterized by declining production, degenerating racial stocks, and decaying institutions.

It is not surprising, therefore, that even though *The Iron Heel* is supposedly edited by a man living under the reign of the brotherhood of man in the twenty-seventh century, no description is given of how this socialist Utopia is organized or operated, no hint is offered as to the steps that have been taken to avoid social decay. Unable to portray a paradise that he knew in his heart was really a hell, London found it an easier imaginative task to concentrate on describing the defeat of the socialist revolution. To lament the defeat of socialism was infinitely easier than to pretend to rejoice in its triumph.

A third possible explanation of the ferocious violence of *The Iron Heel*'s conclusion is that it reflected London's awareness of all the disappointments that American radicals had suffered in the course of his lifetime. The Greenback movement had gone nowhere, except to oblivion; the Supreme Court had reversed the Granger cases; the Populists had never become anything more than a regional movement; in the climactic election of 1896, Bryan had been badly beaten; and Eugene Debs had polled a disappointing number of votes in the presidential elections of 1900 and 1904. London's socialist hopes were simply overwhelmed by his inability to forget the bitter lessons of recent American history: in the new era of the Standard Oil trust and other big-business combinations, American radicals could scarcely be optimistic.

All three explanations of London's novel are equally compelling. Unquestionably, London was neurotically fascinated by tests of mental and physical endurance; long before his suicide, his mind was thronged with images of violent death. To literary critics interested in establishing the sickness of the American psyche, London's personal life simply reinforces their thesis that his novels and stories are obsessed by violence. Because it damages their thesis, these critics ignore the fact that violent endings offered London a means of resolving his contradictory ideological commitments to success and socialism—and that therefore the conclusion of *The Iron Heel* ought to be understood as a literary strategy which enabled a philosophically troubled writer to resolve his ambivalence and complete his books. Equally damaging to the interpretation of *The Iron Heel* as symptomatic of an author's (and a nation's) psychological illness is the fact that a socialist novelist who foresaw the continuing hegemony of capitalist combinations in America was simply being realistic. Can we really be sure that the ending London gave his novel represented anything else than his unwillingness to fool either himself or his readers about the chances of building a socialist utopia in twentieth-century America? The apocalyptic fury with which *The Iron Heel* concludes may well have been the sign of London's sanity as a social prophet, rather than of his psychological imbalance.

Writing about the experience of modern war begins in American literature with Stephen Crane in 1895. Our first modern conflict had ended thirty years before, but for a generation after the Civil War American writers had either ignored or romanticized that terrible struggle. The one exception was John W. De Forest's novel, *Miss Ravenel's Conversion from Secession to Loyalty* (1867), which had portrayed the fighting in grim and realistic detail. However, *Miss Ravenel* had been a failure, commercially speaking, and in the wake of its failure there arose a genre of writing called the intersectional romance, which typically told of a wounded Union army officer being nursed back to health by a predictably beautiful southern belle, whom he finally led to the altar. Even the literary reminiscences of soldiers who had served in the war told a good deal less than the whole truth. Thus the *Century* magazine's notable series of military recollections, "Battles and Leaders of the Civil War," represented only an officer's eye view of what had in fact been a democratic war won by a mass army. The same fault afflicted Ambrose Bierce's otherwise superbly honest *Tales of Soldiers* (1891). Before Crane published *The Red Badge of Courage* (1895), only a very minor writer named Wilbur F. Hinman had recorded, in a comic novel, entitled *Corporal Si Klegg and His "Pard"* (1887), how the violence made possible by modern military technology had affected the men in the ranks.

That Crane should have been impelled to measure the impact of the war on ordinary Americans was certainly not the result of his own experience of violence, for he was not even born until 1871, six years after the close of the war, and in the course of his middle-class New Jersey boyhood had never heard a shot fired in anger. What fascinated him about the Civil War was what also fascinated him about the submarginal world of the Bowery, which he had come to know during his salad days as a reporter on the New York *Herald*. Like the seamiest of New York's slums, the most tragic war in our history represented American life in extremis, and such representations suited Crane's subversive frame of mind.

Political and social events of the early 1890s had revealed to Crane an enormous disparity between the official version of American life as conveyed by such popular authors of the day as James Whitcomb Riley and Thomas Bailey Aldrich, and the often brutal realities that were attendant upon the nation's transformation into an urban and industrial civilization. The effect of this revelation on a young man who had already been engaged throughout his youth in a Tom Sawyerish rebellion against his middle-class upbringing was to turn him against all the optimistic beliefs in the pursuit of happiness, the inevitability of progress, etc., which most Americans cherished. Revolted by blandness and complacency, Crane went in search of misery and violence—in the lower depths of Manhattan; in sleazy bars down Mexico way, where he was nearly murdered one scary night; on the battlefields of Greece, where he served as a correspondent covering the Greco-Turkish War; and again as a war reporter in Cuba, where he differentiated himself from Richard Harding Davis and other correspondents by the risks he took, by the deliberate way he exposed himself to the fire of Spanish rifles.

In the world of his imagination, Crane craved the same experiences, and he often wrote of them before he had lived them. *Maggie, A Girl of the Streets* (1893), the story of an East Side girl whose descent into prostitution concludes with her descent into the East River, was largely worked out before Crane quit college and went to live in New York, just as *The Red Badge of Courage* was published before he saw Greece or Cuba. For his books were not *reportage;* they were works of art which endeavored to make the American novel relevant to a new generation of socially skeptical readers, as the works of Zola, Crane's literary idol, had done for the French novel. The restlessness, the guilt, and the itch to change things that impelled middle-class, urban Americans into the Progressive movement of 1901-1917 were first manifested in the fiction of Stephen Crane in the mid-1890s. Paradoxically, a body of work dominated by a black humor and an ironic style and by scenes of violence often culminating in horridly detailed descriptions of dead bodies had a life-giving effect, a revitalizing effect on American art and politics. For all his mordant skepticism about official American culture and all his efforts to flee—both spatially and spiritually—from the world he had been brought up in, Crane was really a middle-class spokesman. Unlike the Whig humorists of the 1830s or the utopian novelists who were his contemporaries, Crane was not a loser in American life. He was, rather, an outsider who had assumed his critical role by choice rather than necessity. Whereas Judge Longstreet and his fellow humorists had lamented a way of life, a scheme of values, that was irrevocably passing out of the national scene, and whereas Jack London and Ignatius Donnelly were lamenting an American civilization that would never come to be, Crane offered violent versions of a modern war we had already fought and would fight again, and of a city which has been the archetype of our collective life from his own time to the present. As with most outsiders in American life, including the runaway Tom Sawyer, rebellion was a halfway house for Stephen Crane and violence a means of ultimate accommodation.

The violence of Ernest Hemingway's early novels and stories are expressive, so we have been told, of a far more cruel, pointless, and degrading war experience than the Civil War that Stephen Crane conjured up out of talking with veterans and reading the *Century* magazine. Why this should be so is not entirely clear, inasmuch as the Civil War was infinitely more costly to our soldiers and to our people. Indeed, the violence of Hemingway's fiction has become so famous as to obscure the fact that none of his stories, and none of the stories of Dos Passos or E. E. Cummings or any other American writer who served overseas in World War I, come anywhere near matching the butchery described in Erich Maria Remarque's *All Quiet on the Western Front*, Henri Barbusse's *Under Fire*, Guy Chapman's *A Passionate Prodigality*, and other European chronicles of the Great War. In only one way are the novels of the Americans more nightmarish than those of the European writers. Hemingway, Dos Passos, and company did not, and indeed could not, outrival the details of endless horror that four years in the trenches had etched in Guy Chapman's or Erich Remarque's memory. Yet Remarque and the other European writers also paid grateful tribute in their books to the psychological comforts of mass comradeship, whereas the heroes of Hemingway and Dos Passos are loners who feel lost in the midst of the crowd. They may find one other kindred spirit, generally Italian, or possibly a girl friend, generally British, but they know nothing of the group feeling that Remarque and the European writers were grateful for. A desolate sense of alienation is the special mark of the best American fiction to come out of World War I. In seeking to assess the meaning of the violence expressed by the ''lost generation" writers, we must therefore reckon with the loneliness which accompanies it and which gives it its peculiarly devastating and memorable effect.

Perhaps the alienation may be explained by the very special role which our writers played in the war. For the striking fact is that unlike their literary equivalents in England, France, and Germany, the American writers were not soldiers but ambulance drivers or some other kind of auxiliary. Malcolm Cowley worked for military transport; Hemingway was with the Red Cross in Italy; Dos Passos and Cummings were with the Norton-Harjes ambulance unit, and so were Slater Brown, Harry Crosby, and other young men who would achieve some kind of literary distinction in the 1920s. They were in the war, but not of it; involved and yet not involved. They could not pay tribute to the comradeship of the trenches because they had never really experienced it, they had never really belonged.

But this is only a partial explanation of the loneliness recorded in their fiction. For it does not answer the question of why they became ambulance drivers in the first place. And here we come to the heart of the matter. Their enlistment as ambulance drivers was not so much a cause of their alienation as an expression of it. They were outside the mainstream of American life, already suspicious of what Hemingway would later call the "sacred words," before they ever landed in Europe. The war did not cause them to feel lonely but rather confirmed and intensified a preexistent feeling of not fitting in. When these future ambulance drivers had been high school and college students in the period 1900-1917, they had been disgusted by the discrepancy between the consistently idealistic theory and often grubby practice of America in the Progressive era. Ironically, the young men whose imaginations had been kindled by the violence of Stephen Crane in the 1890s had become the adult establishment ten years later, and thus in turn became the target of a new generation of rebels—who also chose to express their dissent from the going values of society by means of violence. That the younger literati of 1917 sought out the war did not mean that they were patriotically responding, as millions of other young men in America were, to the highflown rhetoric of Woodrow Wilson. Dos Passos, a political radical, went to Europe in order to witness the death throes of capitalism. Hemingway, who already knew that the woods of northern Michigan contained truths undreamed of in the suburban philosophy of his native Oak Park, Illinois, made his way to the front line at Fossalta di Piave because he knew that that line offered a great opportunity to a young writer who was seeking—as Stephen Crane had before him—for materials with which to rebuke his middle-class American heritage. When fragments of an Austrian mortar shell hit him in the legs, and he was hit twice more in the body by machinegun fire, he found his materials with a vengeance. Thereafter a wound was to become the central symbol of nearly all his work and the consequences of a wound his recurrent theme. In many ways a highly personal testament, Hemingway's work also captures, in hauntingly symbolic terms, the permanently scarring effects of World War I on American society. In so doing, the violent expression of an outsider has become the means by which generations of modern Americans have understood themselves. Originating as a criticism of peacetime America, Hemingway's violence turned into an explanation of what twentieth-century warfare has done to us as a people. Leslie Fiedler would have it that Hemingway's concern with violence signifies a pathological inability to deal with adult sexuality, but this interpretation ignores the fact that violence has an intrinsic importance in our history, especially in this era of global wars—as Hemingway precociously understood from childhood onward.

The literature dealing with race relations is very different from all other expressions of violence in American writing. Even in Hemingway's most tragic stories, his protagonists make a separate peace which for a fleeting time is a genuine peace; the universe of pain inexorably closes down on them again, but the memories of happiness remain as a defense against despair and madness. However, with the notable exception of *The Adventures of Huckleberry Finn* (1884), in which Huck's memory of his life on the raft with Nigger Jim sustains him against all his sordid encounters with the slave-owning society on shore, the important American books on race are unredeemed by such recollections. The sanative qualities of southwestern humor are also missing from this literature, as are the long-range hopes of social justice that arise out of the ashes of *The Iron Heel* and *Caesar's Column*. "Benito Cereno," Melville's brilliant short story of the early 1850s; Mark Twain's mordant novel, *Pudd'nhead Wilson* (1894); and Richard Wright's smashingly powerful *Native Son* (1940): these three representative works offer us no hope whatsoever for believing that the violence and the hatred, the fear and the guilt that separate black and white Americans from one another will ever end. As I have tried to indicate, the nihilism that has been imputed to works dealing with other aspects of American violence is highly debatable, as is the charge that the violence of American literature is sick, sick, sick, because it really stands for our alleged maladjustment to sex or some other cultural sickness. In the literature of racial violence, however, terms like "nihilism" and "sickness" seem very applicable, indeed.

What hope, for instance, does Melville offer us in telling the story of "Benito Cereno"? The kindness and the compassion of Don Benito are not sufficient to keep his black servant from putting a razor to his master's throat, and while Don Benito does manage to escape from violent death, he is unable to shake the shadow of his racial guilt. Haunted by the hatred that the revolt of his slaves has revealed, but powerless to expiate a crime that is far older than himself, Don Benito dies, the very image of the impotent white liberal, on the slopes of the aptly named Mount Agonia.

The tragic hopelessness of Melville's story becomes in *Pudd'nhead Wilson* one of the later Mark Twain's bitterest jokes. With his superior intelligence, Pudd'nhead Wilson is able to solve a bewildering racial crime: his exposure of the fact that the "Negro woman" who has murdered one of the leading white men of the town is in reality a man, Tom Driscoll, whose entire life has been a masquerade in white face, is a masterpiece of detective work. Even more impressive is Wilson's discovery that the masquerade was made possible by Tom Driscoll's light-skinned Negro mother, who switched a white baby and her own baby into one another's cradle, a deception made possible by the fact that both babies had the same white father. Yet finally, Pudd'nhead Wilson is a helpless man. His superior intelligence is powerless to overcome the accumulated racial crimes of American history. To be sure, his trial testimony sends the Negro masquerader to jail and thence to the auction block, where he is sold to a slave trader from "down the river." But if Wilson's testimony succeeds in condemning a black man, it does not succeed in freeing a white man. For the real Tom Driscoll, who has been a slave for twenty years, is not restored to freedom by being given back his identity. Thanks to what society has done to him, he can neither read nor write, nor speak anything but the dialect of the slave quarter; his walk, his attitudes, his gestures, his bearing, his laugh—all are the manners of a slave.

Mark Twain's awareness of the interwoven strands of sex and violence in the racial tragedy of American life is amplified in *Native Son* into a terrifying story of sexual temptation, murder, and legal revenge. The crippling fears of the white man that dominate Bigger Thomas' mind have their white counterparts in the hysterically anti-Negro editorials in the Chicago newspapers and the demonic racism of the police. Nowhere in this implacable novel does the author give us any grounds for belief in the possibility of genuine communication and mutual trust between the races.

It is, of course, possible that "Benito Cereno" has no other reference than to the darkness into which Melville's mind descended after 1851, *Pudd'nhead Wilson* no other reference than to the celebrated misanthropy of the later Mark Twain, *Native Son* no other reference than to Richard Wright's own tortured soul. Yet it is significant that these three extraordinarily gifted writers, two white, one black, agree so completely about the insolubility of American race hatred. Conceivably, their fictions reveal not only the tragic thoughts of three authors but the tragic truth of American society as well.